The Spirit of Design

To Joe and Ben

The Spirit of Design

Objects, Environment and Meaning

Stuart Walker

publishing for a sustainable future

London • Washington, DC

First published 2011
by Earthscan
2 Park Square, Milton Park, Abingdon, Oxon OX14 4RN

Simultaneously published in the USA and Canada
by Earthscan
711 Third Avenue, New York, NY 10017

Earthscan is an imprint of the Taylor & Francis Group, an informa business

Earthscan publishes in association with the International Institute for Environment and Development

Trademark notice: Product or corporate names may be trademarks or registered trademarks, and are used only for identification and explanation without intent to infringe.

British Library Cataloguing in Publication Data
A catalogue record for this book is available from the British Library

Library of Congress Cataloging in Publication Data
Walker, Stuart, 1955-
  The spirit of design : objects, environment and meaning / Stuart Walker.
      p. cm.
  Includes bibliographical references and index.
1. Product design—Environmental aspects. 2. Sustainable design. 3. Human ecology. 4. Material culture. I. Title.
  TS171.4.W35 2011
  745.4—dc22   2011000740

ISBN: 978-1-84971-363-4 (hbk)
ISBN: 978-1-84971-364-1 (pbk)

Typeset in Futura
by Safehouse Creative
Cover design by Rob Watts
Cover photograph by Stuart Walker
Printed and bound in the UK by Bell & Bain
The paper used is FSC certified.

MIX
Paper from
responsible sources
FSC® C007785
FSC
www.fsc.org

Contents

Figures and Tables

Figures

ix

Tables

Acknowledgements

The author wishes to thank Helen Walker for her editing, patience and unwavering support throughout the development of this book. Thanks also to Roger Whitham for transforming my spidery sketches into the renderings featured in Chapter 10, and to my colleagues and those anonymous peer-reviewers who have provided such thoughtful comments and reviews of earlier drafts of the chapters included here. My sincere thanks also to Claire Lamont and everyone at Earthscan and Taylor & Francis for their support and enthusiasm in bringing this to publication. I am grateful to all my students for their questions, discussions and insightful perspectives. Many thanks to the Social Sciences and Humanities Research Council of Canada for supporting much of the research that led to this book.

Acronyms and Abbreviations

CAFOD	Catholic Association for Overseas Development
CSR	Corporate Social Responsibility
e-waste	Electronics waste
GDP	Gross domestic product
ICSID	International Council of Societies of Industrial Design
IDSA	Industrial Designers Society of America
IPCC	Intergovernmental Panel on Climate Change
LED	Light emitting diode
MAMAC	Musée d'Art moderne et d'Art contemporain, Nice, France
STWR	Share the World's Resources
SOMO	Stichting Onderzoek Multinationale Ondernemingen (Centre for Research on Multinational Corporations)
UITP	Union International des Transports Public
UNEP	United Nations Environmental Programme
UNFCCC	United Nations Framework Convention on Climate Change
USB	Universal Serial Bus (electronics)
WEEE	Waste from Electric and Electronic Equipment (European Union directive)
WHO	World Health Organization

1
Introduction

The study in which I write is a small upper room in the east wing of a large Georgian building that once served as the county lunatic asylum. The now tranquil grounds continue beyond the nearby road where they transform into an extensive graveyard arrayed with damp, stone-shrouded Victorian ornament, plain military headstones, marble and flowers. And everywhere yew trees – those age-old symbols of renewal and immortality. Time pervades this place. One cannot help but be reminded of the fleeting nature of existence – and this heightened sense of transience gives the present a vital beauty tinged with a melancholy hue.

Close behind the town rises the high moorland hill of Clougha Pike. If the early residents of the asylum ever made this climb and looked to the southeast they would have seen on the distant plain before them the smoke-billowing mills and factories of the Industrial Revolution. Here was industry writ large – rationalized production, commerce, unimagined wealth, exploitation and urban squalor. Here was the world of James Brindley, who reshaped goods transportation through the canal system, and Richard Arkwright and Samuel Crompton, who pioneered large-scale cotton manufacturing. Here was technology, instrumental reason and progress.

If those same early residents had turned around and looked to the northwest, a very different scene would have met them. In the distance, across the sands of the broad bay, rise the spectacular fells of the English Lake District – the home of British Romanticism. This was a world of art, poetry and literature, of human imagination and aesthetic experience and was, in many ways, a reaction to the rise of industry and trade to the south. Here Wordsworth and Coleridge roamed and wrote of daffodils and the up-springing lark, and Turner and Constable captured the soul of nature.

While the great poets and painters of Cumbria are long dead and the 'dark satanic mills'[1] of Lancashire are now but silent sentinels of a triumphant past, the sensibilities they each brought into sharpened focus remain. In this place, reason, objectivity, advancement and pragmatism rubbed shoulders with aesthetic sensitivity, intuition and imaginative experiences that lie beyond the realm of intellectual understanding. If there can ever be a geographic spot that epitomizes the spirit of design, it is surely the top of this windswept hill where these two vistas meet.

Design as a form of inquiry

2   A particularly prominent feature of today's society is the emphasis placed on monetary concerns. Even in our universities cost-effectiveness, competitive funding and 'real world' economic benefits have become dominating themes. This has grown to such an extent that the very notion of exploring ideas for their own sake is regarded by some as almost quixotic.

Despite the current of the times and the short-term agendas of government and market, it remains crucial to explore areas of interest, irrespective of their immediate usefulness or prospects of turning a profit. This is the nature of academic inquiry. However, in my own experience, having lectured and given conference talks all over the world, the questions I have been asked time and time again centre on how my propositional designs might be produced and sold, whether they are feasible as commercial products, and whether I collaborate with companies to put them into production. Such concerns have no place in this type of creative investigation.

After a century or more of product design for mass-production, we have developed the means for making a plethora of ever-changing goods readily accessible to many. We are well aware that, in doing so, we have also contributed to unprecedented environmental devastation and unconscionable social exploitation and inequity. Ironically, however, there is little evidence to suggest that all these developments in design, production and acquisition have made us any happier. On the contrary, the unremitting messages of product advertising combine to create a pervading sense of discontent.

It becomes important, therefore, to reflect upon the implications of product design and how its undesirable effects are embedded in the very nature of how we conceive of and produce functional objects. And we must explore alternative forms that manifest quite different sensibilities and values. Eventually, some of these explorations might be developed into a material culture that is not only in closer accord with environmental and social responsibilities but also with more meaningful understandings of human happiness. Such aims tend to be ignored or severely distorted within our present system. International fanfare surrounding minor 'improvements' to small electronic gadgets, product launches that promote endless variations on a theme, and the media spotlight placed firmly on the putative benefits rather than the devastating costs are merely some of the indications that product design, as well as the system of which it is a part, is ripe for fundamental change.

A new direction

If change is needed, we require at least some indication of a new direction. This is where design can make a contribution – by imagining and visualizing new forms of functional objects that are not only less damaging to the natural environment but also are in accord with more meaningful understandings of human well-being.

Such forms are explored here through a series of discussions and propositional objects. Environmental considerations are part of this, but the main focus is on the development of functional objects that are consistent with substantive values and profound notions of human meaning. It is surely self-evident that the former cannot be pursued without due account of the latter.

The following chapters combine reasoned argument and the development of theory with speculative design explorations. These tangible propositions both inform and embody the theoretical concepts. Taken together, the discussions and objects constitute a form of creative academic design practice.

A particular challenge today is the design of functional objects that rely on rapidly advancing, and therefore highly transient, digital technologies. Current approaches favour product replacement when technologies become outmoded, which results in a destructive legacy of electronic waste. However, digital technologies enable functionality via software applications and, as such, the physical form of the object becomes far less relevant to the achievement of everyday tasks than was the case with mechanical devices. Effectively, this liberates much product design from the constrictions of function, allowing it to explore areas of significance that lie outside the virtual realm and giving it a new, much needed stimulus to reconsider its purpose and contribution.

The propositional objects presented here include explorations of design and place, electronic artefacts that incorporate unmodified or 'raw' natural materials, and product concepts that encourage considered use. In addition, hybrid objects combine technologies with archetypal forms to reach beyond prosaic functionality and allude to deeper, enduring notions of human meaning and spiritual understanding.

3

Together these explorations yield a robust basis for a fresh approach to product design. The early 20th century's influential principle of 'form follows function' is superseded not by the black boxes of late 20th century product design, the whimsical forms of postmodern experimentation or fashionable variations whose justification is merely change for its own sake, but by a rationale for form beyond function anchored in enduring understandings of human realization. Such a direction, which we might summarize as 'form follows meaning', takes design beyond the instrumental logic of production efficiencies, in which the product too often becomes simply a means to economic growth and shareholder profit. Here, design embraces not only substantive values but also matters of ultimate concern; those facets of our humanity that encompass but transcend reason. These, at least, are the aims – the fact that they are never fully achievable, makes their pursuit no less worthy.

The results of such practice can serve as a catalyst for discussion and the advancement and maturation of product design as a discipline. The work draws on a heritage of human values and understandings of meaning to take design beyond the often superficial and damaging characteristics it has developed over past decades; characteristics that successfully stimulate consumerism but with insufficient regard for consequences.

4

2

Sambo's Stones
sustainability
and meaningful
objects

it is impossible for you to take up the most insignificant pebble at your
feet, without being able to read, if you like, this curious lesson in it
You look upon it first as if it were earth only. Nay, it answers, 'I am
not earth – I am earth and air in one; part of that blue heaven which
you love, and long for, is already in me; it is all my life – without it I
should be nothing, and able for nothing; I could not minister to you,
nor nourish you – I should be a cruel and helpless thing; but, because
there is, according to my need and place in creation, a kind of soul
in me, I have become capable of good, and helpful in the circles of
vitality.

John Ruskin

On the northwest coast of England, a narrow, poorly maintained road leads
out across marshy tidal flats. The withdrawing tide sucks at the mud, scouring
deep channels. At high water, the way becomes impassable, cutting off the old,
weather-beaten houses huddled on the higher ground at the far end of the spit.
It is a wild, wind-blown place – a constantly shifting landscape of tidal pools,
quicksands and coarse salt-grasses – home to lapwings and curlews and rotting

hulks that are slowly being claimed by the sea (Figure 2.1). Cows, their haunches and bellies caked black, wade through the sodden earth at the edge of the track, seeking clumps of moist, green growth.

Figure 2.1 *Low tide at Sunderland Point, Lancashire*

At the end of the surfaced road, a footpath leads up to the houses. Some are inscribed with dates – bearing witness that in the 18th century this remote, cloud-laden place was once a thriving seaport that sent ships to Virginia and the Indies. Among the houses, a narrow lane leads to the windward side of the point and here, in unconsecrated ground at the edge of a blustery field, lies a solitary little grave (Figure 2.2). It is a poignant reminder of a shameful history. The name inscribed on the brass plaque of the gravestone is Samboo, itself an offensive slur – not so much a name as a label. It marks the last resting place of a young black boy buried here in a period when England profited well from exploiting other human beings.[1,2]

Sambo, which is the name more commonly used, arrived at this spot in 1736. It is thought that he was the servant boy of a ship's captain; and he most likely died from cold and fever.[3]

Figure 2.2 *Sambo's Grave, Sunderland Point*

Memorial stones

Visiting Sambo's Grave today, one usually finds painted pebbles placed around the simple wooden cross (Figure 2.3). These are the work of children; school-trip gifts to a long-dead fellow innocent. The local poet, Edward Calais, in his poem 'Samboo's Grave', calls these decorated stones 'mawkish'[4] – perhaps they are, but this seems a harsh judgement. These stones can tell us much about the nature of objects and how we find, express and ascribe meaning. They can also contribute to our understandings of sustainability, and the environmental and social responsibilities this term invokes.

These painted stones are the result of a teacher's class about history, with simplified stories about events that today we regard as reprehensible and dishonourable. Children express their own interpretations of regret and sadness in these sentimental pebbles; but the process is not complete until the trek is made to the gravesite, which is especially moving because of its bleak isolation.

Figure 2.3 *Memorial stones created by children*

The meaning and significance of these stones can be interpreted from several angles. Firstly, there is the relationship of these artefacts to our own history and sense of identity – a history of empire and expansionism, trade and the economic development of the Americas, together with the inhumanity of the slave trade, which wrought such devastating and enduring effects. So these stones, an outcome of children learning something of this history, are linked to our own cultural identity. Reflecting on this history and identity, these memorial stones inevitably raise thoughts about morality – that ever-changing system of ideas by which a society judges good and virtuous conduct. In hindsight, we judge our predecessors who took part in or were supportive of the slave trade, as having a lower or inadequate sense of morality. Yet, at the time, people whom society judged to be upright citizens were open supporters and politicians spoke out in the Houses of Parliament, decrying any attempts to abolish it.[5] Are these simply the actions of a less enlightened age? Or are we, today, also pursuing activities that will leave lasting scars and which future generations will also judge immoral and reprehensible?

Secondly, there is the intention behind their creation. Far more poignant than generalities about empire and slavery, these stones are created for one particular person. Each is a commemorative act from one child to another; a gift that connects across time and demonstrates a fundamental notion of empathy between two human beings. In effect, the intention behind the act of gift *making* imaginatively ascribes to the object feelings present in oneself and, through the act of gift *giving*, whereby the stones are placed on the grave, passes these feelings on to the dead child. It matters not that the recipient is deceased and therefore

Figure 2.4 *Discarded memorial stones*

unable to appreciate this act of fellowship. The virtue lies in the empathetic connection – manifested through a creative act and through giving.

Thirdly, there is the relationship of these simply-painted objects to the individual act of creativity itself and personal artistic expression. The act of making gives the child a sense of creative accomplishment. And the resulting object may have qualities that others judge to be aesthetically pleasing.

These objects have no practical use and no economic value. Indeed, to create such artefacts for monetary gain would diminish the intent and injure the unaffected personal expression of the outcome. Furthermore, these objects are not lasting; they reside only for a short period on the gravesite. Eventually, to make way for fresh contributions, they are returned to the shoreline, where they are scrubbed clean by the waves and where remnants of older artefacts can be found among the flotsam and muddy grasses (Figure 2.4).

The meaning of these stones lies in their symbolic value – they can be understood as symbols of history, cultural identity and human empathy. There is also meaning in their artistic value – to the child, through the creative act, and in any aesthetic attributes they may possess. An important aspect of their meaning is related to the stories that can be told about them. It is through such stories that we can find, express and recognize meanings, and it is one way of endowing inanimate things with significance and value.

Plumb line

In contrast to the memorial stones, the simple plumb line shown in Figure 2.5 is intended for practical use rather than creative expression. It is made from locally available materials and could last indefinitely by occasionally replacing the worn-out cord. While it is of little or no commercial value, unlike the memorial stones, it

9

Figure 2.5
Plumb line
hemp cord and a pebble

could, conceivably, be produced and sold without diminishing its meaning in any way. Hence, despite being essentially the same as one of the memorial stones, the meaning and significance of this rudimentary tool are very different. It has no symbolic meaning and it has no story. If such an object is unable to be practically useful, it ceases to have value and meaning. (I shall return to this artefact in Chapter 7, where I discuss mass- and locally-produced artefacts.)

These simple objects, the memorial stones and the plumb line, illustrate important aspects of how we ascribe meaning to our material culture. We see that non-utilitarian, expressive objects, which may only last a short time, can relate to profound issues such as ethics, empathy, history and cultural identity. On the other hand, long-lasting utilitarian objects may only retain their meaning and significance as long as they continue to function according to their intended purpose.

This notion of meaning and significance resting in an object's utility is, of course, typical of many contemporary products, especially many of today's electronic consumer goods. When their functionality is deemed no longer satisfactory, such products are easily discarded and replaced – because of how they are produced and because they lack additional forms of meaning.

So let us now consider an example of a contemporary electronic device where an attempt has been made to combine the various cultural notions of meaning we saw in the memorial stones with utilitarian meaning, as illustrated by the plumb line.

Les clés USB Provençales

A local designer in Provence has created a USB memory stick (Figure 2.6) that incorporates cultural elements from this region of southern France.[6,7] Each USB circuit board is encased in locally grown olive wood, which is engraved with

Figure 2.6
Provençal USB stick by Thiery Aymes

symbols of the area. In the example shown, the wooden casing is decorated
with the Cross of the Camargue – a symbol that integrates a Christian cross
embellished with the three-pronged trident of the Camargue *Gardians* or cowboys
and indicative of faith; an anchor, reflecting the seafaring traditions of the region
and symbolizing hope; and a heart, calling people to live with charity. In addition,
the olive wood is infused with the scent of lavender; lavender-based perfume
being an important facet of the local rural economy. And finally, each stick is pre-
loaded with several traditional Provençal songs.

11

We see that this object brings together many elements that are relevant to the
traditions of the region and we might be tempted to conclude that this helps create
a more meaningful and culturally significant artefact. However, the relationship of
these elements to a USB flash drive is completely arbitrary. They are incongruent
additions to its essential utility – additions that exist quite separately, even though
they are physically bonded to the electronics. The additional encasing elements
are purely decorative, they have no connection to the idea of a computer memory
stick. And while the songs make use of the drive as a data storage device, they
could just as easily be stored on a tape, CD or MP3 player. So here, too, there is
no culturally relevant relationship between the songs and type of storage device
used, it is simply a utilitarian relationship. As a physical thing, the various elements
are not integrated into a unified whole and a dissonance is created because of
this lack of aesthetic coherence. Nevertheless, even though such products may be
characterized as kitsch, there is no doubt that they have a certain appeal as an
alternative that reflects something of one's region or as a souvenir of a visit.
These shortcomings raise important issues about our current approaches to the
design and production of contemporary electronic goods. For example, if a fault
developed in the USB's electronics or if technological advancement meant that
its functionality had become superseded the product would be rendered useless

Figure 2.7
Leather walking shoes – more than 40 years of service

and without value. As it cannot be repaired or upgraded, it would be discarded and replaced. In the process the olive wood embellishments, despite their cultural significance, would be discarded along with the circuitry. While the relinquishment of these cultural elements might be considered regrettable, there would be little point in retaining the product once its essential functionality had broken down or become outmoded.

The fate of this USB stick is representative of the enormous amounts of electronic waste that are discarded each year around the world – estimated at 20 to 50 million tonnes annually.[8] The addition of decorative casings and other culturally relevant extras will do little to staunch this squandering of resources or to reduce the devastating social and environmental impacts associated with our irresponsibly wasteful system of production and consumption.

A final example suggests a potential direction for integrating personal, social and cultural meanings with utilitarian meanings in a manner that is not forced or a superficial 'extra', but fully part of, and inseparable from, the object as a whole.

Old shoes

If the leather is regularly fed with polish to retain suppleness and prevent cracking, a well made pair of shoes can last for decades. The leather walking shoes shown in Figure 2.7 are over 40 years old. They have been worn regularly, have been passed on from one generation to another, and they are still perfectly serviceable. These shoes are of an eminently practical design. They exhibit minimal decorative qualities, which are restricted to the slightly stippled finish of the leather and the stitch work, and yet their associations with craftsmanship, and with people and places, imbue them with a host of meanings. Moreover, their continued usefulness is not because their durability is invulnerable and static. Rather, it is related to a

Figure 2.8
Shoe sole with layers of maintenance and repair

system of production and consumption that is fundamentally different from that which is prevalent today.

These particular shoes, which date from the mid-1960s, were made in England. They were purchased by their original owner at a local retail outlet in the English Midlands in 1966, in preparation for a walking tour of Snowdonia. The first owner passed them on to another family member and since then they have had four owners within the same extended family. Many parts of the shoes are relatively new. The heels have been repaired many times, with new rubber replacements. The insoles, inner leather lining and outsoles have all been replaced a number of times, together with the laces and much of the shoes' stitching. The leather uppers and the midsoles are original. Thus, a significant proportion of the materials has been changed over time, which has allowed the functionality of the shoes to be maintained, together with their enduring presence and usefulness (Figure 2.8).

To attain this level of durability in a product a number of factors are needed. Firstly, the product needs to be well-made and worth repairing. Secondly, the design needs to be such that it can endure over time in terms of its aesthetic attributes and be relatively unaffected by the vagaries of fashion, this implies a relatively subdued design devoid of the extravagance associated with short-lived trends. Thirdly, it has to be designed and constructed in a manner that lends itself to repair or improvement. Fourthly, although the location of manufacture could be virtually anywhere, to retain its usefulness a local maintenance infrastructure is needed and product repair or refurbishment has to be economically attractive. Furthermore, and importantly, in the case of leather shoes, the manufacturer and the purchaser must be cognisant of the availability of this product maintenance infrastructure when respectively creating and purchasing these relatively expensive products. Finally, such a product requires regular attention by the owner – what Borgmann refers to as 'engagement'.[9] To prevent the leather from cracking, the shoes have to be regularly polished, and to maintain their shape when not in use, they need to be fitted with shoe trees.

An 'endure and evolve' scenario

These various artefacts, some of which are extremely basic, tell us much about the meanings that can be attached to objects and how these meanings are related to design, manufacture, use and maintenance. They include symbolic meanings, with their connections to culture, identity and history, as discussed in the example of the memorial stones at Sambo's Grave. They also include utilitarian meanings, as in the plumb line, the disconnected relationship of cultural meanings and utility found in the Provençal USB stick, and the seamless integration of aesthetics with utility, and production with maintenance and product care, as illustrated by the leather shoes.

From these examples, we can draw a number of conclusions that can inform our approaches to the production, use and disposal of contemporary products – the aim being to develop a version of material culture that is not only less destructive but also more meaningful. In addition, and as I have already mentioned, electronic devices are a particular concern because of their extraordinarily brief useful lives and the significant harm caused by their high rates of production and disposal.

From the foregoing, it seems that a fruitful way forward would be one in which products are designed to *endure and evolve*. This relatively simple notion could lead to a more mature and more accountable manufacturing and economic system that would be radically different from most current practices. The critical business imperative would no longer be to make the cheapest possible product, then sell and forget it. Instead, the aim would be to develop a high quality product that, as in the example of the leather shoes, may well have a relatively high initial retail price. However, for such a product to be viable, it would have to last much longer than cheaper equivalents; be capable of being maintained and repaired; be flexible enough to be incrementally improved, changed and upgraded over time; be supported by more expansive notions of corporate social responsibility than are presently evident; be part of a more responsible production/use/post-use cycle; and be supported by government policy through appropriate incentives.

Achieving these requirements has a number of implications for designers and producers, as well as many potential social, environmental and economic benefits:

- **Design for maintenance and repair**: In terms of their design, products would have to be conceptually very different from those of today. They would need to be constructed from higher quality components and designed in a manner that facilitates economic and environmentally

14

responsible maintenance and repair. Designers would also have to develop products that are adaptable and capable of accommodating incremental changes and component upgrading over time. Significantly, products would have to be designed in ways that allow new, more advanced technological elements to be integrated, even though the precise form of such elements cannot necessarily be anticipated.

• **A product maintenance infrastructure**: Currently, national and international manufacturers are dependent on an established infrastructure of regional distributors and local retailers. In an 'endure and evolve' scenario, they would also be dependent on an effective product maintenance infrastructure of regional and local enterprises that offer a range of post-retail services for product recovery, repair, incremental change and upgrading. In such a scenario, large international manufacturers could maintain long-term economic interest in their products through the supply of parts and upgrade components and, potentially, through developing local product-service outlets.

• **Local employment and economy**: Local economies, which are so critical to the idea of sustainability, would benefit through the development of many diverse, and thereby potentially more robust, product-service enterprises and job opportunities.

15

• **Environmental benefits**: Products that are retained for longer periods, and serviced and upgraded locally, would help reduce the throughput of virgin materials and energy resources associated with product replacement, along with their distribution and packaging. Moreover, when products eventually do need to be discarded and replaced, perhaps when a substantial technological advance causes them to be no longer upgradable, there would already be a developed service infrastructure in place that would provide an effective means for recovering parts and materials for recycling. In addition, products designed to be easily repaired and upgraded would also be capable of being readily disassembled for parts recovery and recycling.

• **Valuing our material culture**: A higher initial retail price for a good quality, long-lasting, maintainable product is commensurate with the notion of valuing and caring for our possessions and with reducing overall product disposal/replacement levels.

Thus, an *endure and evolve* scenario would reduce product disposal and enable companies to comply with post-use legislation and extended producer responsibilities, such as the European Union's Waste Electrical and Electronic Equipment (WEEE) legislation,[10] which are only likely to increase as environmental and disposal problems become more acute. As we shall see in Chapter 8, such a scenario, developed from a design perspective, is also in accord with economic propositions for a more sustainable society.

Enduring and evolving meanings

Creating products that, physically, are capable of enduring and evolving will allow a significantly different relationship to develop between people and their material culture – particularly with respect to electronic goods. Many of these products are for personal use, such as laptop computers, portable music players and mobile phones. However, because of how they are currently conceived and understood, the meaning and value of these products lie primarily in their utility and their newness, and rapid rates of technological advancement quickly render them obsolete. Consequently, their short useful life prevents them accruing a host of other potential meanings – through stories, accumulated history and personal memories and associations. In contrast, high quality, long-lasting electronic products would have the potential to become precious and meaningful personal items. Such products could be maintained and cared for, and develop with us as our needs change and as new technologies become available. If imaginatively designed, and like a comfortable pair of old leather shoes, such products could improve with age rather than being out of date and out of fashion almost before they are taken out of the box. Conceptually, this is far from current versions of what are essentially disposable electronic consumer goods.

16   The potential benefits of an *endure and evolve* approach to design and production go much further than the pragmatic, instrumental reasoning that underpins product take-back laws. Within such a scenario, personal electronic products would offer permanence *and* change – a sense of stability and continuity along with transition. In this way, our everyday things, which comprise our more intimate sense of material culture, would be allowed to accumulate additional facets of significance and value and attain symbolic and personally relevant connotations that link to ideas, memories, stories and emotions. In addition to, but certainly concomitant with, any environmental or broader social benefits, a more enduring and evolving version of contemporary products would enable us to develop far more personally meaningful relationships with our material culture together with attitudes that are consistent with product retention and care.

In subsequent chapters, I explore aspects of design and meaning through the development of conceptual artefacts. These explorations include locally achievable functional objects that make use of local materials in combination with mass-produced components, and they examine different facets of design – such as enduring values, technological change and form – in relation to substantive notions of human meaning.

No regrets?

I began this discussion with a description of a child's grave in a lonely field on the northwest coast of England – a grave that marks a period in our history that is forever tarnished by the inhumanity of the slave trade. In the opening decade of the 21st century, commemorations of the 200th anniversary of the abolition of the slave trade in Britain were marked by public regret and apologies for the injustices committed by our forefathers.[11-13] We regard this period as a shameful aspect of our heritage, one that created untold damage and misery. And we tend to see these violations as reflecting an inadequate or distorted sense of morality – as the actions of a less enlightened age.

Today, there is massive environmental damage being wrought by our activities, many of which are directly or indirectly related to manufacturing and consumption. The impacts on ecosystems and the social effects are enormous and many will be long-term. As we have looked back at the disgraceful activities of our predecessors, we must ask ourselves if future generations will look back at our age and judge our actions as immoral and reprehensible. Will we have created lasting harm and will our activities be regarded with shame – as the actions of a less enlightened age?

3
Following Will-o'-the-Wisps and Chasing Ghosts

re-directing
design through
practice-based
research

'I must go to the Botanical Gardens.'
'Why?'
'To see the ivy.'
It seemed a good enough reason
and I went with him.

Evelyn Waugh

Since its earliest days, designing for industry has been inseparably linked to the economic viability of products and the financial requirements of mass production. The discipline of industrial design emerged during the early years of the 20th century to address the then new idea of designing consumer goods for high-volume, mechanized manufacture. It quickly became employed to distinguish one product from another, to create market appeal and to spur consumerism.[1] In those early days, the subsequent environmental and social side effects of mass production and mass consumption, on a global level, were not widely foreseen.

Just as in the first decades of the 20th century there was a need to redefine material culture for the new context of mass production, so we have to redefine material culture for the context of today. To do this, we must set aside, at least temporarily, some of our traditional notions of product design and its ties to industry and economics. Without this detachment, conceptualization will be restricted and the advancement of new ideas will be hampered. The creativity of designers can be employed in many ways to develop directions that responsibly address vital environmental and socio-cultural issues. As new insights emerge, and some are already emerging, there may well be hitherto unforeseen possibilities for wealth creation and opportunities for industry.

Designing for a new context

It is perhaps not uncommon to consider the time in which one lives to be especially fraught with problems and challenges, so we must be wary of disproportionately privileging the present in our critique of conventional approaches. While acknowledging this danger, it does seem to many that our time is one of particularly significant philosophical and existential flux.[2-4] We live in a period of uncertain transition as we move further and further away from the 'modern' perception, which became embedded over a period of several centuries, and towards whatever our current, rapidly changing understandings of the world may eventually yield. This period is referred to by some as late modern, by others as postmodern – both are vague, provisional terms that disclose a lack of definition and assuredness about the present. More than anything, they represent a shifting from the assumptions of the past, spurred by a growing realization that those assumptions no longer work for us. They indicate that something is ending or has recently ended and that new directions are emerging; directions that are often confusing and undeveloped. We no longer have the certainties of modernity, but neither do we have a consolidated and well-understood set of alternatives.

Such periods are particularly significant for the arts, including the applied arts. It is artists and designers who are called upon to consider the nature of this change and to respond in creative ways. They have an obligation to explore alternatives, to embrace the uncertainty and investigate ways of reconciling emerging and evolving understandings with the expressions and artefacts of art and design.

To be both creative and relevant to the new environment, such explorations must be unencumbered by many of the assumptions and conventions of the past. In industrial design, which might be more broadly and more fruitfully conceived as simply the design of functional objects, the conventional assumptions of the discipline have to be challenged. Priorities such as technological innovation, ergonomics, mass production of uniform products for wide distribution to international markets, and even economic viability can, indeed must, be at least temporarily set aside so as to more freely develop design possibilities that embrace and are expressive of new sensibilities – not least of which are the harmful consequences of our current approaches. As Fuad-Luke has observed, design must decouple itself from the existing drivers of the discipline if it is to provide a new paradigm for design.[5]

Contesting conventions

In contemplating the nature of change and the magnitude of the challenge, the kind of work that needs to be done has to be experimental and exploratory. There is a requirement for trial and error, and probing of ideas that are founded on well-considered but continuously evolving arguments. Time is required for reflection and deliberation. Necessarily, the results of such work will be provisional, conceptual and contingent upon changes happening elsewhere. In the first instance at least, results will be more indicative than concrete, alluding to new possibilities but, in and of themselves, inadequate. The focus is on setting the seeds of change in directions that are considered appropriate for a new and emerging context – a context that is ill-understood from our current standpoint. This is not the type of design work that is robust enough to warrant the high capital expenditure necessary for its production or widespread distribution; indeed, such assumptions within a new design milieu may be inappropriate.

In today's mass-production context, design has to be low risk and acceptable to many because it has to be profitable. Moreover, we are now all too familiar with the various arguments and indicators that link current modes of production, distribution and marketing to environmental damage and socio-economic disparities.[6,7] It is not difficult to see that design conventions tied to this type of production are also tied to these exploitative practices. The fundamental character of many contemporary products – embodied in their design, their aesthetics, their relatively low cost and their rapid rates of disposal and replacement – is inextricably wedded to inadequate labour and environmental laws, consumerism, energy use, waste and pollution.[8]

21

To confront these challenges, it is implicit that our material culture – in how it is devised, produced, delivered and used, and what happens to it once it is no longer needed – will have to undergo major change. Whether such change is the result of incremental adjustments, more substantial systemic shifts or a combination of both, it will have to bring forth conceptions of material culture that are very different from the norms of today – norms that in reality are rather recent and evidently precarious. Our present globalized production system is perilously dependent on the availability of inexpensive energy, especially oil, both for its acquisition of raw materials and for the international distribution of its products. An economy that is so heavily reliant on a single commodity tends to be inherently unstable and fragile. For example, in 19th century Britain, the national economy was tightly coupled to the fortunes of its cotton industry. During the latter part of the 1800s, when the rate of growth in the cotton sector slumped, the whole of British industry sank with it.[9]

Today, an increasingly important factor, which is inseparably linked to the availability and use of inexpensive forms of energy, is that of 'externalities'. These are the side effects of industrial activities that, too often, are unaccounted for in the economic models and ignored in the costs of doing business. They include such things as air, water and noise pollution, waste production, health effects, human exploitation, the denudation of landscapes, habitats, wildlife migration routes and biodiversity, and the apparent link between industrial production and climate change.

To develop new ways of creating and producing functional objects that are capable of addressing these concerns, at least conceptually, we have to stand outside or temporarily set aside our usual expectations of design; expectations that assume a product must be desirable, marketable and profitable.

Instigating new approaches for changing circumstances

In considering new design approaches that explore areas outside the current system, the question arises as to who in our society is best equipped to conduct such explorations and posit alternative ways forward. Certainly the requirements indicated above, of time, reflection and deliberation are not characteristics typically associated with current business models. Similarly, terms such as conceptual, speculative, exploratory and contingent suggest priorities that are far too equivocal for the time-is-money, profit-oriented concerns so critical to corporate agendas. Experimental design does not fit well here. It is therefore of relatively little interest to business. While some larger companies may devote resources to so-called 'blue-sky' design initiatives, the expectations are usually constrained, explicitly or implicitly, to the principal concerns of the enterprise. Even with the best of intentions, within the corporate environment it is often difficult to reflect upon and explore the fundamental nature of our material culture and to do this expansively and in a manner that is divorced from the primary focus of the company. Furthermore, small and medium-sized enterprises generally have neither the time nor the resources for such work. Thus, despite the argument that it is the responsibility of those within the industry to tackle these larger concerns, it appears that they are either indifferent to or systemically hampered from effectively doing so. Many of the changes that *are* occurring are relatively minor technological modifications that usually serve to further rather than challenge structural norms.

Design, research and change

Recognizing that change from within the production system is at best inadequate we must look to others to explore alternative approaches. This calls for what might be termed 'pure' or 'fundamental' research in which big picture ideas are explored in a manner that is free from the usual constraints of industry and where ideas can be pursued for their own sake, to see where they might lead. This should be occurring in our universities, among academics and in postgraduate programmes, given the importance and urgency of the issues. However, and for some of the reasons outlined later, this is not happening to the extent one might expect. Consequently the study of design within the academy is missing an important opportunity for debate and contribution. While there are exceptions, the majority of design research studies appear to fall into four main categories, the first three of which, although valuable, do not get to the heart of these contemporary issues *through the core activity of designing*.

22

1. **'Research about designing'** – **history, theory and pedagogy**: Areas of important concern for academic consideration include research that focuses on design history, theory and pedagogy. This research about designing covers both the activity and its outputs.[10] The history of design and its development over time, exemplified by the work of authors such as Sparke,[11] Dormer[12] and Heskett,[13] is vital to our understanding of the discipline. Similarly, design theory, its relationship to contemporary issues and insights from other disciplines, inform the practice of design and address phenomena relevant to the creation of material culture. In this area, authors such as Verbeek,[14] Buchanan and Margolin[15,16] provide critical perspectives that enrich our understandings of design. However, it is also important to recognize that history and theory research, while critical to our understanding of the subject, is generally conducted by academics who are not themselves designers. Additionally, research into learning methods and process, design pedagogy, the role of visualization methods and the use of technologies in the studio is also essential to understandings of design, and Cross[17] and Hannah,[18] among others, have contributed in this area. Within such research, however, if the underlying assumptions about the nature of product design are not challenged, its findings might only yield more effective methods for continuing, rather than critiquing and re-inventing design conventions.

2. **'Research for designing'** – **acquiring data**: Another area might be characterized as research for designing. It refers to research that is needed for the design process to begin and advance. The focus is on the acquisition of data that:

- helps define the design requirements, prior to the commencement of designing,
- informs decisions aimed at achieving those requirements, made during the process of designing, or
- informs design decisions made in response to additional matters that arise in the course of design activities.

Qualitative research methods typically used in sociology or anthropology are often adopted to investigate particular areas of interest. Ethnographic, observational and market research are commonly used in design investigations.[19] Other methods might be more quantitative and scientific, for example, if investigating the most appropriate materials for a certain application. These kinds of research are necessary and important for informing design in specific areas but they are somewhat peripheral to the creative activity of designing. Frequently, such research could be, and might best be, carried out by non-designers. Important as it is, such research does not draw on the nature of design itself in furthering our understandings. It does not take into account the manner in which information and knowledge affect form within a transmutative, integrative process; a process in which the relationship between generalized data and tangible, specific design outcomes are explored. This relationship is especially important today because our increasing knowledge about the ramifications of current approaches to design

23

and production suggests that new types of outcomes are needed – outcomes that are fundamentally different from traditional notions of 'products'. Furthermore, emphasis on these kinds of qualitative and quantitative studies and on cognitive knowledge, especially at the postgraduate level, can often mean that this crucial transformative step, which occurs within the focused activity of designing, is given insufficient attention. In turn, this means that expressive knowledge, that is, knowledge about effectively embodying and conveying meaning or feeling through the creative process of designing, remains underdeveloped.

3. **'Research for industry'**: A further area is that of research for industry or industry-related design research. Frequently, this is the type of work that might be more appropriately conducted within the research and development department of a large company or by an independent consultancy. Its legitimate place within academia has to be treated with considerable caution. For example, I recently saw a presentation by two academics in which sponsored research instigated by a major corporation examined user perceptions about the interface design of a domestic appliance. While such work can lead to improvements in certain products, it fails to adequately distinguish between the priorities of design research within academia and those of industry. That is not to say that research projects between academia and industry cannot be productive and mutually beneficial. However, the parameters of such research have to be very carefully considered if the privileges and responsibilities of academia are to be upheld. Unless this distinction is maintained, the danger always exists of a Faustian bargain being struck where academic principles are progressively eroded in order to both secure research funding from the private sector and to seek worldly relevance. Finding the appropriate relationship between industry and design research in academia is a thorny issue. Some prefer to locate at least part of a design research project in the real-world, and argue that it is not a case of *either-or* academic versus worldly research, but *both-and*.[20] However, given the relatively early stage of design research within academia and especially the nascent level of practice-based research (see below), it would seem that, until a stronger and more confident foundation for academic design research has been established, the *both-and* solution may yet be a little premature.

'Research for designing' and 'research for industry' can yield certain insights, inform the design process and lead to improvements in particular design outcomes. However, neither specifically aims at tackling the bigger picture, design-related questions concerned with the advancement and re-definition of manufactured products for a new context. Nevertheless, such questions do need to be asked if we are to reflectively consider the essential nature of our material culture and its reconciliation not only with environmental responsibilities, but also with fundamental notions of human happiness and purpose; as Grayling has pointed out, none of the things worth having in life – kindness, wisdom, affection – can be purchased at the shopping mall.[21] Furthermore, a particular responsibility for the design disciplines is that any attempts at such a reconciliation must transcend generalities and become manifest, at least at the conceptual level, through the specifics that are inherent to the activity of designing itself.

4. **'Research through designing' – practice-based research**: Waters stresses that the marketplace should not be seen as the definitive structure for the free play of ideas. Rather, it is in our academic institutions that flights of fancy and the flourishing of ideas should be nurtured and encouraged. Referring to Kant, he explains that theory exists at the boundary between the human mind and the world, and it develops when our ways of creating the world run up against the world itself.[22]

Clearly, the business of design is of the world, but it is the responsibility of design within the academy to focus on pursuits that contribute to the advancement of design as a discipline. Research through designing, or practice-based research, has a critical role to play in this, not only in expanding knowledge and developing theory but in transforming such knowledge and theory into material expressions. In turn, the outcomes of these transformative activities can be reflected upon to inform theory. There is a fundamental responsibility within the academy to not only tolerate but to encourage experimentation, to follow, as Waters has put it, will-o'-the-wisps and to chase ghosts.[23]

More than anything, practice-based research is an activity that requires our engagement with ideas; to set ourselves the task of questioning, clarifying, challenging, proposing and developing new perspectives.[24] For design, however, this is not yet enough. Design is distinguished from many other disciplines by studio engagement and it has the particular responsibility of both articulating the results of such inquiry through form and recognizing the activity of designing itself as a means of inquiry. This integrative, reflective process of thinking-and-doing is fundamental to the nature of design. It can be appropriately informed by the kinds of research discussed above – design history, methods, quantitative and qualitative information, and knowledge about industry. However, there is the need to deliberate and carefully critique such information, to challenge assumptions and conventions and to continually posit questions and ideas that can be productively explored within the distinctive and core activity of the designing process. By this means, the particular contribution of design within academia can be appropriately realized and advanced. Such inquiry is inherently a practice-based approach that respects both the perspectives and the working methods of designers.[25]

One cannot learn to drive a car or play the violin simply by reading about methods and theory. Repeated and dedicated practice also has to be included as a core element of the learning process. Through such practice, certain kinds of knowledge and insight are gained, experience is built up and, over time, tacit understandings of the activity are developed. The same is true of design; through active engagement in practice, one gains knowledge, insights and experience. Hence, if these core aspects of the discipline are to contribute to its advancement, design practice must be included as a key element of the research approach. Moreover, given the significant issues we are facing today, design within academia has an important role in supporting and developing such practice-based research. Unencumbered by the conventions and expectations of the market, particularly its short-term economic imperatives, practice-based design research can more freely and expansively explore the longer-term possibilities and potential of material culture.

Practice-based research and sustainability

Research that focuses on sustainability, which also gives a central place to the particular skills and knowledge of the designer within the research approach, is relatively rare within academia. On the face of it, this might seem surprising, but on further consideration the reasons become clear.

Firstly, industrial design is a discipline in which academic research of any kind is a rather recent phenomenon.[26] In this context, the development of robust, practice-based research methods is still at a formative stage. Seago and Dunne, early proponents of practice-based research, have suggested that the process of invention can be used as a form of discourse to generate a different notion of the purpose and responsibility of the design researcher.[27] Even though such discourse is vital, research examples are few and far between, as are practice-based examples which address the multitude of considerations covered by the term 'sustainability'.

Secondly, opportunities for academics with design expertise to involve postgraduate students in their research, in order to substantively advance the work in a timely manner, remain fairly restricted. Established PhD programmes in industrial design are not widespread and, given the diverse range of research possibilities within the discipline, there are comparatively few design academics with the necessary locus of concentration to supervise theses in the specific area of practice-based research for sustainability. Master's students can productively contribute in particular instances, through studio explorations and cap-stone projects, but there is insufficient time and usually insufficient funding for them to be able to engage in any substantial practice-based design research investigations.

Within the discipline of industrial design, the establishment of a sound basis for practice-based research in sustainability requires a host of complex issues to be combined into a coherent, albeit conditional, research agenda. Many of these issues are interrelated, ill-defined and ill-understood, and many are not only outside the product designer's area of expertise but are also, themselves, in a constant state of flux. Moreover, within such an agenda, the activity of designing has to be included as a legitimate element of the investigation.

To advance this type of research, various factors have to be taken into account. Theoretical foundations are needed to create the necessary conditions for engagement in the process of designing. Such foundations will themselves be provisional and can be developed in a number of ways. For example, the qualitative and quantitative methods of design-related research referred to earlier, which can include research related to industry practice, can be used to provide information and insights. So too, the work of design historians, and perhaps especially the work of theoreticians are necessary for establishing a starting point. These various contributions must be brought together to develop a line of inquiry that can be productively investigated through engagement in the activity of designing.

In the field of design for sustainability this might mean that primary source data, from surveys or interviews, together with research information from other fields, provide a basis for practice-based investigations. However, in contrast to the aims of conventional design projects, the goal of such investigations is not to create well-defined product solutions. Instead, the aim is to develop propositions that offer new perspectives on the potential and possibilities for a more sustainable material culture. Reflecting on the results of such investigations can stimulate further lines of inquiry, which might require further primary data and theory development and additional practice-based explorations. Thus, the process becomes one of rolling iterations of practice-based studies in conjunction with data acquisition and theory development. Importantly, it is a process in which the activity of designing becomes an intrinsic element in the advancement of knowledge.[28]

Given these requirements of theoretical synthesis, primary data collection, iterative design investigations and reflection, such research lends itself to the longer-term studies that are possible within academia and especially among PhD students working with faculty members.

Practice-based investigations of meaning and sustainability

For some years I have been developing practice-based research along the lines described above. This research, which includes the creation of expressive artefacts, explores underlying approaches and principles rather than practical application. For this reason, it is a form of research through designing that can be best described as practice-based fundamental research. It is a type of research in which the end product comprises propositional artefacts in combination with documentation that articulates some of the *thinking* that accompanies and is integral to the *doing*. Hence, the outcomes are both expressive and cognitive – a dual form that aptly reflects the twofold nature of the discipline, which might be summed up as 'reason + imagination'.

These practice-based investigations, examples of which are included in subsequent chapters, explore the potential for developing more meaningful notions of material culture. Frequently they include an increased role for localization in the design and production of functional objects; localization being an important aspect of sustainability. Particular attention is given to consumer electronics because rapid technological advancement renders such products functionally obsolete within an exceptionally short timespan. A number of the approaches included here re-envision such artefacts so that functional change is facilitated within a framework of continuity. In turn, this allows more enduring product narratives to evolve.

These various investigations draw on information and data from a wide variety of secondary sources in areas that include sustainability, philosophy, design history and design theory. Some also make use of qualitative research methodologies for acquiring and analysing primary data. All the investigations emphasize design engagement as a critical aspect of the research approach and as a key element in the advancement of knowledge.

Essentially, this kind of practice-based research explores new ways of conceiving of our material culture. Critically, the research is not driven by technology, functional benefit or economic imperatives. Instead, objects are considered within a broader, more holistic system that includes production, distribution, environmental considerations and personal, social and cultural meanings. Such explorations begin to point towards a material culture of dynamic and continual evolution. One that is capable of embracing local initiatives and diversity alongside the benefits of mass-production and technological advancement.

As we have seen, practice-based design research is at an early stage of development, and such research that explores the relationships between functional objects, meaning and sustainability is even more embryonic. It therefore seems both fruitful and appropriate to disconnect design from the bottom-line, as well as other conventional constraints, in order to more freely and more imaginatively explore the contributions that creative design can bring to these challenging and complex areas of contemporary culture.

4

After Taste
the power
and prejudice
of product
appearance

Their colours and their forms, were then to me
An appetite: a feeling and a love,
That had no need of a remoter charm,
By thought supplied, or any interest
Unborrowed from the eye. – That time is past

William Wordsworth

In this chapter I turn to the subject of taste – its meaning, its relationship to convention and innovation, and its associations with cultural elitism. Rather than continuing its role as arbiter of a rather narrowly defined idea of good taste, design can broaden its compass to effectively engage with many of today's most pressing issues, including ethical and environmental concerns and considerations related to meaning. These ideas are illustrated through a series of conceptual objects created through practice-based design research. They demonstrate that taste can be a powerful but often highly prejudicial aspect of design and they highlight issues about the design process and the assumptions we make when developing contemporary products. The discussion, together with the conceptual objects, suggest a direction that contests 'designerly' preconceptions about taste in order to address contemporary issues within a broader and richer aesthetic palette.

Our initial visual impression of a product has a powerful influence on our judgement, and our response will be strongly related to factors such as convention and personal notions of taste. Convention allows us to place a product within a known milieu and thus understand it. Taste refers to the kinds of associations a particular aesthetic will prompt; it allows us to decide if the product supports our idea of ourselves within the socio-cultural grouping to which we belong or to which we aspire. The potency of this first impression raises two important points. Firstly, convention and taste tend to hamper acceptance of design innovations that depart significantly from current norms, which, in turn, can hamper productive change in design practice. This point is especially important today because there is an urgent need to develop new, less harmful directions in product design and manufacturing, and it may well be that such directions do depart significantly from what has gone before. Secondly, the overriding influence of a product's appearance can create a false impression of its contribution. For example, if an eco-friendly product is given a simple, clean appearance, then there will be a causal association set up in the viewer's mind between 'clean and simple' and environmental responsibility. Furthermore, if a simple, clean appearance aligns with one's own personal taste, it is likely that a strong positive impression will be created that environmental responsibility and one's personal taste are congruent. However, associations between product appearance, taste and ethical and environmental principles are not determinate and appearances can be deceptive. There is a need to go beyond appearances and to carefully consider the product as a whole, not only in terms of its production, materials, use and after-use, but also in terms of its meaning and contribution.

Taste and its prejudices

Taste is not universal but is related to our personal associations with, or aspirations to, the conventions of particular social groupings. It can be understood as a collectively negotiated but highly individual sense of aesthetic discernment that affects our choices in clothes, music, furnishings and so on.[1] Hence, taste is a function of both personal perceptions and social mores.

Our notions of taste are highly influential in the judgements we make. Things that violate our sense of propriety, be they works of art, modes of behaviour or styles of dress, we speak of as 'being in poor taste'. Those who make choices that differ significantly from our own sense of taste sometimes leave us bewildered, exemplified by the common expression, 'there's no accounting for taste'.

This highlights two important considerations for design. Firstly, judgements of taste are related to the conventions of social groups. Secondly, these judgements lead us to categorize – and subsequently accept, reject or be indifferent to – the artefacts in our material culture.

Convention and creativity

The alliance of taste with the conventions of social groupings means that inherent to our personal notions of good taste is a predisposition to aesthetic expressions that conform to established norms. Consequently, our acceptance of designs that embody new sensibilities and considerations may be impeded. For this reason, many highly creative and innovative people have scorned notions of 'good taste'; Pablo Picasso called it 'the enemy of creativeness'.[2]

For the design professions, notions of good taste can impose a straightjacket of conformity that hinders the development of new directions. If we are to advance design in ways that can more readily embrace important contemporary issues, it becomes necessary to place greater emphasis than is currently evident on exploratory and critical practices that challenge norms and demonstrate alternatives. When the results of such practices enter the public arena, through exhibition, publication and the internet, the unfamiliar becomes familiar and thence part of the milieu or 'norms' of material culture against which people make their judgements of taste and aesthetic discrimination. Hence, one role of critical design is to challenge aesthetic conventions that are linked to damaging practices; in doing so it can make an important contribution to positive change.

Convention, discriminating judgements and prejudice

The relationship between taste and our allegiances to particular social groupings leads to a further consideration. It is an unfortunate but common tendency within human society to associate the discriminating judgements that are influenced by these allegiances with a sense of cultural superiority. Notions of good taste are closely related to ideas of social merit and elitism. For example, Hughes has outlined the tastes and habits of social distinction that became prevalent during the settlement of Australia.[3] In the early years of colonization, the free settlers and 'upper crust' tended to place considerable value on activities, foodstuffs and products that set them apart from convicts and poorer settlers. Convicts went to the beach, washed in the sea and their skin was tanned by a life of outdoor labour. Consequently, free settlers avoided the beach, did not swim in the sea and it was especially important for women to maintain a pale complexion. Convicts ate fresh fish and salt meat, so free settlers ate salt fish and fresh meat – to do otherwise would have been considered in very poor taste. Carey[4] has suggested that for some, especially adherents of high art, taste is so strongly linked to self-esteem that it is virtually impossible to separate personal identity from a sense of superiority over those with 'lower' tastes. Similarly, O'Doherty[5] has criticized the exclusivity of high art audiences with accusations of social elitism and intellectual snobbery. By contrast, Hughes[6] is quite frank about being elitist when it comes to aesthetic discrimination, and Scruton,[7] in a discussion about kitsch, is particularly disparaging when he alludes to the easily assimilated choices of the 'steaming herd'.

In terms of the relationship of taste to contemporary design concerns, it is perhaps enough to recognize that those who tend to enjoy what is regarded as high art and the more avant-garde examples of design have usually been privileged with a certain education about that genre – be it in literature, painting, music or design. Such work is not the readily understood world of popular culture. Indeed, the very intention of the more advanced forms, such as the avant-garde, is to be unorthodox and experimental in order to challenge conventions, provoke discussion and influence ideas. Appreciation of this type of work requires more practised, nuanced and demanding consideration, and the rewards it offers require time, effort, pertinent education and inclination.[8] Many people are simply preoccupied with other activities and interests and may have neither the opportunity nor the appetite for such pursuits. This is not to say that considered critique is not valuable and important. However, it is entirely inappropriate to bolster one's own views and social place through overblown rhetoric and a language of exclusivity that is too often derisive of the preferences of others.

Despite these arguments for or against popular culture and 'higher' forms, it is clear that tastes and preferences span a broad range. If design is to make any serious inroads into ameliorating the severely detrimental effects of production and consumption, it must not only be capable of spanning this range but special attention must be given to those more popular forms that are so often vilified by cultural critics. Indeed, if it is to become more relevant to locale and to cultural preferences – vital aspects of sustainability, identity and personal meaning – it will have to be capable of accommodating a wide variety of values, priorities and tastes. Design has to explore and develop directions that are flexible enough to absorb such diversity, but without compromising sustainable principles. New directions are especially important in those sectors undergoing rapid technological change, particularly consumer electronics. The success of these products is often due in large part to their aesthetic attributes. They are seen as 'cool', which is simply another way of saying that they conform to one's sense of taste. Here, design is being used to enhance the market appeal of products that are inherently short-lived and damaging. The challenge for the discipline is to employ its creative and critical skills to take product design in new, more constructive and more meaningful directions.

Taste and mass-produced products

The mass-production of consumer goods requires large audiences for the same kind of thing. This means that the design of the product must appeal to a wide spectrum of tastes. This is considered essential, not only because of the economic necessities of capital intensive production, but also because of the economic aspirations of companies and their desire to maximize growth and shareholder profit. To meet these needs, the outer aspect of mass-market products, as defined by the industrial designer, tends to be of a type. Things begin to look the same – they are generally inoffensive, acceptable to most, even boring.[9] Furthermore, it is implicit within the current production system that the designer of such products will be physically, culturally and economically 'removed' from the people who will actually be using them. There is a distancing from the particularities of place and local culture because of the system in which design exists. Consequently, there is both an assumption and an imposition of 'taste' within the process.

When it comes to the promotion and marketing of these goods, suggestions of social elitism and exclusivity are, somewhat paradoxically, interwoven with popular preferences and tastes in order to encourage consumerism. So, even though mass-produced products tend to be uniform and bland and have to be affordable to many, their marketing often suggests privileged lifestyles and exclusivity. The implication being that one's expression of good taste, through the purchase of the product, somehow aligns the purchaser with such lifestyles.

Setting aside the patent hollowness of such connotations, the constrained homogeneity of contemporary product aesthetics is characterized by glossy perfection, newness and impeccable surfaces that are extremely vulnerable and, therefore, inevitably fleeting. Also, due to the methods and materials used in their design and production, there is a remoteness and inscrutability to many contemporary products. They lack warmth and character and are largely impervious to cultural difference and local expression. Nevertheless, advertising and lifestyle magazines promote these offerings as the height of good taste. Generally absent from such accounts, however, is any critique or discussion of the social and environmental ramifications of their production and use, not least of which is the continuance of a culture of dissatisfaction and inordinate waste based on transient novelty. Within this culture, there is heavy reliance on the power of the initial visual impression of the product, which has a major influence on our judgement. The designer Richard Seymour has succinctly summed up its potency. Referring to the work of psychologists, he suggests that judgements about products are made almost instantaneously and a design that is capable of making an emotional tie spurs the viewer to make three subconscious statements, namely: 'I like it. I want it. What is it?'.[10] Such preoccupations within contemporary product design, tied as they are to impact and enticement, conflict with more enduring understandings of beauty and they highlight the need to consider further the relationships between design, taste and human fulfilment.

Taste, beauty and the moral dimension

Notions of beauty have long been associated with goodness, virtue and truth. Throughout history, many artefacts of human creativity and design – from fine art, architecture and gardens to poetry and music – have been regarded as inspiring and in some way informed by and expressive of ethical or spiritual underpinnings.[11-15] Accordingly, in addition to any intrinsic merits, it seems that aesthetic discrimination must be based, in part, on our knowledge about the artefact, what Muelder Eaton has termed its extrinsic qualities,[16] and the relationship of these qualities to our understandings of goodness and truth.

33

Knowledge about an artefact can affect how we see, experience and respond to it. If we learn that a painting by an artist we admire is a fake, this knowledge will diminish our view of it. Such a revelation affects and, justifiably, alters how we see the painting because fakery is a form of deception and is considered morally reprehensible. The singer Brian Ferry, who studied art at the University of Newcastle under Richard Hamilton,[17] was once criticized for comments he made during an interview in which he praised the aesthetic effect of the mass marches and flags of Hitler's regime. He later apologized, explaining that his remarks were made entirely from an art history point of view.[18] However, it is unreasonable to think that Nazi banners and marches can be seen purely in terms of their formal artistic qualities; these spectacles and regalia cannot be separated from their meaning. If aesthetics is linked to notions of goodness, truth, love and higher meaning, then clearly something cannot be seen as beautiful while also being known to be a symbol of heinous crimes and malevolence, at least not within this traditional understanding of beauty. From this perspective, judgements of beauty and taste are inseparable from knowledge about the artefact under consideration.

This relationship of beauty and taste to our ideas of goodness and virtue is highly relevant to the ways in which we advance our understandings of design and to the processes we employ in producing our material culture. There is a moral dimension to taste and beauty that is too often obfuscated in the one-sided rhetoric of product marketing. The social exploitation, environmental damage and culture of discontent associated with contemporary consumerism belie the aesthetic perfection of today's industrially designed products and point to a moral vacuum at the heart of our globalized production system. It is a system in which decision-makers are too often indifferent to its damaging, potentially ruinous, practices. The following example is symptomatic of a more general malaise. A prominent New York industrial designer recently responded to a question about the current challenges facing designers and the problems associated with contemporary products by saying: 'We produce more and more for consumer lifestyles, so I try not to think about it too much.'[19]

Design after taste

It becomes apparent that taste plays an important role in our judgements about material culture. It is associated with social distinctiveness and notions of elitism and can be used in very manipulative ways to encourage consumerism. Although it is often a highly dynamic characteristic of modern culture, it can also impede creativity and the advancement of design in directions that address contemporary concerns. However, it is also the case that the dominant characteristic of taste is outer appearance and it is here that an opportunity exists for designers to move beyond the vagaries of styling to address substantial issues. New forms of functional objects that represent different values, different processes and address contemporary concerns in significant ways will require different kinds of visual language. Design must develop to reflect these new sensibilities. In doing so, it can employ the influential effects of appearance and taste to both embody and convey new priorities.

Design for sustainability does not necessarily imply any particular type of product aesthetic, in fact quite the opposite. The relationship of sustainability to localization, cultural expression and use of regionally available skills, knowledge and resources suggests a diversity of expression that is concomitant with local preferences and capacity. In addition – and contrary to the current uniformity of product appearance that relies so heavily on 'newness' – design must also embrace the aging of products, the accumulation of meaning over time and more profound notions of attachment and empathy.

Today, design is part of a system that produces and markets discreet, beguiling, short-lived, usually unrepairable products. Clearly, such a system is highly damaging and incredibly wasteful. Design must therefore contribute to the development of products that are capable of being continually adapted and upgraded. And, as we saw in Chapter 2, this can support a system in which local resources, local capacity and cultural and personal preferences can play a far greater role. Such a system would yield forms of material culture that are less wasteful and better able to accommodate differences in conditions, needs and culture.

A system in which everyday functional objects are in continual state of adaptation and revision, and that is informed by social and environmental responsibilities, has significant implications for design. Among other things, design priorities must be amenable to varying degrees of change, continuity, ephemerality and endurance – and all these have implications for 'taste'. It would be simplistic and even counterproductive to merely design products to last longer; needs change and evolve, while advancements in technology can offer new functional benefits as well as more efficient use of materials and energy. Instead, approaches are required that explore a variety of routes for developing a material culture that is capable of being continuously revised and renewed, and that seamlessly integrates older, still useful elements with new. Designs can be developed that allow elements to be maintained, renewed and reworked in order to sustain a product's value, both in terms of its functionality and its visual attributes. Other approaches can explore ways of revaluing the plethora of out-of-fashion but still functional products that are so prevalent in modern society. Such products can be regarded as a resource and an opportunity for creative design. For one thing, they provide fertile ground for coming to terms with product aging. Older, unfashionable products offer a challenge to designers to develop imaginative frameworks that either overcome these shortcomings in the initial design, or are able to find a valued place for such products within contemporary material culture. Without such developments, today's 'cool' products will simply be added to the ever-growing waste pile, only to be replaced with the next new thing.

Together with my research students, I have explored several of these directions, and various propositional designs have been developed. The examples included

35

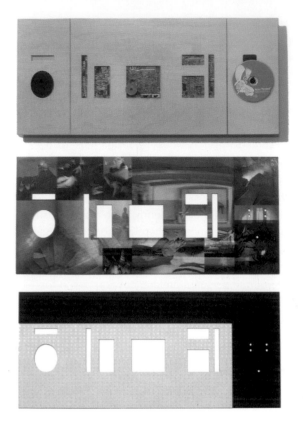

Figure 4.1 (a, b, c)
'Panel Play'
conceptual music product designs
by Çagla Dogan
courtesy of Çagla Dogan

here demonstrate that sustainable principles can be addressed in very different ways. They also show that preferences of taste and details of product appearance can be highly variable, ranging from clean minimalism to decorative kitsch, without compromising sustainable principles. Indeed, this diversity in product appearance – which can be locally adapted to suit local sensibilities – is to be welcomed as an important aspect of progressive design.

'Panel Play' (Figure 4.1) is a conceptual design for a music player. A rectangular panel, which can be made from locally available sheet-stock materials such as plywood, acrylic or MDF, is pierced by a series of apertures. The size of the panel and the arrangement of the apertures are highly variable; the functional circuitry is mounted on the reverse side, portions of which are revealed through the apertures, which are fitted with clear acrylic windows. When elements of the circuitry need replacing they can be easily changed, and the simplicity of the design allows variations in the size of substitute circuitry to be readily accommodated. The surface of the panel can be treated in many different ways, to suit individual tastes or to be expressive of cultural mores. Hence, this design integrates, in a flexible manner, mass-produced functional elements with locally

Figure 4.2 (a,b)
'Continuity in Diversity'
*one of a series of designs to reinstate
older families of products,
by Anne Marchand
courtesy of Anne Marchand*

produced expressive elements, both of which can be incrementally maintained and upgraded. The fundamental concept is based on sustainable principles but the appearance is highly adaptable.

A different approach is illustrated in the next example, 'Continuity in Diversity' (Figure 4.2). This design is part of a series that explores how older products can be reinstated through locally achievable design interventions. The emphasis here is on families of objects – in this case, chairs. An assortment of old, battered, low-value dining chairs are given aesthetic continuity through the design of a simple slip-cover for the back of each chair. Figure 4.2a illustrates how this addition transforms a diverse assortment into a useful collection or set. Front view and rear view photographs of one of the chair backs have been printed onto each side of the slip covers. The lower parts of the chairs are still visible, revealing their differences and something of their scarred history, the upper parts are covered to provide continuity. Thus, a simple, low-tech, but imaginative design intervention that uses relatively few materials enables an assortment of old products to be reinstated and revalued.

This example reveals an aspect of design for sustainability that is perhaps a little uncomfortable for designers. In terms of sustainability, the main design contribution is the development of an adaptable, locally achievable concept for creating aesthetic continuity among disparate, used products; the designer has developed other, similar concepts for drinking glasses, tableware and cutlery. However, for this concept to take effect and have impact, the particular aesthetic treatment applied to the covers has to be relinquished by the designer and handed over to others at the local level, so that it can be adapted to suit local preferences. The treatment shown in Figure 4.2a can be judged as having aesthetic merit because it is consistent with the idea of 'chair' and is an artful and light-hearted way of providing visual continuity. One can appreciate that the choice is not arbitrary but intentional to the reinstatement and renewal of the aged objects. But this need not be the case. It is perfectly possible to give the concept a very different appearance, without compromising its sustainable basis. Figure 4.2b shows the same concept, but in this case the rendition is sentimental and kitsch, with no reference to 'chair'. This again illustrates that design for sustainability can address product aging, endurance and aesthetic revision while simultaneously spanning a wide range of tastes.

The final examples are based around a simple, locally producible frame, constructed from softwood timber and sheetstock. 'Winelight' (Figure 4.3a) combines re-used bottles with standard, off-the-shelf electrical parts to create a wall sconce rendered in a crisp, clean, minimalist aesthetic. Again, this concept can be executed in a manner that has a very different appearance, without affecting any of the sustainable principles, as illustrated in Figure 4.3b.

Despite their apparent simplicity, these examples represent a complex and substantial readjustment of design and production to better address sustainable concerns. They integrate old and new, innovation and continuity, and mass-production, regional sourcing and local production. Aged or re-used products become elements within a larger composition that constrains the field so that they can be seen anew. And aesthetic expression is achieved through a combination of mass-produced elements and local involvement. They demonstrate that a system of design and production capable of accommodating local contributions and continual change can include a variety of sustainable principles in the conceptual basis of the object. Product appearance is an aspect of this – both in reconceptualizing our notions of 'products' and in being flexible enough to accommodate a wide variety of visual treatments, to appeal to a broad range of

Figures 4.3 (a,b)
'Winelight'
*an exploration of product re-use
and localization, by the author*

preferences and tastes. Beyond any particular visual treatment however, there is a deeper notion of aesthetic experience that responds to the fundamental basis of the artefact – a basis that is perceived by the viewer or user through its overall visual construct, the materials employed and the tangible aspects of the object. In addition, if the sustainable basis of the object is known, this can also affect one's appreciation and aesthetic experience of it.

Conclusions

Design for sustainability requires that far greater attention be paid to locale and distributed production and reproduction, compared to current globalized, and evidently highly damaging, modes of manufacturing and distribution. Forms of design and production that allow products to be continually renewed, locally or regionally, offer opportunities for products to be manifested in new ways, where old and new components are combined and where, periodically, products are technically and aesthetically updated. In this way, everyday functional objects can become more permanent, but ever-evolving, elements of our material culture. In turn, such products would not only represent less profligate modes of providing for our material needs but, through their added endurance, they would also be capable of acquiring new layers of meaning and value.

Clearly, such concepts require a rather different design and production system from the one we have today. Rather than simply providing a continuous, but highly wasteful, supply of new, mass-produced products to local retail outlets, there would be a need for a more distributed system. Local investment and the development of supply chains to provide particular, especially technological, components, would allow product production, maintenance and upgrading at a local or regional level. Moreover, within such a scenario, design would have to relinquish its acquired role as an arbiter of taste, because distributed acts of creativity would enable products to be continually defined and redefined at the local level, to suit local needs and preferences. In this way, products would become more varied and taste would be more diversified and in a continual state of flux.

Given the urgency and import of sustainability and the damaging legacy of mass-production, such a direction for product design is to be welcomed. Product design has the opportunity to reach beyond its traditional preoccupation with the 'look' of products to develop functional objects that are socially and environmentally responsible and, potentially, more enduring and more meaningful contributions to material culture.

5
Extant Objects
seeing through
design

Looking is a marvellous thing of which we know but little. Through it
we are turned absolutely towards the outside, but when we are most of
all so, things happen in us that have waited longingly to be observed;
and while they reach completion in us ... their significance grows up in
the object outside.

Rainer Maria Rilke

In re-imagining some of our most fundamental notions of material culture, the
purpose of design has to become far more compatible with sufficiency and with
conserving and valuing natural resources and existing products. To this end,
design can be directed towards creating 'new' products that enable us to re-see
and re-appreciate. Such a direction can create new opportunities, especially
in terms of the local economy and local employment. In this way, design and
manufacturing can assimilate the environmental and social consequences of
production and consumerism in a more substantial, constitutive manner than has
been evident to date. This would take design beyond style-based, technology-
led novelty and in a direction that is more meaningful and apposite. If our
conceptions of manufactured goods are ever to become compatible with these
broader and deeper obligations, changes must occur throughout the design and

production system. In stimulating such changes, designers have a responsibility to envision alternative directions and to make new possibilities more tangible and more comprehensible. Designers can develop a range of incremental adjustments or they can offer more radical responses. Both approaches are discussed here. This is followed by design explorations that emphasize the second while incorporating elements of the first. The basis of these explorations is described and several propositional objects are presented to illustrate the ideas.

This discussion and its accompanying design work extend the ideas presented earlier but with a particular focus on still-useful electronic goods. These are the products that are being so rapidly discarded and replaced – because minor technological advancements render them less useful and/or because they are no longer considered desirable for aesthetic reasons. The concepts included here represent ways of revaluing such objects, thereby increasing their useful life and, in the process, mitigating the need for replacement.

Design and sustainability

The continuous production of consumer goods with new aesthetic expressions, accompanied by relentless marketing campaigns, is intended to create a sense of dissatisfaction with one's possessions, leading to the replacement of older products with new.[1] Even though the older product may still be perfectly serviceable, it becomes prematurely obsolete because, over time, its appearance grows shabby and outdated and because fresh, new styles are made available. While the production and consumption of new products satisfies economic objectives, spurs business growth and gives temporary pleasure to the user, there are a multitude of well-documented problems associated with this conception of material culture that render it fundamentally unsustainable; sustainability, in its basic form, being simultaneously attendant to environmental, ethical and economic considerations.[2]

Ironically 'design for sustainability', as the name implies, is often pursued by designing shiny new products – albeit products that in some respects address sustainable principles. Perhaps they use materials that are more benign or incorporate up-to-date, cleaner technologies. In recent years, a number of incremental strategies have been developed to improve the environmental performance and, in some cases, the social ramifications associated with current manufacturing; these include The Natural Step,[3] Cradle-to-Cradle design,[4] Product Life Cycle Assessment,[5] and Factor 10.[6] Such programmes offer pragmatic solutions for modifying current practices in order to reduce the negative impacts of product design and production. They are important models for implementing improvements within the existing system. However, incremental change models can often result in even more, but slightly 'improved', products being manufactured – using more resources and more energy. So this interpretation of design for sustainability, while it may contribute to the improvement of products over time, has some inherent problems. To varying degrees, such approaches

42

tend to endorse and bolster, rather than challenge, the current consumerist model of a totally commodified material culture – a model that is manifestly destructive. Within this system, product marketing, of which product design has always been a part,[7] is based on creating dissatisfaction with what we have. It fosters discontentment and tells us, unremittingly, to want more and that we deserve more. It promotes consumerism and desire for novelty, and gives rise to disquiet and yearnings that can never be sated. When we fall victim to this, we can never find happiness; happiness, in many traditions, being synonymous with the notion of human satisfaction.[8] Thus, it could be said that our contemporary market system sells, more than anything else, discontent and unhappiness.

Incremental improvement models do not address this problem in any significant way. They may ameliorate certain negative effects but they do not offer a way out of a production system that is not only environmentally damaging but also socio-culturally and personally corrosive.

It is important to acknowledge that there are many new developments in science and technology that can lead to genuine and extremely valuable changes. However, the concern here is with design and the role of the product designer. In the current system, a vast range of products are continually being restyled and repackaged, perhaps with the addition of some relatively trivial updates and features to grab our attention. This kind of design can boost profits but, in the context of sustainability and of more profound understandings of human happiness, it represents an immoderate use of resources, inordinate amounts of waste and pollution, and the continuance of a pervasive culture of dissatisfaction.

43

A changing role for design

If, as I have suggested, the creation of new products is part of the problem rather than the solution, then what is left for the designer? Does the designer still have a contribution to make? On the face of it, and within the conventional parameters of product design, it would seem that the answer would be no, or at most, relatively little. However, if we are prepared to broaden our horizons and think of designers not simply as the creators of novel products, but as creative individuals who think about and contribute to the nature, meaning and design of material culture, then they will have an important role to play in reconceptualizing and redefining our notions of functional objects. Potentially, the creative abilities of the designer can be critical in a world where excessive consumption and waste are leading us down a self-destructive path. As I pointed out in Chapter 3, in developing this role, design within academia can make a significant and reflective contribution, removed as it is from the pressures of the business environment.

If designers are to face the challenge of sustainability in a more substantive manner, they must question the ways in which they design, the assumptions they make, and the products of design. Some academics and designers are already doing this – by developing innovative strategies and new understandings of the function and contribution of the designer. Several of these can be seen as more fundamental explorations of our understanding of material culture, compared to the incremental approaches mentioned above. For example, Wood et al have proposed the concept of 'attainable utopias' for envisioning a systemic shift,[9] Scharmer has developed 'theory U' for revolutionary change,[10] and Manzini, Meroni et al have developed 'sustainable everyday' strategies for 'creative communities' that allow people to become more involved and self-determining in the development of their products and services.[11] Compared to incremental improvement models, these approaches are more demanding, more difficult to envision and often less comfortable. They suggest new priorities and, in doing so, they challenge contemporary conventions and assumptions, including our assumptions about production and consumption.

Integral to many of these more radical approaches is the use of design as a way of thinking about, developing and manifesting alternative ways of living, together with different notions of material culture. Hence, it is through the creative design process itself that designers and design-centred academics, often working with people from other fields, can imagine and visualize potential change. By confronting the relationships between contemporary products, consumerism and environmental and social impacts, designers can explore new directions and develop alternative ways of conceiving and defining the functional object.

Extant design

44

Here I explore a direction for product design that leans towards these more radical approaches. I consider our relationship with objects and seek to develop concepts that offer an alternative to the novelty-based, voguish notion of design that is still so prevalent. The perception of designer as master of chic is becoming increasingly inadequate and irresponsible. It serves only to maintain product design as a branch of advertising and a spur to consumerism.[12] In doing so, it prevents it from becoming a more substantive discipline – one capable of applying its particular knowledge and skills to important contemporary issues. Even though this conventional notion of design may allow it to contribute to the continuous growth model of market economics, in terms of sustainability it creates a host of undesirable impacts. Moreover, the yearnings it helps stimulate do little to enhance our sense of fulfilment and personal happiness.[13]

Another way of thinking about design, and the products of design, can be based on *acceptance of what is*, rather than continuing to propagate the new, the novel and the short-lived. The first of the three 'r's associated with environmental responsibility is *reduce*, which can be applied to consumerism as much as to the use of materials and energy in particular products. A reduction in consumerism is logically related to the second of the three 'r's, *re-use*. If we reduce consumerism, then we have to re-use what we already have. Reducing and re-using are both more important than the third 'r' of *recycling*, yet it is recycling that has received far more attention. This is because recycling can be readily accommodated in our current design and production system; consciences can be soothed while maintaining 'business as usual'. Reduction and re-use require a much more drastic reassessment of the nature and norms of contemporary material culture.

In addition to reduction and re-use, the design examples included here take into account a variety of associated sustainable principles such as product longevity, localization and self-determination, and they recognize the social and environmental costs of large scale product manufacturing, distribution and waste.[14–16] These various considerations are interlinked and directly related to how we design and the production system we design for. They raise questions about the nature and meaning of design, the place of design and our understanding of what it means to be a designer in a world straining under the pressures of consumerism.

Hence, these propositional objects represent explorations and discrete manifestations of reduction and re-use. Each includes a product that had been discarded due to its low perceived value. Two of the concepts also incorporate new microchip-based components that allow the older, technologically outmoded products to find renewed usefulness. In the third example, an aesthetically dated, but still functioning product is simply re-presented, allowing it to be seen anew and re-valued. The fourth example is a wall-mounted composition created from two aesthetically outmoded products. All these concepts integrate old with new, and link mass-production with the benefits of reduction and re-use. Through modest design interventions, older, rejected products are given new life and, in doing so, the need for product replacement is eliminated. Thus, all four propositions contribute to re-use and reduction, and all have been designed in a way that is suited to the diversity and constraints of local production.

It is through these kinds of design explorations that the designer is able to encounter and grapple with issues of aesthetic obsolescence, product revitalization, moderation in resource use, waste reduction, localization and self-reliance. In doing so, questions are raised about the fundamental nature of products and their relationship to sustainability and ideas of human fulfilment. These issues are directly confronted within the creative, synthesizing process of *designing*. It is only through such practice-based inquiries that design can bring this creative core into play. However, it is vital that it does so if it is to make an effective, discipline-appropriate contribution to these contemporary concerns. Practice-based inquiry can yield concepts and prototypes that exemplify different priorities and values, and which stand outside current norms of newness and novelty. Through such means, the discipline of design can play its part in developing functional objects that are more meaningful, more lasting and can contribute to a culture of moderation and acceptance.

Explorations in extant design

The approach taken in this present series of works begins to illustrate aspects of the changing role of product design – one that reaches beyond the priorities of unfettered production and consumption. Today, design has a responsibility to wrestle with a host of important contemporary concerns and use its creative

45

skills to envision a more benign and ultimately more satisfying and meaningful conception of material culture.

The focus of these explorations is on what we might term 'the lost products of contemporary society'. These are unwanted consumer goods that are regarded as out of date but which are not yet old enough to have any sentimental value as retro objects or antiques. These are the products that are so readily cast aside and replaced. Using the discarded, finding a place for the rejected and reusing the broken are ways of treasuring, honouring and respecting not only the resources of the Earth, but also the time, thought and ingenuity that have already gone into these objects. Exploring how to use them again, beyond their first use, is a way of further justifying and valuing their presence in the world. It may seem unfashionable to say so, but it is a form of appreciation and a way of respecting, even sanctifying, the world, its people and its resources. More than this, re-presenting older, existing products in a new light can allow us to accept them *as they are*, and despite their unfashionable styling and their wear and tear, be content with them, to see them as *enough*.

Figure 5.1
'Replay'
a personal MP3 player linked to a
re-used, old-fashioned cassette stereo,
set on a white frame with shelf to form
a 'functional composition'

There are admirable models in the world of art for these types of explorations, from the ready-mades of Duchamp in the early years of the 20th century,[17] to the work of Rauschenberg in which found objects are incorporated into sculptural pieces. Rauschenberg's work in particular, while not addressing utility, nevertheless salvages and resurrects the discarded, the abused and the lowly objects that are so carelessly abandoned in today's affluent societies.[18]

The first artefact in this set of exercises, 'Replay' (Figure 5.1), links a personal MP3 player to a re-used, old-fashioned cassette stereo. These are composed on a rectangular panel with shelf. In this example, the black casing of the original stereo is matched with black electrical cords and MP3 player and contrasted against a stark white background, resulting in a crisp, clean figure-ground relationship. However, compositions will vary, depending on the available recovered products, and can be adapted according to local needs and aesthetic preferences. 'Replay 2' (Figure 5.2) utilizes similar elements but takes a very different direction. Here, a simulated woodgrain finish on the plastic casing of

Figure 5.2
'Replay 2'
the Replay concept can be adapted to various old products found locally. Here, an old wood-grain effect radio becomes a speaker unit for a personal stereo

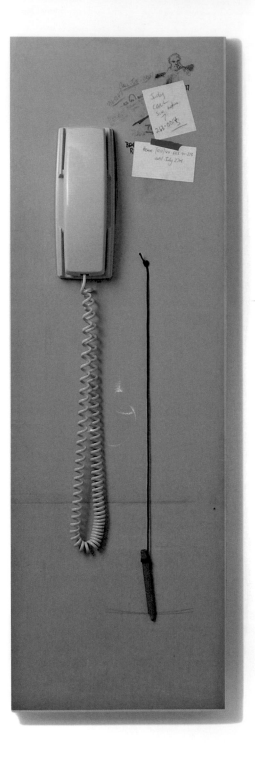

Figure 5.3
'Re-Call'
aesthetically outdated wallphone mounted
on a painted panel

an old radio is set against a wallpaper of similar vintage. An iPod is held in an old envelope, which is pinned to the backboard along with a period postcard. The resulting composition illustrates that the approach can be customized at the local level to accommodate a wide variety of older products. This is an essential aspect of the design concept. These kinds of discarded objects come in all shapes and sizes and are widely distributed. Therefore, any design propositions that seek

49

Figure 5.4
'Re-Call 2'
an old-fashioned wallphone and radio
composed on a white frame with shelf

to incorporate such items must be highly flexible and be achievable at the local level. 'Re-Call' (Figure 5.3) is an unfashionable wallphone mounted on a painted rectangle, which evokes a previous time and place. In this case, no additional technologies have been added and no modifications have been made to the original product. It has simply been presented anew within the confines of the painted panel. Similarly, 'Re-Call 2' (Figure 5.4) incorporates an old-fashioned wallphone, here composed on a white panel alongside a radio of similar vintage.

In these examples, the objects are mounted on specially built armatures that serve to, quite literally, reframe the outdated products. In effect, this places them on a pedestal, separates them from their surroundings and recontextualizes them so that they may be seen and appreciated anew. The approach is one in which the individual, re-used objects become elements within a larger whole. In this way, the emphasis is shifted – the focus is no longer on an out-of-date, imperfect old product but instead is on the entire composition. The re-used objects are not disguised or refinished to hide their previous use or their unfashionable styling. Within the larger compositions, they 'work' as they are and for what they are. Thus, they attain a renewed dignity and a new value by becoming integral components of a contemporary composition.

These explorations are intended to contribute to the development of a new role for design – a role that is more attuned to the needs of people, society and the environment. These examples are not presented as viable commercial products, but simply as small steps along a road of rediscovering a new, perhaps more valid and more profound role for design – one that stands outside the destructive system of immoderate production and waste that has become so dominant. The approach also implies a rather different design process than is common today in industrial design; the process here being more akin to collage or assemblage, rather than the *ex nihilo* methods of contemporary practice.

It is pertinent to point out that this approach does not ignore technological development or innovation, instead it attempts to use it where it seems appropriate to do so. In the first two concepts, the re-used products have been modified to allow the use of MP3 technology. In this way, the benefits of the MP3, which dispenses with the need for cassette or compact disc production, with their attendant packaging and distribution, are combined with the existing and still serviceable amplifier and speakers of the older product. This is a more moderate solution than discarding the old product and replacing it with a new speaker system designed specifically for the MP3 player. The older product is adapted, re-used and, through re-presentation, revalued.

This example differs in intention from somewhat similar explorations carried out by Droog designers Wolf, Bader and Oschatz. In their 'Bootleg Objects' series, classic designs from the past were updated to use MP3 technology. The chosen products included Dieter Rams' 1962 Braun Audio, a 1973 Bang & Olufsen system and the Technics SP1210 record deck from 1980.[19] All these products are now recognized for their design excellence and therefore already have value; these products were chosen precisely because they are regarded as classics. Hence, they are not typical of the kinds of products that end up in charity stores or landfill. They have passed the transitional period that renders products undesirable and have reached an age and a rarity that makes them, once again, sought-after items.

By contrast, the products used here have no such design cachet. This is perhaps best illustrated by the cassette player in the 'Replay' composition (Figure 5.1). This product was selected precisely because it was no longer wanted. Its cassette technology was outdated. It was no longer regarded as aesthetically pleasing or fashionable, and it had no 'retro-chic'.

In summary, the functional compositions featured in this chapter attempt to:

- **See** objects as they are – by re-presenting familiar products in a new frame, through design interventions that can be achieved modestly and locally.
- **Accept** objects as they are – with their faded, unfashionable aesthetic and their scars of use.
- **Value** objects as they are – for the benefits they still offer.
- **Respect** objects as they are because in doing so we show respect for the thought, ingenuity, time and effort that have gone into their design. We also show respect for the resources and energy that have already been used in their production.
- **Moderate** our acquisitiveness – by re-presenting and revaluing what we already have, rather than simply discarding and replacing older objects with new.
- **Slow** the culture of distraction that acquisitiveness engenders. A distracted culture, *ipso facto*, cannot be self-reflective and this, in turn, tends to reinforce the present model of consumerism.

Ultimately, however, these compositions have to speak for themselves – the language of design is not words, it is not arguments and criteria. It is simply design itself. Words can take us some of the way but the artefacts themselves have to do the rest.

51

6
Sermons in Stones
argument and
artefact for
sustainability

And this our life exempt from public haunt
Finds tongues in trees, books in the running brooks,
Sermons in stones and good in every thing.

William Shakespeare

Transforming our modes of living away from our highly consumptive lifestyles and
towards ways that are both preferred and less damaging, will not only require
considerable changes in our activities but also a shift in our attitudes, values and
priorities. What would be the nature of such a transformation and what would
it imply for our approaches to product design and production? In this chapter, I
contemplate these questions and illustrate their potential implications through the
creation of a symbolic artefact. This functional object is not only entirely consistent
with sustainable principles in its production, use and eventual disposal, its
essential purpose is linked to profound understandings of human meaning.

The dominance of technology in contemporary society presents a particular
challenge with respect to sustainability and raises a number of concerns.
Technological development is inextricably connected to consumerism, growth,
the promises of industrial capitalism and our understandings of 'progress'. Here,
an alternative perspective is explored based on 'being' rather than 'having',

which is rooted in long-standing philosophical and spiritual traditions. This places sustainability firmly in the here and now – rather than seeing it as a goal to work towards in the distant future. The relationship between changing our activities in the world and inner change, in our attitudes and perspectives, is related directly to sustainability and linked to the role of 'the local'. These concepts are then translated into a set of considerations for the product designer and applied through the development, design and production of the illustrative artefact. The result is a functional object that can be considered sustainable and meaningful, and the issues it raises offer a basis for rethinking many of our priorities and approaches to product design. Thus, the process of creating the object and the object itself both serve to inform the discussion and throw light on the relationship between functional objects, sustainability and deeper considerations of personal meaning and fulfilment.

Techno-utopia

One of the most emblematic features of our current age is the prominence given to technological development. It commands enormous efforts, resources and investments in our universities, in private corporations and in government priorities. Advanced technology fills the homes, cars and even the pockets of most people living in the affluent countries and, increasingly, in the less-economically developed countries. It is seen as a major factor in wealth creation, jobs, security, competitiveness and progress, and has become virtually synonymous with the term 'innovation'.

54

The development of technology is strongly linked to the potential for profit through the manufacture of consumer products – which in turn is linked to resource and energy use, waste and pollution and, all too often, social injustices. Hence, technological research and development are not neutral activities but are, in many ways, significant aspects of the sustainability question. As I mentioned in Chapter 5, 'sustainability' is generally understood to refer to social, environmental and economic concerns and their interrelationships. In addition, and as will become apparent in the discussions that follow, deeper questions of meaning and purpose will have to become much more central to this debate if significant, lasting and desirable change is to occur.

Advanced technologies have brought enormous benefits to many areas of our lives – from medical research to communications, and some new technologies help reduce environmental impacts by offering more energy efficient solutions and less polluting products. However, it must also be acknowledged that the emphasis given to the development of consumer goods based on advanced technologies, and their consequent production and global distribution, is creating severe environmental problems together with many social injustices and inequities.[1,2] Therefore, if we are to seriously address the challenge of sustainability, it will be important to consider the emphasis placed today on the development and proliferation of such consumer goods.

Furthermore, technological research and development tend to be well supported by government funding through research councils and regional development agencies. When preferential support is given to science and technology over, say, the arts and humanities (in the UK by a factor of more than twenty to one[3]), based on a rationale of creating competitive advantage, growth, jobs and wealth then, despite the benefits, there arises an imbalance in our priorities and our efforts — one in which instrumental value tends to be favoured over intrinsic value.

Unsustainable development

The relationships that exist between technological development, short-term government agendas and the production of short-lived, hi-tech consumer goods, all serve to encourage consumerism and reinforce a fundamentally unsustainable system. It is irrational to think that we can reduce our environmental impacts and advance social and economic well-being, equity and justice through unbridled development of increasingly sophisticated technologies. Within a free market, capitalist system, investment in research and development is only justified if it is likely to turn a profit in the future. This invariably means the commercialization of the technology through saleable products, often in the form of mass-produced consumer goods, which, in turn, intensifies environmental damage and is frequently associated with social exploitation. This route to economic prosperity and societal well-being is based on:

55

- the fallacious, increasingly precarious and damaging ideology of *continuous growth* – in production and consumption – and hence, too, in resource and habitat depletion, pollution, waste and human exploitation;[4]
- the misguided attempt to attain happiness through ever higher material standards of living; and
- aggressive competitiveness within a global economy.

To continue to pursue such methods only maintains the same kind of thinking that has characterized the past century or more. This is not innovative thinking. It is merely carrying on the convention of developing and producing ever new, often trivial and always fleeting consumer goods. At one time it may have been justified to produce any and every kind of product we could imagine as long as it created wealth and jobs. Today the cumulative impacts and harmful effects are only too evident, making the continuation of such practices increasingly difficult to support. However, the messages of marketing persistently tell us that we need these technological 'marvels', and the shrewd talent of the advertising industry is to even turn critique of consumerism into persuasive advertising copy. A collaboration between the UK department store Selfridges and American artist Barbara Kruger is one example,[5] where in-store banners boldly proclaim, 'Buy me, I'll change your life' and 'You want it, you buy it, you forget it' (Figure 6.1). Similarly, the US auto manufacturer Hummer, which received much criticism for its oversized vehicles aimed at the consumer market, once launched a TV commercial that focused on a man buying vegetarian produce who is later seen at the wheel of a Hummer, accompanied by the line 'Restore the balance'.[6] By employing irony and humour, such examples demonstrate the infinite adaptability of industrial capitalism, which allows it to undermine virtually any form of critique.[7]

Of course, a major objective of commercial corporations is to create and continually grow shareholder profit, and technology linked to consumerism has become a primary means for creating such profit. Governments usually support this, seeing it as positive for the economy. However, despite the profusion of 'green' rhetoric that emerges from corporations and governments alike, approaches based on continual growth in consumerism, resource exploitation and energy use are clearly at odds with any serious understanding of the term 'sustainability'.

Flawed perfection

When manufacturing is combined with marketing the result is often a technocratic version of societal well-being. The implicit message is that some kind of future state of sustainable perfection is actually achievable, where our environmental and social problems will be solved through the ingenious application of advanced, super-efficient, non-polluting technologies. Such a notion is plainly naïve and flies in the face of both logic and the teachings of all the major philosophical and wisdom traditions down the ages. Yet, the unwavering message of corporate commercialism is, in effect, that this product or that service will fulfil your dreams and make you happier.

These flawed notions are being taken ever further as corporate interests remorselessly create dissatisfaction and stimulate desire – from the gaudy trappings and superficial 'splendours' of the modern shopping mall (Figures 6.2– 6.4) to the increasingly exclusive and outlandish goods and services on offer. Both are meant to appeal to our vanities through their suggestions of elitism and status. At one international design conference I attended,[8] keynote presentations included a high performance electric sports car[9,10] and designs for the commercialization of space tourism.[11,12] While a high priced electric sports car may appear to address concerns about auto emissions, the problem is simply transferred from the exhaust pipe to the electricity generating station, which could be coal fired – creating carbon emissions, nuclear – creating a radioactive waste problem, or hydro – creating an environmental impact problem. Such exclusive products do little to seriously address environmental concerns but they do serve to stoke our desires and maintain our addiction-like behaviour towards consumption.[13,14] They also bring with them their own problems. In this case, for example, no mention was made of the relatively short life or the disposal problems associated with thousands of batteries. The space tourism presentation concentrated on the 'experience' being offered – the excitement of acceleration, three or four minutes of weightlessness, the views of Earth and stories to tell your grandchildren.

Such thrill rides, whether in a sports car or spacecraft, have little to do with fostering meaningful notions of contentment; instead they offer a false idea of happiness based on consumption. While such aspirational products, available only to the few, may cultivate vanity, envy and discontent, the proliferation of less expensive products creates even broader problems. For example, the launch of the world's cheapest car, by Indian automaker Tata Motors,[15] serves to further transform India into a high consumption society.

These kinds of products and services exacerbate already severe environmental problems – directly through their contribution to cumulative effects and indirectly through the dissatisfaction and cravings they foster.

Philosopher Charles Taylor explains that a particular characteristic of the modern, secularized worldview is that 'meaning' is sought through self-realization, which is based in concepts of progress, reason, freedom and so on. He suggests that, unlike in previous times where meaning was found in higher or transcendent understandings, in the modern world a sense of meaning in one's life is based in the idea that individual efforts can contribute to human progress across time. Thus, human efforts related to advancement and material progress have become central to contemporary notions of 'meaning'. Criticism of this relatively recent idea is rooted in the fear that our notions of progress yield only meaninglessness, either through an unexceptional sameness, a 'levelling down' of humanity or that the denial of the transcendent results in vacuousness – the threat of an empty life, inspiring 'nothing but ennui, a cosmic yawn'.[16]

Progress, meaning and unsustainability

This highlights some of the most fundamental problems associated with our contemporary efforts to address sustainability. Modernity, with its ideology of progress, sought to advance human happiness, meaning and fulfilment through industrialization and the consumption of material goods. Its rationalizations led to a severe attrition in traditional sources of meaning in most of the economically developed countries of the West and, as Northcott has pointed out, the imposition of this ideology on developing nations, through institutions such as the World Bank, has led to environmental and social destruction on a massive scale.[17] Pope Benedict XVI has expressed a similar view, suggesting that technical and material aid from the richer nations has pushed aside indigenous social structures, values and beliefs and imposed a technocratic mindset on developing countries.[18] Moreover, it is important to recognize that there is no evidence to support the implicit assumption of modernism that technological and material advancement is accompanied by moral progress – the industrialized genocide of World War II and the consequent advance of technology for arms development belie any such claims.[19]

Challenges to the assumptions of the modern view gave rise to postmodernity. On the one hand, this holds the promise of a renewed sense of meaning, through its apparent tolerance of diverse forms of expression, including religious expression and the acknowledgement of meaning via the transcendent. On the other hand it couches religion, along with other forms of expression, in relativism, thereby denying any claims to universal truth or authority[20] and rendering them banal and ineffectual; a factor that is not unrelated to the rise of fundamentalist reaction, both religious and secular.[21]

The undermining of modern assumptions about progress and the relativism of postmodernity has contributed to the emergence of what Beattie calls the 'voracious consumer' who constantly seeks 'novelty, innovation and change',[22] but who, in lacking a sense of overall meaning and purpose, is highly vulnerable to the persuasive messages of corporate marketing where meaning is always to be found in the *next* purchase.

Having or being

Neither modern notions of progress in general, nor technological progress in particular, can claim to have brought us closer to more sustainable ways of living; in fact, the evidence points in the opposite direction. Similarly, the multifarious and confused concerns of postmodernity mean that calls for more sustainable directions, for limiting the emissions associated with climate change and for improvements in social equity and justice, emerge from the very same government and business leaders who simultaneously espouse the mantra of growth and free trade and who, to achieve these goals, effectively promote 'voracious consumption'. There are inherent contradictions in such messages and in the perplexities created we simply continue our frenzied stripping of the planet. In the affluent countries especially, human well-being has become synonymous with the accumulation of products and, as people increasingly associate their sense of identity with what they own rather than who they are, '*having* takes precedence over *being*'.[23] When this is accompanied by a sharp rise in entertainment products, as has been the case in recent times, acquisition is combined with ever greater opportunities for distraction and atomization – further eroding a reflective sense of self within a larger, meaningful social context .

An emphasis on *having* rather than *being* and the dangers it holds for our welfare is echoed by theologians such as Williams, who says, 'There is something about Western modernity which really does eat away at the soul'.[24] Similarly, De Botton has said: 'Our minds are susceptible to the influence of external voices telling us what we require to be satisfied, voices that may drown out the faint sounds emitted by our souls and can distract us from the careful, arduous task of correctly tracing our priorities.'[25] Hence, the cult of 'progress' and opportunities for distraction from reflection, self-knowing and the search for meaning have become key features of our contemporary age. Both are linked to acquisitive lifestyles and, thus, to unsustainability.

Universities are not immune to the rhetoric of the times, indeed, as governments impose increasingly prescriptive measures on university research budgets, they have little choice but to toe the line if they are to secure funding.

Two recent university marketing strategies have proclaimed, 'It's not where you are, it's where you're going' and 'It's not where you are, it's where you want to be'.[26] Such slogans parallel commercial agendas that foster dissatisfaction with the 'now' by emphasizing the potential and allure of what's coming 'next'. These are unfortunate messages to be sending out to young people about to embark on their university careers – education is promoted as a means to some other end, rather than having merit as an end in and of itself. It is marketed solely as a ticket to a good job rather than for a love of learning. Such messages implicitly denigrate the value of the present, of living fully in the here and now. They also demonstrate how insidious the ideologies of our age have become – because if there is one institution in our society that should be examining, challenging and critiquing such assertions it is our universities. As Chesterton once put it: 'It is always easy to let the age have its head; the difficult thing is to keep one's own.'[27]

Another voice

Those who tell of a different way tend not to be politicians, business leaders, economists or technologists, but poets, artists, philosophers and those dedicated to more spiritual pursuits. This alternative path is represented in the Long Now project of artist and musician Brian Eno et al;[28,29] in the religious understandings of the 'eternal now' spoken of within monastic traditions;[30] it is alluded to in paintings such as *L'esperança del condemnat a mort 1-111* by Miró;[31] and in the words of Longfellow[32] when he writes:

> **Trust no future, howe'er pleasant!**
> **Let the dead past bury its dead!**
> **Act – act in the living present!**

Emphasis is placed on living fully in the reality of the present, rather than constantly anticipating or yearning for the next thing.

This suggests a rather different way of understanding sustainability – not as some future way of living to strive towards, but as something to address now – in our attitudes, thoughts and actions as individuals; in our *being* rather than our *having*. It challenges our assumptions, our desires and our behaviours. Living fully in the 'eternal' present is not about momentary thrill rides or continual consumption. As such, it represents a significant change in priorities and values. Undoubtedly, without such an 'internal' change we will be unprepared and unwilling to make the necessary systemic changes that are required; changes that could steer us away from our current highly consumptive and destructive behaviours. Indeed, if our contemporary modes of living really are environmentally unsustainable, then sooner or later we will have no choice but to change. However, without a shift in priorities and values such enforced change will be viewed as a continuous imposition of undesirable deprivations that inexorably impede our progress towards still-desired but increasingly elusive lifestyles.

59

Sustainability: values and localization

Sustainability does not simply represent a problem 'out there' to be fixed – through new technologies or legislation or policy. Without a clear sense of inner purpose and meaning such 'external' activities can, and do, create a host of contradictions. External change has to be accompanied and steered by inner change. As Armstrong has said: 'Unless there is some kind of spiritual revolution that can keep abreast of our technological genius, it is unlikely that we will save our planet. A purely rational education will not suffice'.[33]

Realistically, we cannot hope to reduce environmental degradation if we are not prepared to reduce our levels of consumption. This is only likely to occur if we can develop other ways of finding fulfilment that also provide for economic confidence and security. For such change to occur, we need to consider what it means to prioritize *being* over *having*, and the effect this might have on our ways of living.

Such notions are anything but new. Emphasis on living fully in the present, or 'being', has always been a principal teaching of the world's major philosophical and spiritual traditions. These traditions – from Lao Tsu to Thoreau and from Socrates to Gandhi – not only speak of inner development through selflessness and rejecting egocentric desires, they also teach that concern for wealth, status and possessions hinders 'inner' growth.[34] They are therefore completely consistent with contemporary sustainability concerns related to the damaging effects of consumerism. These teachings, however, could not be in starker contrast to today's corporate messages (see Table 6.1).

Despite their wisdom and their relationship to inner development, the 'narrow path' of which these teachings speak[35] has always been sidelined in the everyday busyness and business of society; striving for worldly comforts, distractions and personal gain too often takes precedence. In the past, the effects of such behaviours on the planet itself were relatively minor, even though they may have been socially or personally harmful. However, this is no longer the case. The drastic rise in urban populations over the past century, accompanied by massive growth in industrialization, mass marketing and mass consumerism, have contributed to environmental impacts that in recent times have become extremely serious in their projected implications.[36]

Thus, the teachings of the traditional wisdoms represent many essential considerations for sustainability, especially: focusing on the present; reducing acquisitiveness; and being concerned for others. Placing greater importance on *localization*, also a key aspect of sustainability, ties in well with these traditions.

Firstly, 'the local' addresses that which is proximate. Consequently, people become more directly aware of the impacts of their activities on their environment and there are obviously individual and communal benefits in looking after one's own local environment – to ensure an attractive and healthy place to live and work.

60

Table 6.1 Traditional teachings and 21st century marketing messages

Teachings of philosophers and spiritual leaders down the centuries	Corporate messages in the 21st century
'There is no greater sin than desire, No greater curse than discontent.' Lao Tsu, ca.500 BCE, China[37]	'[The photos] never show the entire car but still arouse desire for something new.' Mercedes-Benz, Europe[42]
'…those who buy something [should live] as if it were not theirs to keep; those who use things of this world, as if not engrossed in them.' St Paul, 1st century, Europe[38]	'Its yellow, white and Everose gold are timeless symbols of prestige and luxury.' Rolex, Europe[43]
'Our inventions are wont to be pretty toys, which distract us from serious things.' Thoreau, 19th century, US[39]	'With an anodized aluminum and polished stainless steel enclosure and a choice of six colours, iPod nano is dressed to impress.' Apple, US[44]
'…present-day industrial society everywhere shows this evil characteristic of incessantly stimulating greed, envy, and avarice.' Schumacher, 20th century, England[40]	'Google profits disappoint market' Google's profits were up 17% to $1.21bn (£608m) for the three months to the end of December. Some analysts had been hoping for stronger profit growth and its shares fell sharply in after-hours trading. BBC News[45]
'Civilization, in the real sense of the term, consists not in the multiplication, but in the deliberate and voluntary reduction of wants.' Gandhi, 20th century, India[41]	'Glacéau smartwater: the water with all the answers.' Bottled water ad, US[46]

61

Secondly, through direct encounter at the local level we are less inclined to objectify other people. When we fail to see and treat people as full human beings, but think of them merely as 'users', 'consumers' or 'labour', then we help create 'the other'. When this happens it represents a failure to empathize. Globalization would seem to exacerbate this tendency because of physical distance or differences in language, class, ethnicity, religion or skin colour. We may hear about exploitative labour practices 'over there', in economically developing countries that manufacture goods for the more affluent nations, but the physical separation also distances us mentally and can lead to objectification and the acceptance of practices and conditions that are inequitable, unjust and that we would not be prepared to tolerate ourselves. While certainly not impossible, it is more difficult to objectify people with whom we have direct contact – our neighbours and colleagues, and the people we encounter in our everyday lives. Therefore, in addition to efforts that seek to reduce human exploitation in other countries, a shift towards greater localization in manufacturing would encourage direct encounters and therefore practices that conform to the sustainable principles of social equity and justice.

Thirdly, focusing on local practices, activities and solutions can rein in our tendency to consider sustainability as something to be worked towards – as something to be achieved *in the future*, where there will no longer be inequity and injustice or environmental degradation; this is utopian and counterproductive. We are obliged to act in the present, to challenge our destructive norms and to develop practices that lead away from environmentally and socially damaging conventions. Irrespective of some future condition, each one of us, in our current activities, should be contributing constructively within our own sphere of influence – and with the understanding that the notion of 'the local' may vary considerably from one individual to another, depending on one's role and contribution.

For these reasons, a shift towards greater localization would mean that prices of consumer goods would better reflect their true costs. The people making the goods would be receiving a living wage and working in decent conditions, and it would be in everyone's interest to ensure that environmental standards were upheld. Thus, it seems that a shift towards localization would encourage those attitudes and behaviours spoken of in the world's great wisdom and spiritual traditions and, in the process, would better address many social and environmental principles,

Artefact: a symbolic sustainable object

The potential difference these concepts might make in the field of product design becomes clearer if they are made more directly relevant to the design process. Therefore, this present study includes the creation of a functional object. The design and production processes, and the resulting artefact, serve to embody and exemplify the principles being explored; the aim being to effectively encapsulate the *general* concepts and ideas discussed above within the design and creation of a *specific*, tangible object.

The practice of design is itself a form of inquiry that connects 'thinking' and 'doing' within an iterative, mutually informing process. Therefore, the creation of a physical artefact, which emerges from and contributes to the ideas, can bring an important design-centred element to our understanding of the issues.

A number of design objectives can be identified from the foregoing:

*   The functional benefit of the object should be consistent with, or contribute towards, the shift in values that have been described, including a shift from *having* to *being* and an emphasis on the present. It should contribute positively towards a reorientation in priorities – away from those that maintain a socially harmful and environmentally damaging production system, that tend to concentrate economic gains and that encourage dissatisfaction, consumption and waste, and towards those that are in accord with the ethical and sustainable principles of socio-economic equity and justice and environmental responsibility.
*   The object should be capable of being produced wholly or partly at the local level by making use of the materials and skills readily available within a place, and with a minimum use of energy resources.

62

- The environmental impact of the object during its creation, use and post-use should be negligible. Its concept as a thing, its materiality, its process of production, its function, its use and its disposal should all be entirely consistent with the ethos of sustainability.

Thus, the goal is not simply to achieve an object that *aims towards* sustainability by reducing its impacts compared with other similar objects but which, itself still has a negative effect. Instead, the goal is to produce something that actually is *a sustainable object* in its very conception as a thing. This means it must be sustainable not only in its mode of creation, its function, its aesthetic and in its eventual disposal, but also in the way that its presence and use contribute to positively developing and reinforcing an attitude of sustainability.

Several other factors were considered in the development of this illustrative object:

- The place that was to yield the object had to be local to where I, as the designer, was living and working.
- The determination of what the functional object was to be, and its specific definition, would be a result of combining a familiarity and consideration of place with the factors related to purpose, materials and skills discussed above. Thus, the artefact was to emerge from a negotiation with *locale* rather than being externally imposed.
- An emphasis on the fitness or aptness of the object to 'purpose-and-place' overrode other factors that might be important in a contemporary design practice. Commercial viability was not a factor; the aim being to inform and to be illustrative.
- Novelty and originality were not considered to be important and were not sought after when deciding on the type of object to be created or when designing its form. Unusual as this may seem, modern consumerism is so strongly associated with and promoted by novelty and so called innovation, that an attempt was made to eliminate such factors from this design project. There are precedents for such an approach. For example, in the creation of the icons of Eastern Orthodoxy the subject of the icon is painted (or 'written', as is conventionally said) by reference to previous depictions, and composition and style are determined by tradition rather than through individual expression.[47,48]

Bearing in mind these priorities and considerations, I visited the rural area immediately adjacent to my home. It is a place of high moors and deep fertile valleys (Figure 6.5). The main occupation is farming, and the predominant sight is dry stone walls enclosing pastures filled with different varieties of sheep. Streams and rivers cut through the moor land, with gravel beds and ancient stepping stones, while stone farmhouses and barns stand out on the horizon (Figures 6.6–6.9). Research about the area revealed a small cottage industry of rare-breed sheep rearing, together with the spinning and weaving of their wool.

Reflecting on these experiences and findings, and referring to a previous study that looked at objects used as aids for inner development and contemplation, such as the Buddhist prayer wheel, prayer beads and the Jewish prayer shawl[49] I was reminded of references to an ancient type of tallying device used for keeping track of meditative sayings or prayers.[50-52] The 'device', used since the 3rd century, consists of a simple pile of stones. To keep track of the spiritual exercises, each time a saying or mantra is completed, a stone is moved from the pile, to form another adjacent pile. Combining such a device with the local cottage industry of weaving would enable a simple, illustrative, functional object to be produced that would fulfil all the priorities set out for the project.

Revisiting the area, I collected small stones from a stream bed. These I later cleaned and dried and piled in a manner suitable for use as a tallying device. Moving the stones one by one into a second pile prescribed a comfortable 'use' area, which I defined in terms of specific dimensions. I visited the local weaver and commissioned a piece of woven cloth, which was to be made from wool she had spun from the rare breed Teeswater sheep that she rears (Figures 6.10 and 6.11). Several weeks later, the cloth, woven on a small hand loom, was ready (Figure 6.12). I placed the stones on the cloth to form the simple 'tallying device', and the artefact was complete (Figures 6.13–6.15).

A symbolic artefact

64 Clearly this object is very simple and its significance as a useful tool for a contemporary audience is marginal to say the least. However, as an artefact it fulfils all the objectives described earlier.

In terms of its function, these types of devices are used in conjunction with meditative practice – which is related to a shift in priorities. Such practices have been carried out in many cultures all over the world for thousands of years. They can be based in religious tradition or they can be entirely secular. Frequently they centre on the repetition of a passage of scripture, a short phrase or even series of meaningless syllables.[53] Significantly, such practices can lead to greater attentiveness, and freedom from compulsions and cravings,[54] which are the kinds of behaviours associated with consumerism. Therefore, this type of object is related to the shift in priorities that seem to be needed to counter our susceptibilities to the messages of modern marketing, impulse buying and so on. Hence, the conceptual nature of the artefact is consistent with sustainable principles and with more profound notions of meaning and happiness.

In terms of its definition as a thing, its materials, and the manner by which it was produced – these are all intimately related and responsive to locale and the particulars of place. While its actual usefulness may be marginal, its relevance lies more in what it represents, in terms of its concept, its process of creation and its materiality. It signifies a sort of sustainable ideal because, by conceiving it as an object that is related to a shift in priorities and by intentionally keeping it very simple and local:

- its use is associated with the development of values that are in accord with sustainability
- it offers an opportunity to employ local people and locally available skills and resources
- it takes little to create in terms of materials and energy resources
- its use produces no adverse waste
- at the end of its useful life it can be easily reabsorbed back into the natural environment with no detrimental long-term effects

In this sense it is symbolic. Even though this degree of sustainability may be unattainable in the creation of most other objects, it provides an example of what a fully sustainable functional object can be.

In addition, the creation of this object demonstrates the ability of the design process itself to contribute to knowledge. It exemplifies well how the experiential process of designing can inform our understanding of the relationship between the conceptual notion of an object, its design and production, the nature of the resulting artefact and the priorities of sustainability. In this case, the consideration of aptness to place comes to the fore, which expands and deepens our understanding of 'the local' in the context of manufactured functional objects. It is not simply a case of doing things locally for instrumental benefits – to create local jobs, reduce transportation and so on. The difference is also qualitative, aesthetic and cultural. The functional object is no longer an alien artefact that is imposed upon a place. Instead, it is an artefact of place, which emerges from a gentle rearrangement of the elements within the local environment – like the art works of Andy Goldsworthy or Richard Long, or the vernacular architecture of traditional cultures such as the adobe houses of the American Southwest, the reed houses of the Marsh Arabs, or the stone cottages of rural England. These vernacular forms, and this 'tallying' object, are not concerned with novelty, individual expression or 'making a splash'. They are quiet, familiar forms based on traditions that are centuries old and processes that have been contributed to by many over time. The resulting artefacts are both refined and fitting – in many important aspects, they 'work' effectively within their social and natural environments.

65

Thus, 'the local' is a critical element of design for sustainability and the nature of sustainable objects. It contributes to important extrinsic factors, such as reducing environmental impacts and providing work and economic benefit through local employment. However, it also contributes to the intrinsic qualitative and aesthetic aspects of objects, as well as to the qualitative and aesthetic aspects of the culture in which the objects are produced. These intrinsic factors, so easily forgotten when discussions focus on environmental performance indicators and targets, are vitally important if we are to shift our values and priorities and develop a new kind of cultural relationship with material 'goods'.

Sermons in Stones

a photo essay

Figure 6.1
Marketing banner 'Buy Me'
Selfridges department store,
Trafford Centre, Manchester

Figure 6.2
Main concourse 'Palm Court'
Trafford Centre, Manchester

Figure 6.3
Food court 'Ocean Liner'
Trafford Centre, Manchester

Figure 6.4
Grand marble and brass staircase
Trafford Centre, Manchester

Figure 6.5
Countryside adjacent to author's place of work

Figure 6.6
Dry stone walls

Figure 6.7
Sheep pasture

Figure 6.8
River stones

Figure 6.9
Stone barn

Figure 6.10
Teeswater rare breed sheep

Figure 6.11
Wool from Teeswater sheep

Figure 6.12
Woven cloth on hand loom

Figure 6.13
'Sustainable artefact'
a tallying device – 33 river stones on a woven cloth

Figure 6.14
'Sustainable artefact'
detail 1

Figure 6.15
'Sustainable artefact'
detail 2

7
Gentle
Arrangements
artefacts of
disciplined
empathy

there is a condition of lived experience, where what we might call a
construal of the moral/spiritual is lived not as such, but as immediate
reality, like stones, rivers and mountains.

Charles Taylor

Here I begin to integrate a number of the themes introduced earlier. In Chapter
3, I discussed research through designing – a form of creative, practice-based
inquiry that includes intuitive, subjective elements. Ensuing discussions brought to
the fore ideas about meaning and self-knowledge, locale, the natural environment
and a more comprehensive interpretation of design for sustainability. What starts
to emerge from this is that if design research, and thence design, is to effectively
address issues of environment, social concern and meaning, it has to move
beyond the evidence-based methods and intellectual arguments so favoured by
policy-makers and researchers. Cognitive knowledge takes us only part of the way.
Design's contribution has to go further than analysis and rational methodologies
because a large part of it is about creativity and expression. These intrinsic
features of designing involve the imagination, emotion and aesthetic experience.
Therefore, it is not only entirely appropriate that these aspects be embraced, their
inclusion is absolutely vital for developing what might be termed a 'designerly'

approach to research, sustainability and the making of a meaningful material culture. Such developments will not result simply from instrumental reasoning and single-minded purposefulness, but by enfolding factors that have no such ambitions – beauty and aesthetic experience, appropriateness within a place and culture, and correlation with understandings of goodness and truth.

Bringing these to bear in our approaches to design research can lead to a rather different sensibility. In this discussion they result in propositions that are characterized as *gentle arrangements*. However, no attempt is made to discover or advance a formula for sustainable design that can be universally applied. Rather, the process relies on the specifics of place and an empathetic appreciation of what a place may yield. As illustrated in the previous chapter, developing a practice of design that is embedded in locale begins to yield a perspective, and hence a process and objects, that point towards the sustainable; the term 'design' being used here to refer simply to a process of defining functional objects, with no implication of commercial viability, market need and so on. It is an appropriately open and flexible usage for exploring new, more fundamentally sustainable directions.

Critical to such an understanding of design for sustainability is a foundation of inner development, which through the ages has been variously referred to as the examined life, self-realization and spiritual development. Such a foundation enables the process and products of design to be enriched by that critical aspect of our humanity that seeks meaning, and it helps foster a design ethos that we might refer to as *disciplined empathy*.[1] Taylor reinforces this idea when he says that there is a need to recognize something more profound and fuller than reason, that reason alone may well lead to human and environmental destruction.[2]

Hence, the approach explored here fully recognizes the integrative nature of design, which seeks to reconcile pragmatic, utilitarian requirements with aesthetic, emotional considerations. Advances in design for sustainability must incorporate these two, very different aspects (see Table 7.1).

Table 7.1 **The integrative nature of design research**

	analysis	+	synthesis	
	intellect	+	intuition	
	objectivity	+	subjectivity	
Instrumental Value	cognitive	+	expressive	Intrinsic Value
	descriptive	+	imaginative	
	global	+	local	
	rational	+	emotional	
	function	+	meaning	

Directions that acknowledge deeper considerations of meaning, over and above instrumental criteria, suggest a notion of 'right attitude', which can lead to new priorities and a shift in perspective. In turn, this resonates with contemporary critiques that call for radical change in design processes and practices[3] and more holistic ways of thinking about design.[4,5]

A design-based approach that is necessarily creative and specific will also be partly polemical as well as indeterminate and rhetorical – meaning that the products of design can be understood as vehicles of arguments and viewpoints that are always open to discussion and debate.[6] Research through design, which features 'designing' as a key ingredient, differs from many traditional forms of academic research in that it focuses not on looking at or analysing what has been or that which already exists – it is not historical. While this may play a part, the primary concern is with how things can be designed – it is inherently creative, not purely objective, and certainly not definitive. Moreover, aesthetics and individual design examples are concerned with concrete particularities, not abstractions and generalizations. Thus, the products of such design research will be illustrative rather than prescriptive. They can be understood as discrete, tangible contributions to ongoing arguments and discussions; as such, this type of design work is not primarily concerned with practical utility or economic viability.

A key point that emerges from these directions is the need to expand upon our approaches to sustainability, not simply in our practices, but more importantly in our attitudes. Currently, most attempts to address sustainability are *reactive*, which regularly puts them in conflict with contemporary behaviours, business priorities and government agendas. As a consequence, progress towards more sustainable modes of living is often inordinately slow.

A far more significant shift is needed, and while such a prospect may seem optimistic, even unrealistic, design researchers within academia are in a position to explore and illustrate what such a shift might mean in terms of *what* and *how* we design. This kind of research requires a sound theoretical foundation, engagement in the creative design process and the development of tangible artefacts that transmute general theoretical ideas into specific, concrete propositions for reflection and debate. Thus, practice-based design research is an iterative process of *theory development – conceptual design – reflection – theory development*. It is an approach that is eminently well suited to the complex, integrative nature of so called 'wicked problems', where no single, correct solution exists.[7]

Methodologies, legislation, targets and moral arguments

Let us now briefly review the principal ways in which sustainability is currently being addressed. By considering the contributions and weaknesses of these various methodologies, legislation, targets and moral arguments, a clearer view of a potential role for design can be revealed. The implications of this role will then be explored, and illustrated through simple propositional objects.

Methodologies: A wide range of methodologies and tools are now available to assist private and public sector organizations, including local, regional and national governments, in reducing the negative impacts of their activities.[8] I mentioned some specialized programmes, such as life cycle assessment, in Chapter 5. In addition, Corporate Social Responsibility (CSR) policies help facilitate ethical, economic and environmental accountability. Although the particulars vary considerably from company to company, in broad terms, CSR is concerned with corporate citizenship, sustainability and corporate compliance with national or international regulations. There are also methods for measuring progress in sustainable development[9] against a range of indicators that cover:

- environmental issues (e.g. energy use, air emissions, water quality)
- economic considerations (e.g. economic growth, productivity, investment)
- social factors (e.g. quality of employment, community participation, social investment relative to gross domestic product (GDP))

Generally, these programmes, policies and methods have been developed *in response to* problems and the recognition that the pursuit of business interests, shareholder profit, and economic growth frequently conflict with broader considerations identified with the common good.

Legislation and targets: Legislation, targets and binding commitments represent specific responses to problems or symptoms of damage arising from human activities. They include emissions targets, such as the Kyoto Protocol,[10] and the European Union's Waste Electrical and Electronic Equipment (WEEE) legislation.[11] These kinds of targets and controls are based on intellectual arguments around conflicting sets of issues – for example, on the one hand *energy-intensive, consumer-based lifestyles* and on the other *climate change due to greenhouse gas emissions*. Such arguments, founded on oppositions, tend to encourage *reactive*, rather than *proactive*, methods for dealing with sustainability.

Moral arguments: While moral arguments underpin much of the legislation related to environmental and social issues, they go further than mere legalities and appeal to our conscience and society-established norms of just behaviour. Sustainability is often presented in such terms.[12,13] Arguments are made to reduce the environmental impacts of our activities for the sake of future generations,[14] to preserve natural habitats,[15] and to improve the conditions of those suffering from injustices caused by social disparity.[16] Moral arguments fall partly within legislative frameworks, to which compliance is mandatory, and partly outside them, where they become a matter of conscience and personal choice. As with legislation and targets, appeals to our sense of moral obligation are usually presented in the form of intellectual arguments and rational analysis, which again depend on two opposing sets of issues, such as low-cost, affordable goods (which are linked to lifestyle, spending, and economic growth) versus labour exploitation and social inequity.

Complexities and contradictions

The complexity of the sustainability issue – and its global reach – means that despite moral arguments and the increasing implementation of methods, laws and targets, progress is constantly frustrated by competing priorities. For instance, governments tend to endorse sustainability while simultaneously encouraging economic growth via consumerism. They also have a poor record of assent and support for international agreements that would foster sustainable practices and allow businesses to compete on a level playing field.[17] In the meantime, greenhouse gas emissions continue to rise.[18-20] Furthermore, advocating and maintaining moral arguments is often difficult for several reasons, including:

- the relatively slow, incremental pace of environmental change compared to the more urgent day-to-day issues that face businesses and governments;
- damaging developments often occur in places that are geographically far removed from us; and
- our current times are characterized by diversity and relativism,[21] which means that appeals to moral arguments are perhaps less straightforward than they once were.

So, on the one hand, we encourage growth in productivity and consumption for legitimate reasons of wealth creation and national well-being. On the other, sustainability is a concept characterized by sufficiency and reductions in consumption and waste. For fundamental, lasting change that overcomes these conflicts, a shift in perspective is needed – one that challenges the assumptions at the heart of our highly consumptive, extremely damaging lifestyles.

87

Perspective shift

It would seem appropriate to look at the potential of anchoring change in a deeper sense of personal conviction and significance. The necessary external changes in our behaviours and activities would then be willingly sought, which cumulatively could lead to reductions in consumerism and waste, a slowing in resource use and an alteration in our lifestyles. Instead of responding to the symptoms, such an internalization of the issues would start to deal with some of the root causes of the problem.

The moral arguments discussed above begin to point us in a direction for attaining this sense of inner compulsion. Moral obligations, to which we may initially submit only because of social pressures, can be understood at an intellectual or reasoned level and accepted on that basis. Once accepted they begin to be internalized, at which point they can start to affect how we think and act. Even so, it is important to recognize that our heavy reliance on intellectual arguments may well be an aspect of our contemporary discontented condition. Taylor ascribes modern society's sense of disenchantment, at least in part, to what he terms 'intellectual deviation', which includes a determinedly instrumental stance and helps generate a dualistic view.[22] Humphreys has said that the intellect 'leaves the heart disquieted'.[23] Both authors recognize that there are notions of meaning that lie beyond our capacity to acquire knowledge and beyond the rationalistic, point-counterpoint arguments that characterize intellectual debate; arguments that rely on oppositions and division rather than synergies and harmony. Moreover, no matter how far we pursue intellectual arguments, reason and knowledge, none of these provide a basis for experiencing life as 'meaningful'.[24,25] A sense of significance and meaning in life is to be found elsewhere.

Despite their import, however, today's cultural climate is not congenial to contemplation and considerations of meaning. The market system within late-capitalism ceaselessly encourages acquisitiveness and selfish thinking, and the digital age has seen a burgeoning of opportunities for distraction, entertainment, advertising and further consumerism. So, while the search for meaning has always required self-discipline to transcend egocentric preoccupations, it is perhaps an even greater challenge today – at a time when, arguably, it is needed more urgently than ever.

Disciplined empathy

As I mentioned in the previous chapter, for millennia, the vital aspect of our humanity that seeks meaning has been the domain of philosophy and religion, and while the great traditions may differ widely, the ethical teachings common to them all encourage outer actions that are characterized by consideration and compassion for others and all creation.[26] Yet, it is not outer actions that are their primary concern. Rather it is inner transformation and the development of a fundamentally different viewpoint – a shift in perspective.[27] Taylor calls this a 'sense of fullness' that is markedly different from our ordinary sense of the world and helps give direction and meaning to our lives.[28] This inner transformation is critically related to our sense of morality because it is both cultivated by and leads to outer actions that are considerate of others. In turn, this implies a shift away from self – and this shift, which lies at the heart of the sustainability issue, has significant implications for how we go about designing and producing our material culture.

Teachings and practices that lead to self-realization and a change in perspective have long been associated with the world's religions. There are also philosophical traditions, such as those of ancient Greece[29,30] and China,[31,32] which do not fit easily into what we commonly refer to as religion, as well as contemporary atheistic interpretations of spirituality and ultimate meaning.[33] The important point to recognize is that, whatever one's beliefs, we all see our lives as having a moral/spiritual character.[34] The development of this character requires personal discipline and adoption of behaviours that are less self-oriented and consumptive – both of which appear to be necessary conditions for, and tend to result from, an authentic striving for self-knowledge and meaning. Notably, the compulsion to take this path must come from within oneself, through intuitive apprehension or direct awareness.[35] Moreover, this 'examined life' is *not* based on intellectual arguments,[36–38] nor is it pursued for instrumental reasons, because it can reduce environmental damage or lead to greater social justice; even though such benefits would be the natural outcomes of taking such a path.

> **This sense is closed to all except the senseless,**
> **and words are all the ear can ever purchase.**
>
> Rumi Persia, 13th century

Intuitive ways of knowing that transcend reason and inference are given less credence in our rationalistic, instrumental age. Nevertheless, they are vital ingredients of human understanding and can be critical aspects of systemic change. Indeed, Gladwell argues that a major challenge of our time is to learn how to combine intellectual arguments with intuitive judgements.[39] And, if there is one pursuit in particular that demands this combination it is design, which brings together aesthetics and utility, form and function, intellectual reasoning and intuitive apprehension and, ideally, productivity and meaning.

To better understand both our world and ourselves, it seems that we have to pay far greater attention to our often fleeting, intuitive insights and judgements, and less to grand themes;[40] and certainly one of the grand themes of our age has become sustainability. Consequently, it may be both unwise and fruitless to look so intently upon the highly complex and ill-defined notion of sustainability as the *goal* that we should be striving to reach via the implementation of specific methods or measures, or by imposing targets and legislations. It would seem more important to see the goal as far closer to home and in terms that are more personally relevant and challenging. This entails the habitual pursuit of self-knowledge, adherence to the ethical life and consideration of others and leads, we are told, to a greater sense of contentment, where acquisitiveness and desires are curbed. Clearly this would, in turn, lead towards values and priorities that are in closer accord with sustainability.

Such a direction begins to re-orientate our perspective of the issues. No longer would the sustainability question be seen as one that arises from the dualisms inherent to intellectual arguments – such as striving to improve and increase our material standards of living while also seeking to preserve the natural environment; wanting more convenience while also trying to produce less waste. Viewing the issues in such terms simply continues the *reactive* way of thinking discussed earlier, where irreconcilable opposites are maintained. Instead, this re-oriented perspective offers a way forward that is generative and proactive. It is a perspective that sees us as part of a larger whole with which we seek to be in accord, it is inherently creative,[41] and it is a path characterized by disciplined empathy.

89

Implications for design

it bugs me when people try to

analyze jazz as an intellectual theorem.

<u>it's not</u>. it's a feeling.

Bill Evans, jazz pianist, US

Intuitive ways of knowing are, of course, very familiar to artists and designers. Intuition is an essential ingredient of the creative act and a critical aspect of the human imagination. Intuitive insights can occur suddenly, seemingly out of nowhere. When a particular issue or creative problem has been preoccupying one's mind for some time, often a potential solution will occur out of the blue – when one's mind is on other things entirely. But such insights are fleeting and easily lost – which is, perhaps, why so many artists and designers constantly carry a small sketchbook – lest an idea be forgotten.

These insights, or seeing with the mind's eye, provide an instantaneous apprehension of the whole – a complete solution to a design problem. They are integrative, holistic and a critical feature of our imaginative abilities. They are also closely associated with concepts of meaning and spiritual development. This sudden, intuitive 'seeing' is a long recognized aspect of Zen Buddhism, and its enigmatic koans or sayings (e.g. the sound of one hand clapping) are intended to stimulate sudden intuitive insight by deliberately confusing, and thereby transcending, the intellectual mind and reasoning.[42] In fact, Zen Buddhism is known as the religion of sudden insight.[43] Similarly, Beatty talks of spiritual insights that arrive 'in a flash', but which are easily forgotten.[44] Here we see that creativity, which is so dependent on seeing the world in new ways, is crucially linked to fleeting, intuitive and holistic modes of thinking.

It seems that these notions of meaning are also associated with aesthetics. Creative endeavours and ways of living that emerge from the 'inner path' often bear a somewhat characteristic quality and appearance. Outer expressions are not simply matters of choice, fashion or fad, but are rooted in and representative of deeply held beliefs, values and meanings. For example, the way of life within monastic orders from Eastern Buddhism to Western Catholicism are characteristically plain and simple.[45,46] Such frugal beauty is also apparent in the Haiku poetry of the 17th century Japanese master Basho,[47] and the minimalist music of contemporary American composer Philip Glass[48] – both influenced by spiritual traditions.

Of course, there is no guarantee that greater recognition of intuitive ways of knowing will lead us in more fruitful directions. However, if we:

- exercise discipline and rigour, and engage in constructive debate;
- ensure activities are informed by ethical considerations and broader understandings of meaning and purpose; and
- complement intuitive approaches with objective, rational decision-making, which is also a necessary aspect of design research,

then intuitive ways of knowing can deepen our understandings of design for sustainability. Furthermore, what we might refer to as spiritually informed expressions, artefacts and modes of living, such as the examples mentioned above, offer insights into creating ways forward that are, potentially, more meaningful and less damaging than our current approaches. These kinds of aesthetically austere expressions are symbolic of ways of thinking and knowing that are inherently respectful of others and the world. Their plainness stems from an ethos that is common to all the great wisdom traditions – one that urges the seeking of inner joy rather than worldly pleasures. It seems that the path of wisdom, inner contentment and true happiness, according to the longest-standing philosophical and spiritual traditions, are unanimous in their teachings of disciplined empathy, moderation and compassion, and they counsel against profligate indulgence and wastefulness – not simply because of their damaging effects on the world, but because they distract us from the examined, meaningful life. Many of the ancient cultural and wisdom traditions of indigenous peoples around the world advocate similar ideas.[49]

This heritage of human understanding can enable us to see our present activities from a somewhat different perspective, which can lead to new attitudes – so that we *willingly* reduce our consumption by wanting less, taking less, spoiling less and exploiting less. In the process we can become more empathetic to what a particular place, and the world in general, can comfortably yield.

Taking from the natural environment is, of course, an unavoidable necessity for our survival. It is not a question of ceasing to do this, but of moderating our activities – of not taking profligately, but with greater consideration and respect.

A gentle arrangement: an artefact of disciplined empathy

> If you make an altar of stones for me,
> do not build it with dressed stones,
> for you will defile it
> if you use a tool on it.
>
> Exodus 20:25

To illustrate how such a shift in thinking can affect design decision-making, let us first consider a very simple functional object. Recalling the plumb line example from Chapter 2, a mass-produced version of this basic instrument can be purchased from any local hardware store. Reflecting on the design of such a product reveals how we tend to think about functional objects in contemporary society and the issues raised here can be extended to far more complex products – from furniture to kitchen appliances to computers.

Typically, a plumb line is purchased as a pre-packaged product (Figure 7.1). It is made from turned steel with a tapped and knurled insert that holds the knotted, bleached cotton cord (Figure 7.2a). It is sold in display packaging comprising a printed card and polymer bubble pack. For the product to arrive in this manner on

Figure 7.1 *Mass-produced plumb line in its packaging*

Figure 7.2 Plumb lines
a) steel/bleached cotton,
b) drilled stone/hemp,
c) bound stone/hemp

92

the store shelf, a vast production and shipping system is needed – iron-ore mining, bulk transportation, arc furnaces, smelting and casting, manufacture of turning and tooling equipment, and hardened steel cutting tools. The packaging requires a pulp and paper industry based on logging, as well as oil wells, pipelines and refineries for the clear plastic bubble pack; to say nothing of the trucks and crates for delivering this product to the store and the power stations and energy resources needed to fuel the various processes. So we see that even such a basic product is representative of a massive industrial complex that is too often unsympathetic to sustainable concerns.

As we have seen, an alternative is possible – fashioned from a selected river stone and a length of organic hemp cord (Figure 7.2b). This locally made solution requires no packaging or shipping and, when the object is no longer needed, it can be discarded with little detrimental effect – the two components being natural. However, even here there are embedded assumptions that are rarely considered, which only reveal themselves when we look more closely at the details of our actions. In this case, the cord passes through a hole bored in the stone. Small as it is, this hole damages or violates the natural stone – so when it is eventually returned to the environment it is marred. More significantly, to create this hole, a tungsten tipped masonry drill bit is required in conjunction with an electrically powered drill. The drill requires a power supply, which in turn implies a power grid, electrical distribution, pylons, power stations, energy use, mining, transportation, pollution and so on. While the damaging effects may be few compared to the pre-packaged, mass-produced plumb line, there remain considerable impacts.

Another solution is possible that overcomes the requirement for a power tool, and all its implications. The stone can simply be bound by the cord (Figure 7.2c). Here, the stone is not damaged, the energy use is minimal and the return of these materials to the natural environment when they are no longer needed has *no* detrimental impact.

Obviously, this primitive object is not intended to be a commercially viable design. However, it *is* a perfectly serviceable, functional tool. Its creation emerges from a consideration of the nature of our actions, the assumptions behind them and their effects. Sensitivity to this level of detail reveals that the most basic of artefacts can embody ways of thinking that can be characterized, on the one hand, as inconsiderate, wasteful and destructive or, on the other, as empathetic, moderate and constructive. Significantly, the object shown in Figure 7.2c is not what we typically think of as a 'product'. Instead, readily available materials have merely been temporarily and tenuously combined to create a useful but ephemeral device. It can be seen as a *gentle arrangement* resulting from disciplined empathy. It flows from a consideration of functional artefacts, human needs, human meaning and sensitivity to the natural environment, which, ultimately, is also a human concern. Its simple definition as a tool necessarily requires intuitive, subjective decisions, which centre on the nature of the artefact and its particular form of expression, as well as more rationalistic, objective decisions related to its required function. The process of creative design always combines these two ways of knowing, which means that there is always an infinite number of possible outcomes. Some of these will be more appropriate than others, but there is never a single 'correct' solution. Moreover, when the intuitive, subjective element of design is empathetic to people and planet – as informed by environmental research and encouraged by 'inner development', then the result can lead to more holistically envisioned, less damaging notions of functional objects.

The rudimentary nature of the plumb line helps focus the discussion on the shift in thinking that is needed if we are to create a more sustainable narrative for the design and development of our material culture. It highlights the differences – both in artefact and impacts – between current, commodified notions of functional objects and more empathetic propositions.

However, this *gentle arrangement* approach to design, based in an ethos of disciplined empathy, can also be applied to more sophisticated objects. It can lead to new kinds of locally attainable combinations that:

93

- use resources sparingly to create utility and beauty;
- marry existing objects with new components;
- benefit from new technologies while also responsibly making use of components that still function but which, nevertheless, are frequently discarded; and
- reflect local cultural and individual needs and tastes (see Chapter 4).

Included here are three further examples, created from within the built environment rather than, as in the case of the plumb line, from the natural environment. Such artefacts are conceptually rather different from typical approaches to sustainability within the field of product design. Not only do these tend to emphasize materials use and technological change related to energy consumption, they do so within the existing expressive paradigm of design. Here, a different sensibility is evident, one in which understandings of sustainability and meaning are embedded in and inseparable from, the conceptual and aesthetic bases of the objects.

Building on earlier explorations,[50] these artefacts combine new elements with older, locally available, low-value components to create temporary functional compositions:

- 'Lite Lite' (Figure 7.3) exposes our extensive use of disposable batteries, through a minimalist lighting concept.
- 'Bucket Seat' (Figure 7.4) seeks a simple elegance from prosaic materials. It is created by arranging a galvanized pail and a pine plank on a rubber mat. The bucket is fitted with a silk cushion and the plank leans against a wall to form the seat back.
- 'Music Box' (Figure 7.5) combines a new MP3 player with old computer speakers contained within a re-used cardboard box.

New functional value is achieved by making use of existing artefacts and finding new applications for otherwise discarded items. They use few or no virgin resources, demand little in the way of energy use or special equipment and create little or no waste. Such explorations strive towards a more moderate and perhaps more meaningful understanding of functional objects – that can benefit from mass-production and from unique, locally rendered creative expression.

These objects were created via an iterative process of theoretical understanding related to sustainability and localization, and *their* relationship to employment, empowerment, self-realization and meaning. Such propositions, along with the examples included in previous chapters, can help foster a better understanding and appreciation of the origins and impacts of functional objects. Developing designs that incorporate older objects and represent them in an aesthetically acceptable manner opens up the possibility of a more enduring, but continually evolving, culture of objects. Through their lasting and changing presence, they can become cherished possessions worthy of our care, and which we associate with meanings and memories.

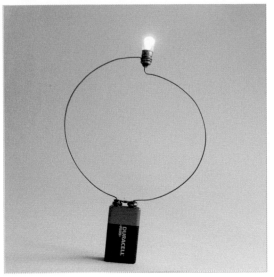

Figure 7.3
'Lite Lite'
9v battery,
copper wire,
torch bulb

Figure 7.4
'Bucket Seat'
galvanized pail, pine plank, silk, rubber

Figure 7.5
'Music Box'
a portable MP3 speaker unit –
cardboard box, electrical cord,
re-used computer speakers

Hence, such artefacts are indicative of a direction that is more holistic in its ethos and more sustainable in its outcomes than conventional approaches to product design. It is a direction that seeks to include in the design process deeper aspects of human understanding and leads to design outcomes that are more ambiguous in their categorization. Conceived as gentle, ephemeral arrangements that are empathetic to sustainable concerns, they are neither mass-produced nor craft, neither rationalized tool nor art. In light of the separation of craft from design-for-industry at the beginning of the 20th century, and the damaging effects such a separation has subsequently wrought, perhaps it is time to consider their re-integration in ways that once again pay greater heed to intuitive, tacit knowledge and long-established understandings of human meaning and purpose.

8
The
Chimera Reified
design, meaning
and the post-
consumerism
object

faced with this world of faithful and complicated objects, the child
can only identify himself as owner, as user, never as creator; he does
not invent the world, he uses it; there are, prepared for him, actions
without adventure, without wonder, without joy.

Roland Barthes

Despite mounting evidence and credible, science-based arguments calling for
change, there have been worrying developments in the manufacturing sector
over recent decades. The design and mass-production of an ever-expanding
range of short-lived, power-hungry, electronic products for global markets is
creating enormous environmental and social damage. Most of these products are
unrepairable and virtually disposable, and their very transience indicates that, as
objects, they possess little enduring value.

In this chapter I look at the design-related aspects of these goods. I will briefly
consider their instrumental value, their social, economic and positional functions,
and their related impacts and implications. However, beyond these broad and
rather familiar issues, it seems there is *something more* to be taken into account
if we are to better understand the extraordinarily prominent position these
devices have acquired in contemporary society and if we are to formulate more
considerate, benign and meaningful design directions.

As an initial response to these concerns, a simple conceptual object was created to encapsulate various aspects of contemporary critique. It can be characterized as a 'post-consumerism', non-functional electronic object – where the term consumerism refers both to a preoccupation with buying products and to the idea that continued growth in their production and consumption is economically desirable. The speculative notion of post-consumerism represents a major shift in priorities and is one interpretation of 'radical change', as discussed in Chapter 7. This object provides a focus for reflection – for considering current electronic goods, their prominence and their consequences – to help throw light on the *something more* referred to above. Its creation stimulated further enquiry into philosophical critiques of technology, environmental economics and developments in conceptual design, to position electronic consumer goods within a broader context of understanding. Such a context is essential if we are to develop more constructive interpretations of design and new directions for design practice.[1]

Electronic consumer products

Electronic consumer goods comprise a range of products that have become ubiquitous within affluent countries and are becoming increasingly common in countries with developing economies. They include laptop computers, printers, flash drives and other peripherals, as well as mobile phones, personal music players, entertainment devices and digital cameras.

One characteristic of these technologically sophisticated products is the relative brevity of their useful lives. Worldwide, the lifespans of such products range from four to eight years,[2] in the more affluent countries they may be less than two years.[3] In addition, all these products require a source of electrical power, usually in the form of batteries, which may or may not be rechargeable.

In terms of the benefits offered by these goods, they all have some kind of instrumental value – they are a means to some end. Also, there is social value associated with laptop computers and mobile phones – they enable us to communicate with family, friends and colleagues. Laptop computers especially offer a host of instrumental and social benefits through the applications they provide and the access they facilitate via the internet. There is also social value to their production, distribution and use – jobs are created and careers are developed. Related to this, there is economic value – in their production and often through their use; they offer opportunities for wealth creation for companies, individuals and, more generally, for society. Furthermore, for some people, there is a certain socio-positional or status value associated with having the most up-to-date mobile phone or video game console. Electronic products may have other values – such as aesthetic value, but the ones mentioned above are especially relevant to this present discussion.

Instrumental, social, economic and socio-positional attributes have long been associated with material goods and with the human-made environment in general.[4,5] As I have discussed elsewhere,[6] forms of dress, jewellery, furniture and modes of transport can all have socio-positional connotations, and traditional cafés and bars have value in facilitating social interaction and communication. Today, however, there are issues to be considered that are specific to our own age and are especially associated with electronic consumer goods.

High rates of technological advancement, spurred by economic incentives, ensure that electronic consumer goods become outdated very quickly. When this happens, the entire product tends to be discarded and replaced, rather than just a few specific components being upgraded. Such practices reveal an extravagant use of resources and result in enormous volumes of waste, and they bear witness to the priorities and attitudes underlying product design, manufacture and distribution. Despite attempts to limit such practices, as discussed in Chapter 7, the production and disposal of these products continue to have a host of destructive consequences. In poorer countries, where labour is cheap and health and safety standards virtually non-existent, appalling working conditions have been revealed,[7-9] and recovery of valuable metals from old circuit boards is often carried out under conditions that are severely harmful to human health.[10] In addition, there are manifold environmental implications. Millions of tonnes of toxic electronic waste, so called 'e-waste', are being created each year – and such waste is often illegally dumped in poorer countries.[11]

Thus, contemporary electronic products have a variety of benefits, as well as a multitude of harmful effects. No doubt cogent arguments could be made to show that the benefits of these products can continue to be developed and expanded and, with time, working conditions improved and environmental effects reduced, by employing more advanced, more efficient technologies. Yet, there still seem to be considerations that are not taken into account by such arguments.

99

Something more?

To develop more holistic renditions of material culture, we have to look at issues that lie beyond utility, technological advancement and instrumental arguments, and beyond the rather narrowly framed notions of social benefit that such arguments tend to foster. These additional considerations are more difficult to pinpoint but they are related to what might be described as 'things that matter'. While electronic products might provide a means to a variety of putatively desirable ends, it is important to recognize that the processes associated with these products can also be seen as ends in and of themselves. The manner in which they are produced, used and recovered can all contribute, in their own way, firstly, to the quality of life of those involved and secondly, to caring for the natural environment. Furthermore, the accumulation of human-made products in our society could enrich our physical environment through their presence – culturally and aesthetically. Our current manifestations of electronic goods fail to do this because they possess little inherent value as objects, over and above their utilitarian value, which results in them being discarded and replaced when newer models arrive.

This raises the question of what we mean by 'quality of life', which is rather different from 'standard of living'. While the latter has implications of material comfort and economic security, the former is a more comprehensive notion that includes personal, social, cultural, environmental and spiritual factors, including a sense of meaning in one's life, a sense of identity and a sense of peace and well-being. When we consider these in relation to contemporary electronic consumer goods, conflicts and contradictions appear and new questions are raised. For example, what are the implications for cultural and personal identity when a significant proportion of our material culture is not only globalized, homogenous and bereft of any specific cultural significance and expression, but is also produced in ways that are environmentally damaging and often unethical? What are the implications of this segment of material culture being increasingly disposable and fleeting? One value associated with material things, and related to the personal and emotional life of an individual, is that of sentimental value,[12] but this is unlikely to have much bearing in a material culture that has become so transient. Also, when we look at the ways in which many of these products are used, we see that they help create situations and environments that can be characterized as diverting and distracting.[13] Such products tend not to be conducive to reflective ways of thinking and living. Mobile phones, email and text messaging frequently interrupt conversations and intrude upon trains of thought and periods of silence. The hypertext facility on the internet, for all its benefits, can lead to a rather frenetic, disconnected, 'sound bite' relationship to information, compared to more considered, contemplative modes in which we are able to absorb, learn and ponder. It was these kinds of questions and thoughts, and their apparent relationship to understandings of meaning, that prompted me to create an initial design response.

Design Response I

In the field of industrial design, conceptual objects are often created to explore design directions and test possibilities. They are generally regarded as steps on a journey that eventually leads to a more refined, potentially viable design outcome. In research through design, the conceptual object has a rather different role. It is not a step on the way to a final design solution but an element, complete in itself, within a broader field of inquiry. However, in both commercial design practice and in design research, the exploratory nature of such objects means that any individual examples can legitimately remain at a rather crude, unrefined level – their purpose often being to expeditiously manifest and visualize unresolved ideas and to stimulate further thought.

In my own practice, conceptual objects are used to explore and express ideas and provide a focus for reflection within a continuing process of academic inquiry. They occupy a different place from those created within commercial design practice because, essentially, they are a critique of it[14] – a role that is entirely consistent with developing definitions of practice-based research.[15]

The process of creation can take many forms — one can begin with a clear set of intentions and criteria or with a rather indistinct notion and allow the creative process itself to integrate, solidify and clarify one's thoughts. It is within this latter form, especially, that the design process itself can become an important primary element of inquiry. The creative process allows us to develop and express ideas in ways that embrace the intuitive, the subjective, the impressionistic and the emotional, and through materials, form and detail, to be sensitive to the aesthetic experience. Further still, even if the final object does not fully or adequately express the ideas one has in mind, its very inadequacy provides a stimulus for additional inquiry. In this way, the conceptual object can be a potent, discipline-appropriate means for exploring and expressing ideas.

101

Figure 8.1
'Technology Can'
conceptual object

As one aspect of this study, a conceptual electronic object was created, entitled 'Technology Can' (Figure 8.1). Intentionally gestural and unrefined, it is a hollow façade that displays features of an electronic product between two natural stones. It was created to encapsulate the idea of the 'designed' electronic product as outer shell – what Borgmann calls the 'commodity' of a product.[16] The stones express the idea that all electronic products are born from the resources of the natural environment. It provides a tangible focus for reflecting on electronic goods, the role of the industrial designer and the insufficiencies of both with respect to contemporary concerns about sustainability and meaning. In creating such an object, abstract, theoretical ideas become concrete within one specific form. The process yields an outcome that is more sense-based than is possible with conventional arguments and because design, like other visual arts, is about holistic communication, the object should be viewed in its entirety.

In this example, although it displays some of the features of an electronic product, it has no utilitarian purpose. It is conceived as a 'memorial' to contemporary electronic consumer goods from an imagined future – a time of post-consumerism, when our priorities and preoccupations have changed, either through our own volition or because the harmful consequences have given us little other choice. This type of design is not market-oriented, but one that responds to a broad set of contemporary concerns. Dunne and Raby have used the term 'critical design' to describe such explorations, which are concerned with future, imaginary contexts and products, that are not necessarily desirable, but could just as easily be cautionary.[17,18]

Thus, 'Technology Can' can be seen as a functionless reminder of a time – the present – when we created a socially and environmentally damaging, highly transient and disposable form of material culture. It represents an attempt to see this through 'future eyes', and to recognize these unsustainable and often unethical practices as a rather grotesque aberration in human development – a chimera reified. In this inquiry, it provides a basis for exploring an alternative, more benign and enriching direction. One that, potentially, could overcome the deficiencies of the product façade, which tends to obstruct a more comprehendible and engaging interaction with things. The future, post-consumerism proposition on which it is based alludes to the inescapable implication of the sustainability question. Namely, if our current ways of producing, consuming, discarding and replacing goods are 'unsustainable', as mounting evidence seems to suggest, then clearly we will have to alter our approaches. Such a prospect is more than mere speculation. Signs of the fragile dependencies that allow us to maintain our consumer lifestyles are many and change is already happening – in our modes of living and working and in academic thinking and education. Further still, 'Technology Can' alludes to questions of meaning and the suspicion that our current conceptions of consumer goods and especially electronic products are, for all their technological ingenuity, somehow hollow and inadequate when it comes to these deeper questions.

Incremental changes to modes of living and working

A variety of indications suggest that our present consumer-based mode of living is beginning to run its course. Although, as yet, these indications are relatively small compared to the magnitude of the issues, they appear to signal the beginnings of change and adaptation. As more countries attempt to achieve the material standards enjoyed for so many years in the affluent, energy-dependent nations, demand grows for finite and increasingly hard-won resources. Consequently, prices escalate and lifestyles are affected. The alterations in behaviours and practices caused by a dramatic spike in oil prices during the first decade of the 21st century are indicative of a general trajectory of change. Some examples are included in Table 8.1, many of which could have both environmental and social benefits.

Table 8.1 Change related to a spike in oil price

Change related to a spike in oil price
Production of large private vehicles, including 4x4 vehicles, reduced Demand rose for small, more economical cars.[19]
Pennsylvania police reduced car use and increased bicycle and foot patrols Officers in cars were told not to run air conditioning while stationary, but to park in the shade. In Georgia, speeding fines were increased to cover extra fuel costs incurred when police chased offenders.[20]
Factories began to relocate closer to markets Tesla Motors had originally intended to produce batteries for its electric car in Thailand. Production was transferred to California to be nearer to its main production and consumer base, reducing shipping distances by 8000km along with associated costs. Swedish company Ikea opened its first factory in the US to avoid the cost of shipping products from overseas. Electronic companies that had moved from Mexico to China to reduce production costs through lower wages began to return to be closer to US markets to reduce transportation costs.[21]
Container ships began to reduce speeds to save on fuel The cost of transporting a freight container from China to the US increased from $3,000 earlier in the decade to $8,000.[21]
Food prices rise due to reliance on air/road freight This results in less disposable income for other goods and services[22] and affects consumerism. High shipping costs can also lead to more regionally grown foods, reducing fuel use and associated environmental impacts and creating new, more local economic opportunities with related social benefits.

103

In addition, high consumption lifestyles place increasing demands on public services and the public purse. Inevitably, ways of coping are introduced that seek to constrain expectations and encourage change; some examples are included in Table 8.2.

Despite these various indications, and the considerable social and environmental ramifications, our current systems of production and consumption remain firmly entrenched as primary means of wealth creation. Corporate

Table 8.2 **Change related to high consumption lifestyles**

Change related to high consumption lifestyles
Urban congestion charges Implemented in London since 2003 and later considered for Manchester, these are attempts to manage problems created by automobile commuting that, in turn, is related to our desire/ability to own a car and thus to our consumer lifestyles. If revenues from such charges are invested in public transport, the overall environmental effects of automobile commuting can be reduced and there can potentially be social benefits; when people travel on buses and trains, commuting becomes a collective rather than an individual activity, that requires tolerance and consideration of others.
Road charging and tolls These are also potential mechanisms for reducing congestion and various forms of traffic charging are now in effect around the world. High levels of congestion in the UK result from relative affluence combined with high population levels and less convenient, inadequate or expensive public transport systems. Shipping of goods via truck adds to congestion, as well as to road degradation. However, congestion has severe economic, social and environmental costs, so measures that lead to effective, well-managed public transportation and reductions in road use are becoming increasingly important.
Public transport In the European Union, there have been calls for greater investment in public transport to reduce greenhouse gas emissions and improve energy efficiency.[23]
Waste and Refuse Other indicators of the problems associated with consumption include municipalities banning the use of plastic carrier bags[24] and restrictions on the amount of refuse thrown away per household.[25]

104

executives and political leaders continue to extol the benefits of consumerism and growth and, consequently, use of resources and fossil fuels, and production of greenhouse gases, continue to climb.[26,27]

Systemic shift

In addressing these concerns, especially those related to environmental degradation, we would be unwise to rely too heavily on technological solutions – doing so can often create even further problems.[28] Such an approach to sustainability is simply a continuation of the mindset of modernism. Davison calls this 'eco-modernism'; it does not represent any significant change in thinking but is simply a continuation of unrestrained technological growth.[29] As we saw in the previous chapter, a far more fundamental change is needed. Moreover, a general direction for such change can be discerned from authors that represent a diverse range of disciplines and interests. For example, Young[30] describes our current age as one in which rationality, logic and science have become detached from thinking based on ethics and values. He argues that the next stage in human development should attempt to unify this split so as to become more sustainable, socially inclusive and equitable. Thackara[31] argues for major structural changes in how markets are organized, modes of transport and how we live and work. Mathews[32] suggests that, whereas modern ways of living can be characterized as materialist, the next potential stage of human development could be post-materialist, representing a shift towards ways that are more holistic, ecological and spiritual. And Rodwell[33] makes the point that current sustainability targets remain resolutely material and fail to include deeper understandings of meaning and spiritual concerns.

Thus, a body of work is emerging that indicates systemic change is required. The conceptual object 'Technology Can' anticipates this shift to what is referred to here as a time of post-consumerism. It represents a major change in understandings, priorities and values.

The role and meaning of electronic objects

We live in a time when the legacy of the modern era – in which empiricism, utilitarianism and instrumental reason rose to prominence – is still very much part of our ways of thinking and acting. However, Mathews argues that modernity can be defined, not so much by its adherence to instrumental reason, but by its emphasis on materialism – a philosophical position based on that which is objectively evident and provable. She argues that, because the scientific method, grounded in an understanding of materialism, is empirical, its investigations are *predetermined* to reveal only those aspects of reality that are observable in matter and, consequently, unobservable, non-material, dimensions of reality are, by definition, excluded from the method and unrecognized. She makes the case that the instrumentalization of reason in modern societies was a development not of abstract knowledge but of empiricism, with its concomitant assumptions of a materialistic explanation of reality. However, once the presupposition of materialism is challenged, there remains nothing inherently instrumental about reason. According to this thesis, the modern view of reality has resulted in a constrained understanding of reason and has become dominated by material progress and utility.

Such arguments are fundamental to our understanding of the place and role of electronic products in contemporary society. Firstly, scientific research seeks to continually advance our knowledge of the observable material world. Secondly, instrumental thinking leads to the development of that knowledge into technologies that have utilitarian value. Thirdly, our economic and market system seeks to develop those technologies for mass markets. As we saw in Chapter 6, these activities are based in the notion that progress, including material progress, is central to contemporary notions of 'meaning'.

With this in mind, if we look at how new electronic products are launched, we see that much is made of supposed improvements and innovations. For example, that the device has a higher screen resolution than previous products, that the screen is comparatively large, and that the product is thinner than its rivals.[34] Such attributes are often forcefully publicized. In the words companies choose to promote these products, they are making the case for how a small electronic product is, in fact, contributing to the human project of progress, which in the modern understanding is an inherently meaningful thing to do. Hence, such devices can be viewed as modern expressions of meaning.[35]

Questions of meaning and purpose are critical to contemporary understandings of technology and consumerism. Borgmann argues that below the surface of technological freedom and the wealth it can create, there is a feeling of 'captivity and deprivation' and that a philosophy of technology should address things that really and finally matter, which he associates with spiritual sources of meaning.[36] Inayatullah argues that spirituality should be an additional element in our understandings of sustainability.[37] Unsurprisingly, these deeper questions of meaning are entirely commensurate with long-established understandings that have been present in all societies throughout history.[38] However, modern materialism is philosophically incompatible with such traditions. Current approaches to sustainability might include environmental and ethical considerations but for the most part they remain at a pragmatic level within the existing production–consumption model.

From the foregoing, we see that propositions from various disciplines point to more fundamental change and the recognition of deeper notions of human meaning. Such a direction holds the potential for a more robust, enduring understanding of sustainability.

Meaning, sustainability and the design of electronic products

Current approaches to product design and production, as we have seen, are intimately related to growth. Given the finite nature of natural resources, this link is inherently incompatible with the notion of sustainability. As an alternative, Daly[39] has proposed the 'steady-state economy'. Necessarily, the priorities of such an economy would be very different from those of the growth model, with significant implications for design, production and disposal. It emphasizes qualitative improvement and sufficiency over quantitative production. Product durability becomes important, together with maintenance and repair, which, in turn, could provide employment opportunities at a local level. This is entirely consistent with philosophical reflections on technology that suggest environmental approaches should a) increase product lifespans by using forms and materials that age well and b) improve product support and repair services.[40] In turn, this is congruent with examinations of the emotional durability of products and its relationship to sustainability.[41]

While such ideas emphasize important new priorities for design by placing greater emphasis on localization and service provision, they do not take us too much further in terms of the relationship of technological objects to more profound understandings of meaning and human purpose. It is here that a significant gap appears in discussions of design for sustainability.

Borgmann's contribution is especially germane in addressing this gap. He has distinguished between a 'thing' that requires our engagement and a 'device' that offers functional benefit but makes few demands on us. He argues that such devices are impediments to the meaningful life because the 'answer' to this search is provided via technology.[42] This, he suggests, contributes to an emerging sense that the promises and benefits of technology are meaningless.[43] He describes two modes of a technological product – 'reference' and 'presence'. The reference mode can provoke endless curiosity, research and analysis and invokes restlessness, whereas the presence mode can foster admiration and appreciation and lead to a sense of peace and affirmation. However, the provision of functional benefit bereft of any significant opportunities for engagement means that the presence mode has become occluded in technological devices.[44] To overcome this shortcoming, new design priorities must be developed that allow room for greater involvement, awareness and product comprehension, together with the stillness of appreciation.

A space heater with adjustable ceramic plates, which people can gather around like a campfire, and a wind-up radio are two examples of technological products that, some have argued, call attention to themselves and invite our involvement.[45] However, unlike a log fire, an electric room heater can function with or without our attentiveness. In the radio, the hand-cranked dynamo is an alternative power source to batteries or mains electricity and, while a power source of some kind is necessary and the specific type selected will have its own implications for the environment, none are fundamentally involving elements in the activity of radio listening. Hence, in both these examples, the nature of 'engagement' is rather supplementary to the primary purpose of the product.

In developing a more pertinent form of engagement, van Hinte's argument for greater functional clarity indicates a way forward.[46] A technological product that is designed to be both beautiful and functionally explicit can offer many positive features. If it is transparent in terms of what it does, how it is to be used, what its various components are for and how they might be replaced or upgraded, it could be capable of commanding a deeper sense of 'presence' – not simply because it might be considered beautiful but because in its object-ness, its functioning and through its use:

- it conveys a causal relationship between its assembly of component parts and its functional benefit – even if the scientific concepts that enable that benefit are not well-understood by the person using it, as may often be the case with technological products;
- it expresses the ingenuity of humanity in its pursuit of advancement through curiosity and research; and
- it reveals the use of nature's resources in the provision of this functionality through the 'wonder' of electromagnetic wave transmission, micro-electronics, and so forth.

If we are to develop more meaningful renditions of technology, these kinds of considerations become vitally important, despite the fact that current market-led product solutions display little evidence of such priorities and relatively few designers are presently addressing such issues. Exceptions are Dunne and Raby; even though sustainability is not a prominent feature of their work, their electronic objects – informed by social, political and cultural concerns – are speculative attempts to embody values and invite reflection.[47]

A technological product designed to disclose rather than obscure those elements that are essential to what it is as a thing could, potentially, enable all the above aspects to be acknowledged, appreciated and admired. Furthermore, if the product commands our attention and involvement during use, it would bring together and manifest both the reference and the presence modes of being.

Design Response II

In an attempt to capture something of these essential qualities, a simple technological object has been created – a 'Crystal Radio' (Figure 8.2). It has been expressed in a manner that exposes the individual components on a plain white background, rather than encasing them within a product envelope. It requires no batteries or other internal power source and its use, typically characterized by very weak signal reception, demands concentration, attention and involvement. The design strips away any artificially imposed surface appearance; its visual qualities rest entirely on the form, colours and assembled composition of its functional components. In this way, the design eliminates the styled 'shell' or

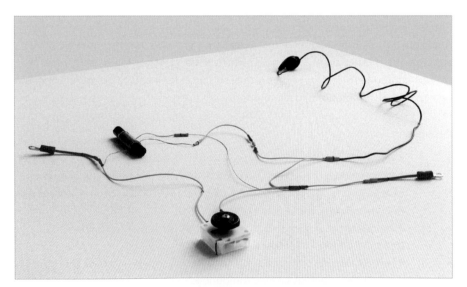

Figure 8.2
'Crystal Radio'
conceptual object

casing that tends to impede a more comprehensive understanding of products. It is also commensurate with arguments for more meaningful products that enable 'engagement'. Because its use requires concentration, it is intended to be in accord with spiritual teachings that steer us away from distractedness and 'multi-tasking', but instead encourage single-pointed attention - as an important aspect of inner development.[48]

Essentially, this object is the converse of 'Technology Can'. There is no obscuring façade, but rather the components are set in place on a simple flat panel. It is open, functional and purposeful, and its use requires attention and engagement. It is but one suggestion for how the priorities of both sustainability and personal meaning might be made concrete in our approaches to electronic product design. Clearly, it is inadequate as a practical product for day-to-day use, but that is not its intent. Rather, it represents an integration of ideas that point in a particular direction. Although there are many interrelationships among these various ideas, they can be summarized as follows:

- **Environmental factors**: Unlike an injection moulded casing, the simple panel can be created locally. Rather than replacing the whole object, mass-produced components can be changed individually, for repair or upgrading, at the local level. No batteries or other internal power source are required.

- **Social factors**: Local manufacture of certain parts together with services that could include design, making, repair, upgrading, remanufacture and recycling provide opportunities for work that would comply with endemic employment and environmental standards.

- **Economic factors**: By integrating social, environmental and health and safety considerations into the costs of manufacture and remanufacture at the local level the price of products would be more closely aligned with their true costs. As I pointed out in Chapter 3, these considerations are too often regarded as 'externalities', which means the true costs – to people and planet – are not included in the price of the product. In addition, wealth creation would be distributed among local communities, thereby contributing to a more variegated, robust and flexible system and to socio-economic equity, both of which are key aspects of sustainability.

- **Personal meaning**: Through its open, transparent design, the conceptual object attempts to convey a causal relationship between its assembly of component parts and its functional benefit and to express the human ingenuity underlying the concept of 'radio'. It also explicitly reveals the use of nature's resources in providing this functionality. The use of this particular object also requires focused attention, and does not easily lend itself to multi-tasking. I will say more on this point in Chapter 10.

109

Conclusions

Contextualizing contemporary technological products within understandings that are capable of embracing a more comprehensive range of sensibilities than those recognized by materialism can contribute to constructive, systemic change. In their conceptualization, purpose, materials, modes of production, use and after-use, products developed in a time of post-consumerism could reflect understandings that are not only far more compatible with the social justice and environmental priorities of sustainability but are also in accord with richer, more complex, multi-layered notions of human meaning. Without such a shift, the consumer-based economic/production system of the modern era – a chimera that is not only highly destructive but, for many, lacking in meaning, will undoubtedly continue on its rapacious course.

110

9

The Spirit of Design

notes from the
shakuhachi flute

All life that is not merely mechanical is spun out of two strands: seeking
for that bird and hearing him. And it is just this that makes life so
hard to value, and the delight of each so incommunicable. And just
a knowledge of this, and a remembrance of those fortunate hours in
which the bird has sung to us, that fills us with such wonder when we
turn the pages of the realist.

Robert Louis Stevenson

When I was at art school, I attended a field trip to the National Gallery in London.
One of the paintings that stood out for me was *The Baptism of Christ* by the 15th
century Italian, Piero della Francesca. It struck me as a rather strange work. The
figures were pale, almost white, their stances unnatural and the composition
was formal and stiff. The overall effect seemed to be pointing the viewer to
something that lay beyond the depiction of a biblical story and beyond aesthetic
appreciation.

Years later this painting was brought to my attention again when the
Archbishop of Westminster called for it to be removed from the National Gallery
and placed in a church (Figure 9.1). The reason he gave was that it was not a

work of art. Instead, he described it as a work of faith and a way into prayer.[1] According to this view, its purpose surpasses those ideas and concerns we normally associate with art; it has a higher level of meaning related to spiritual development. When this kind of painting is placed in an art gallery its purpose changes; implicitly it becomes *no more than* an object for aesthetic appreciation. However, such paintings were not conceived as autonomous works of art but as active elements within spiritual practices.[2] In a highly secularized society, the presentation of such paintings in an art gallery may be better than nothing, as has been suggested by another prominent religious leader and academic,[3] but it is important to recognize that they were created for other reasons entirely — reasons that are rooted, for many, in profound ideas of what it is to be human.

This notion of material artefacts being directly related to understandings that surpass mundane attributes and aesthetic pleasure is the central theme of this chapter. Here, however, the focus is not on paintings but on functional objects that require physical interaction.

Figure 9.1
Cardinal calls for painting to be relocated
The Tablet, 6 December 2008

To appreciate how such objects, in their conceptualization, design, making and use, can be intimately connected to inner development and questions of human purpose, we must go beyond conventional descriptions that consider practical and semiotic functions and aesthetic qualities.[4] As we saw in Chapter 7, more profound understandings are related to long established traditions that include philosophical and spiritual teachings and ethical principles. The relationship of technology to these deeper concerns can inform both the physical definition of an artefact and the nature of its use. A key aspect of this is the reintegration of design and technology with context.[5] Furthermore, the disciplined use of a functional object in which substantive issues have informed its creation can help foster what we might refer to as inner progress or spiritual development. In this way, the functional object links practised accomplishment or 'outer progress' to inner development – in a reciprocal, mutually reinforcing relationship. This is a quite different kind of progress from that which today has become so closely associated with technological innovation, material advancement and consumerism. Importantly, this relationship between the design of objects, their use and inner development contributes to a more comprehensive understanding of human concerns – one that encompasses not only practical needs, material comfort and aesthetic experience, but also notions of meaning, ethical responsibility and environmental care. In other words, it includes those very issues that are proving so problematic to effectively address within our current conceptions of product design and production. This more holistic view of human needs and its relationship to material culture help foster an understanding of sustainability that is more yielding and reflective than technocratic approaches – exemplified by 'green' design and eco-modernism, which tend to be controlling and projective.[6]

113

Rather than attempting to explore these interdependent aspects of material culture in terms of generalities and abstract theories, it is more constructive and more appropriate within the field of design to consider a specific object – from which we can draw conclusions that might be useful in other situations. To this end, I would like to examine a particular functional object that has been chosen because it spans an unusually broad range of issues, including the spiritual. It is the Japanese *shakuhachi* flute. The findings that emerge provide a basis for critiquing many of the assumptions and norms of contemporary product design. They also provide a basis for reassessing our priorities and developing design approaches that take into account sustainable concerns in ways that, hitherto, have not figured prominently in design education or professional practice.[7]

A description of the object and its design is followed by an explanation of its use in spiritual or meditative practice. The discussion explores the relationship of this form of use to the physical design of the object, how we think about it as a thing and the nature of the outcome – the produced sound. It becomes evident that notions of meaning and inner purpose fundamentally shape its conceptualization, design and use and, it seems, the user. It also becomes evident that the characteristics of this particular object resonate with a multitude of issues associated with design for sustainability.

The shakuhachi flute

The *shakuhachi* flute is a heavy, thick-walled, end-blown flute made from bamboo. Its shape, with a slight curve and increase in diameter towards the base, is due to the fact that its design incorporates the root bowl of the bamboo. Typically, it is made in two parts, which allows it to be more accurately tuned, but simpler, one-piece flutes, such as the example shown in Figure 9.2, are also used. It has four finger holes on top and one thumb hole underneath. The inside diameter is precisely regulated, often with the use of filler materials, and the bore is usually lacquered.[8] The flute has a characteristic oblique 'blowing edge' at its upper end made from a bone or horn insert (Figure 9.3). The traditional length is 54.5cm, though today it is made in many different sizes and keys.[9]

The *shakuhachi* is remarkably simple in its design and construction, yet it is capable of producing a broad range of sounds, from the pure notes so characteristic of flute music, to highly complex, expressive tones.[10] It is a notoriously difficult instrument to play and can take a lifetime to master; for the beginner it can be difficult to even produce a sound.

It dates from as far back as the 8th century and the instrument has long been associated with spiritual practices. Beggar priests played an early, thinner

Figure 9.2
A 'jinashi' style shakuhachi flute ca. 1920: This one-piece, unrefined type of shakuhachi is more suited to solo meditation than to musical performance

walled version during the Muromachi period (1333–1358),[11] but it was in the Edo period (1600–1868) that it acquired its characteristic thick-walled design. During these years, the *shakuhachi* was used by a sect of wandering Zen Buddhist monks called *komusō*, who were often masterless samurai or *ronin*. The *komusō* were not permitted to carry swords, but the times were violent and, despite being monks, they were frequently involved in combat. For these reasons, it seems, the *shakuhachi* was redesigned, becoming thicker and heavier, and the root bowl was included in its design – turning it into a substantial cudgel as well as a flute.[12,13]

Today, the *shakuhachi* is used mainly for playing secular music, often in ensembles where it provides only background support to the *koto*, a Japanese zither; there are also large *shakuhachi* massed bands.[14] However, throughout its history the solo instrument has had strong associations with meditation, contemplative practices and the religious disciplines of Zen Buddhism.[15] In recent decades, the *shakuhachi* has successfully transcended international boundaries and has become established in the West.[16] Indeed, while the playing of the solo *shakuhachi* as a form of spiritual or meditative practice is relatively rare today among players in Japan, this type of use has assumed a major role among players in the West, especially in the United States.[17] This change of context also changes

115

Figure 9.3
The characteristic oblique blowing edge of the shakuhachi with bone insert or utaguchi

how it is used. In a monastery, a Zen monk might play the *shakuhachi* as one element within a repertoire of spiritual exercises that are performed in a particular way. It is not simply an individual practice – as is often the case in the West.[18]

We see from this brief overview that the *shakuhachi* flute embodies a broad spectrum of human concerns that, throughout its history, have included:

- physical defence;
- group performance, secular entertainment and aesthetic experience;
- individuality and self-reflection; and
- disciplined meditative practices as a path to spiritual development.

It is an instrument that has transcended time and culture. It has been valued and played for more than 1000 years and, since the latter part of the 20th century, it has become adopted in the West and is now played all over the world.

Design, simplicity and spiritual practice

While the overall form of the modern *shakuhachi* stems, in part, from the fact that it also once served as a weapon, significantly, there are marked differences between the flute used today for secular musical performance and the instrument traditionally employed in meditative practices.

In Zen Buddhism, the playing of the *shakuhachi* is considered a path to enlightenment.[19] For such practices, the preferred type of *shakuhachi* is a rawer form of the instrument known as the *hōchiku*. This is a one-piece flute, in contrast to the 'secular' form that is made in two pieces, and it is simpler and cruder. It is also thicker, heavier and more natural.[20] Often, the mouthpiece of the *hōchiku* does not have a separate insert but is simply an oblique edge cut into the bamboo, and the bore is left natural, with little or no filler or lacquer.[21-23] Thus, the 'meditative' *shakuhachi* is simpler and less refined than versions used for secular purposes.

There are examples of flutes from other spiritual traditions that are also basic, raw and natural. The *ney* is an end-blown reed flute from the Middle East used within the meditative practices of Sufism; like the *shakuhachi*, it is both rudimentary in its design and difficult to learn.[24] The *bansuri*, a simple, transverse bamboo flute from India, is also regarded as a spiritual instrument.[25] Design characteristics of simplicity, absence of ornament and use of natural materials can also be found in other functional artefacts associated with spiritual practices.[26] Such traits are entirely commensurate with ideas and beliefs that place emphasis on the inner life, where material superfluity is seen as a distracting hindrance to spiritual development.[27]

The relationship of artefact design to the nature of use

The rawer design of the *hōchiku* means that it lacks standardized tuning, making it unsuitable for playing compositions within an ensemble or for playing recent compositions that have Western influences. The *hōchiku* is used for

116

the solo practice of traditional meditative or spiritual compositions known as 'original pieces' or *honkyoku*.[28] Its cruder, less refined design gives each flute its own unique characteristics and sound – which means a player develops an individualized form of meditative practice linked to his or her own specific instrument.[29] This fosters an uncommon set of relationships between object, function and user – a set of relationships that are critical to notions of meaningful activity and inner progress. The player becomes attuned to the particularities and idiosyncrasies of his or her own instrument and these affect the nature and discrete qualities of disciplined practice. Notably, in its form and its use, the purpose is not to make music but to produce sound, within a regime of meditative practice. Such practice entails no 'correct' set of sounds and no standard requirements or expectations into which the instrument and the player must 'fit'. Consequently, and in contrast to more refined versions, the simpler *hōchiku* can be regarded as a functional object that physically embodies and prioritizes spiritual value and inner growth over musical value and aesthetic pleasure.[30]

At the beginning of this discussion, I described how *The Baptism of Christ* by Piero della Francesca can be understood as an object for inner development rather than as art. Similarly, through the characteristics of its physical design, and the particularities of its use, the *hōchiku* form of *shakuhachi* can be regarded as a spiritual tool rather than as a musical instrument. The process of creating sound within a disciplined practice of 'non-performance' playing can produce a transformative experience for both the player and the listener and is considered a path of spiritual development that can lead to an enlightened state.[31] This form of practice is known as *suizen*, which can be translated as 'blowing meditation' or, literally, 'blowing Zen'.[32,33]

Thus, in its material form and its use, the Japanese *shakuhachi* flute is an example of an object that is strongly linked to some of our most profound notions of meaning. As such, it is an object that can tell us much about the nature of what might be termed a meaningful material culture, which can in turn provide insights pertinent to the environmental and social challenges associated with our current modes of creating and using products. To understand this more fully, it is necessary to take a closer look at the nature of the functional use that is enabled by the simple, raw form of *shakuhachi*.

The intrinsic value of use

Normally, we regard the use of a functional tool as a means to achieve some other end. A wrench is used to tighten a bolt, a shovel is used to dig a hole. In these cases, the value of the object is primarily instrumental. However, playing the 'meditative' *shakuhachi* is regarded as an end in and of itself; it has intrinsic value. It is done without judgement, without concern for or attachment to the achievement of specific goals or measurable outcomes. Focused attention is given simply to the activity itself, an activity that includes producing sound, breathing and being aware of the silences between sounds. It is an activity that requires patience and setting aside expectations of reward or success. Emphasis is placed on solitary practice and on blowing one note, without appraising its merit or value.[34,35] A similar emphasis on playing one note, and on listening to the silences, is present in the practice of the *ney* flute[36] and in the *Masnavi-ye Ma'navi* or 'Inner Verses' of Rumi [37] in the Sufi tradition of Islam, where silence alludes to that which is inexpressible. Silence, or absence, is also an important element in the musical works of American composer John Cage,[38] the 'White Paintings' of Robert Rauschenberg[39] and the spiritual paintings attributed to Shivdas.[40]

In this form of concentrated practice the player – and, potentially, the listener – becomes immersed in the activity and, by this means, fully engaged in the present moment. This engagement with the present is a critical dimension of many spiritual traditions including Buddhism, in which the *shakuhachi* is used, Christianity and Hinduism.[41,42] It is also apparent in other intuitive, improvisational art forms such as the spontaneous Japanese ink painting known as *hobuku* and extemporaneous forms of Western jazz, as in John Coltrane's *A Love Supreme*.[43,44]

Symbolic meanings

A variety of symbolic meanings have accumulated around the *shakuhachi* and the sounds that it can be made to produce – which serve to reinforce its importance as a culturally and spiritually significant object. Typically, the *shakuhachi* is made from a length of bamboo that has three joints or nodes, and it has five finger holes. The three joints are said to represent the three powers of Heaven, Earth and Mankind, while the five finger holes represent the five elements of earth, air, fire, water and space.[45] The sharp and flattened notes have been likened to the yo and *in,* or *yang* and *yin*, of Eastern philosophy and playing both types of notes symbolizes 'playing the universe'.[46] The *hōchiku* monks who originally played the meditative form of *shakuhachi* wore a basket-like hat that hid the identity of the player – symbolizing the inner life and non-attachment to ego or worldly concerns.[47] Through such traditional associations, the *shakuhachi* has accumulated a rich set of enduring symbolic values that are deeply rooted in spiritual practices and inner development.

The meaningful object and sustainability

In all its characteristics, the *shakuhachi* contrasts markedly with many of today's most technologically advanced functional objects – especially the myriad electronic products that are such popular consumer items. Whereas the *shakuhachi* is a simple object whose use is complex, modern electronic products are highly complex but are usually quite simple to use. The *shakuhachi* requires focused attention, patience and learning over many years, whereas use of the modern electronic product can often be mastered in minutes. The use of the *shakuhachi,* at least within spiritual practices, is an end in itself and thus has intrinsic value, whereas the use of the modern electronic product is primarily instrumental in nature – a means to some other end – such as sending a text message, listening to pre-recorded music or taking a photograph. In addition, the unrefined, meditative *shakuhachi*, because of its associations with profound meaning and its individual characteristics, can itself have intrinsic value as an object; in other words, value lies in its essential nature as a thing and, as such, it can become a cherished, meaningful object for its owner. If properly cared for and maintained, it can last for generations. By contrast, the modern electronic product tends to have little intrinsic value, which results in it being readily discarded and replaced when its instrumental value becomes superseded by a more technologically advanced model.

All these factors are intimately linked to understandings of happiness and a meaningful life[48] and to our contemporary responses to sustainability. In its design and use the *shakuhachi* can be understood as a physical manifestation of, and contributor to, long-established, substantive notions of human meaning; these relationships are shown in Figure 9.4. The link to sustainability is unequivocal. We see from the above comparisons that a functional object, which has been associated with human happiness and meaning for centuries, has, at its heart, priorities and values that are polar opposites of those embodied in many of today's most widely sought after consumer products – products that lack enduring value and are proving highly damaging and unsustainable.

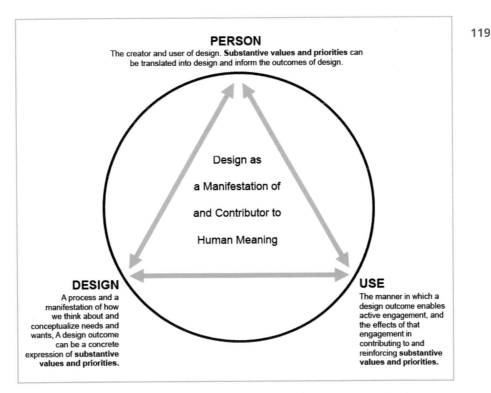

Figure 9.4 Design as an expression of and contributor to human meaning

The shakuhachi in the context of contemporary debate

The *shakuhachi* flute is a pre-technological object, the use and functionality of which demands our full involvement. Indeed, its use and its functioning are inseparable from our activities with it. This obligatory level of engagement is inherent to the nature of the object; it provides an enriching relationship with a material artefact that can reinforce substantive values. As such it can be categorized as a 'thing', as defined by Borgmann (see Chapter 8). By contrast, electronic goods, with their provision of instrumental benefit without a similar level of engagement or even attention, can be categorized as 'devices'. According to this view, our conceptual notions of technological goods, contextualized within a technological culture driven by market values and consumerism, are inadequate because they do not enrich, but rather reduce our experiences and understandings and, in the process, erode opportunities for fully engaged experiences, or 'focal practices',[49] which can develop skills, strengths and more reflective modes of being.

Yet, even though the predominant emphasis of technological goods might be on instrumental benefit, it is important to recognize that they too can offer important and valuable contributions to well-being. They may also acquire a variety of symbolic meanings that may be regarded as positive or negative depending on one's point of view. However, despite these potential attributes, such products generally remain at variance with understandings associated with sustainability and deeper notions of meaning. The instrumental and symbolic values associated with electronic consumer goods include:

- **Use value** – as a means to achieve a certain task.
- **Use related to social value and personal engagement** – as a means to enable social interactions through communication, information exchange, listening to music and so on. Technological objects can offer valued opportunities that transcend the accomplishment of a set of tasks by enabling activities that may be pursued for their own sake. While the use of a laptop computer, a smartphone or an MP3 player may offer untold opportunities for diversion and unreflective modes, it can be argued, also, that they provide for activities that may be considered more socially or personally enriching and which have intrinsic value.[50]
- **Production value** – as a means for a company to make a profit and create wealth and employment opportunities, which can all have an important social role.
- **Symbolic value** – as a tangible indicator of (technological) 'progress' that in the modern view, as we saw in previous chapters, is regarded as meaningful; an understanding that, in today's late-modern or post-modern context, is increasingly contested.
- **Symbolic value** – as a tangible socio-positional artefact associated with competitive individualism and expressed through acquisition of the latest technologies, products and fashions.[51,52]

These latter 'symbolic' elements can encourage consumerism and are, therefore, problematic with regard to sustainability. While some of the activities made possible by modern electronic goods may relate to more substantive values, there can be little doubt that the overarching effect of our current conceptions of technology emphasizes instrumental benefits that are disassociated from deeper, more holistic understandings of fulfilment and meaning. Moreover, the cumulative effects of producing such large quantities of relatively short-lived, energy-dependent products via a globalized industrial system are clearly incompatible with the environmental priorities of sustainability.

It becomes incumbent on the design disciplines, therefore, to envision new ways of conceiving technology – not by rejecting it and retrenching to some romantic idea of simple living, but by imaginatively positing alternative propositions that contextualize technological benefits within a more comprehensive, more profound set of considerations. I have previously mentioned various constructive change directions – but critical to any such change will be technology reform. As Feenburg has explained, this will require a radical reconstruction of practices to reconcile instrumental benefits with substantive values through greater emphasis on democratic forms of technological development that internalize qualitative considerations such as environmental care and healthy, enriching work.[53] Such reform will require a renewal of the role of locale, the realization that production does not have to be global to be successful and that local employment can open up local markets.[54] This would not only contribute to environmental improvements – through product recovery and repair – but also to greater equality in society through more distributed wealth creation opportunities. In turn, greater equality has been linked to economic stability and social and environmental sustainability.[55]

These directions recognize the inadequacies of our current conceptions of technological products – in both the personal benefits they afford and the unsustainable modes of production and disposal they employ. They also indicate that reform is needed, not only to more effectively tackle environmental and social concerns, but also to address more substantive values related to human purpose and meaning. As an artefact that illustrates these latter factors especially, in both its physical design and its use, and which also includes clear distinctions from similar versions intended for more prosaic purposes, the *shakuhachi* flute is an exceptionally germane example.

Developing more meaningful design approaches

The social damage and exploitation related to globalization, together with increasing environmental degradation attest to the ethical shortcomings that accompany our contemporary product manufacturing and marketing system; a system that encourages competition rather than cooperation, greed and wealth accumulation rather than charity and wealth distribution, and which tends to deny, obfuscate or externalize the environmental and social ramifications of its activities.[56,57] Furthermore, philosophical and spiritual traditions from all over the world have, for millennia, emphasized self-knowledge, introspection and reflective modes as key ingredients of human happiness and of living a meaningful life. In stark contrast to these traditions, much of our contemporary material culture is intentionally designed to be distracting – through, for example, a host of often compelling entertainment products and technological goods that interrupt and intrude upon our thoughts, that enable and encourage multitasking, and that absorb our minds and our time, thereby hindering more considered and reflective modes of living.

To address the serious deficiencies in our design conventions and, more generally, our manufacturing and economic systems, a fundamental change in philosophy and motivation will be needed. This consideration of the *shakuhachi* flute, and comparison with contemporary electronic products, help focus the discussion on the particularities of design. It allows the implications of generalized theoretical discussions emerging from the philosophy of technology, the social sciences and environmental philosophy to be considered in terms that are more pertinent to the concerns of the designer. It provides a basis for developing new priorities to tackle those very issues of environmental and social responsibility that are proving so difficult to deal with when pursued via the sophisticated but highly transient versions of consumer goods proffered by globalized capitalism.

The findings from the *shakuhachi* enable us to see our current priorities from a fresh perspective and they challenge many of our prevailing assumptions. While these findings may not all be applicable in the design of a contemporary technological product, they do provide a basis for reappraising many design conventions and for resolving the destructive division that has developed between instrumental and more substantive values. The latter generally fall outside the conceptual frame in which technology-related design possibilities are considered and therefore, as technological goods proliferate and become more significant elements in our ways of living, substantive values become increasingly attenuated and largely absent from our conceptions of and engagement with material culture.[58]

Transforming design

Having described the various features of the *shakuhachi*, and considered some of the more important directions emerging from contemporary discussions on design and technology, it is now necessary to draw these threads together. This will allow us to discern where the distinctive attributes of this culturally rich, spiritually relevant and enduring artefact might contribute to our understandings of design for sustainability, and especially our responses to technology reform.

The *shakuhachi* is a functional object that is wholly compatible with environmental considerations because its material constituents are entirely natural and renewable. As an exercise in learning and understanding the nature of the instrument, some traditional Japanese teachers of the *shakuhachi* require their students to gather bamboo, and make and play their own flute.[59] This firsthand experience – from local resource acquisition to final artefact – imparts a direct and intimate knowledge of materials, process and impacts. The transformation from a living organism to an artefact that is capable of producing sound helps instil a deeper understanding of and respect for the connection between the natural environment and human provision.

In addition, the *hōchiku* type *shakuhachi* is an object in which design, function and application have become fully integrated within an holistic and profound understanding of human purpose. Its raw, natural state is fully in accord with the individualized form of use characteristic of meditative practice, where over-refinement in detailing, finish and making would be superfluous and counterproductive. Conformity to some predetermined, objective standard is not relevant, and the rawness of construction, which imbues each instrument with its own distinctive qualities, strengthens the sense of connection between the user and their own individual instrument. These physical particularities affect both the nature of use and the quality of the sounds produced, creating a unique set of interdependent relationships between the fully engaged user and the material artefact.

In virtually every respect, these various features and processes contrast markedly with those of contemporary electronic consumer goods, which are homogeneous in their design and production, and are based on widely dispersed, segregated decisions and processes remote from – and often largely disinterested in – the social and environmental ramifications. This physical and psychological detachment from human concerns and from the intimacies of place has led to a systemic impoverishment of ethical and environmental responsibilities. It is a system in which people and natural places become viewed in instrumental and economic terms – as units of work or as tonnage of resources. As a consequence, in many countries, factory employees work long hours in poor conditions, have few rights and live in on-site worker dormitories where they are far removed from family and friends, and resource extraction operations create barren, denuded and polluted landscapes.[60]

123

While the damaging consequences of our current conceptions of product design and production are indisputable, recognition of the real and potential benefits of technological goods challenges us to fundamentally re-evaluate many of our assumptions and industry conventions, and to re-imagine what such goods could be and how they might be created and used. As we have seen, to transform our approaches so that the critical, systemic failings are overcome, many are suggesting a significant shift in priorities and processes. A crucial aspect of this is a renewed emphasis on localization, in terms of resource acquisition and use, and in terms of engagement, decision-making and control by the people employed or affected. Such an emphasis, which allows for direct acknowledgement and a vested appreciation of the consequences, would encourage a deeper connection to people and place.

Perhaps more critically, such a transformation requires a rethinking in how we conceive of and design technological goods, in terms of their purpose and meaning. When technological goods are characterized by shallowness of purpose, absence of deeper notions of human capacity and endless opportunities for diversion, the result is an erosion of human potential and sense of meaning. From an examination of the *shakuhachi* we see that, in the way in which a functional object can be manifested and used, it can transcend mere instrumental concerns to include an holistic environment-object-user interrelationship that has intrinsic value by enabling an enriching engagement that nurtures and expands human capacity. This kind of engagement deepens our knowledge, understanding and sense of appreciation and admiration – what Borgmann refers to as the commanding presence of reality.[61] When a technological device is conceived and used primarily in terms of its instrumental value, its presence and our engagement with it are lessened – it becomes simply a means to achieve some end. In the traditions of the *shakuhachi*, this is seen as a corruption of purpose because it fails to recognize the intrinsic value of the 'doing' – the beauty of learning and wonder of discovering through full engagement with the activity in a way that is unmotivated by success or failure.[62] This 'doing' is always conducted in the present moment – the present in which our lives are actually lived, it cannot be otherwise. A sense of delight and meaningfulness can emerge from such engagement; but while this may be the result, it is not a goal. However, when the inherent value of this moment is not appropriately recognized in the design and functionality of an artefact then, effectively, its use will be life-diminishing.

It becomes apparent that a significant part of technological reform will be to develop concepts that combine instrumental benefit with a greater sense of engagement. This will mean designing products in a manner that integrates aspects of mass-production with localization, environmental responsibilities and more profound notions of human purpose and meaning. It also means greater acknowledgement of the impacts of our activities, which must become internalized within product production and use. And it requires a transformation in our conceptions of business towards distributed, localized working communities.[63] Potentially, through such transformations, technological objects could become enduring but evolving elements of our material culture. This would allow them to acquire greater emotional durability and symbolic meanings that are more consistent with substantive values.

Such a prospect requires a new imagining. Necessarily, the products of such a change would be very different from those of today and their development will require a new, revitalized creativity – one that captures the true spirit of design. It is a challenging opportunity that implies a transformation of our processes, our products and, potentially, ourselves.

10

Wrapped Attention

designing products
for evolving
permanence
and enduring
meaning

My mind leads me to speak now
of forms changed into new bodies

Ovid

If we were to walk down a busy street, sit in an airport departure lounge, or take a journey on a train, we would be certain to see many people using a variety of small electronic goods. They might be listening to music on headphones, having a conversation on a mobile phone, taking a photograph with a digital camera or sending an email on a laptop computer. Sometimes, people engage in several activities at the same time (Figure 10.1). Such sights have become ubiquitous and they raise a number of issues related to our current conceptions of products. The conventions that underlie the design of electronic products are not only linked to how they are made, the longevity of their use and what happens to them after their useful life has ended, but also to how these products are used and the kinds of use they encourage. All these factors have implications for the responsibilities of industrial design in the 21st century in addressing sustainability and 'meaning'.

This chapter begins with an examination of the so called 'triple bottom line of sustainability', which is expanded to include 'personal meaning'. The relevance of this fourth element becomes evident in light of research that suggests multitasking and partial attention, as are common in the use of electronic devices, can have detrimental effects on behaviours and values related to social responsibility, environmental stewardship and substantive notions of meaning. These issues raise a number of design challenges and this in turn leads to the development of design priorities that seek compatibility both with more reflective product use patterns and with sustainability. The implications of these priorities are then explored and illustrated via a series of conceptual designs.

The propositional designs that emerge from this study transform general principles into specific, tangible objects. Of course, these are not definitive and many other design outcomes are also possible. However, the examples included here serve to illustrate the potential of an alternative direction – one that not only offers a fruitful way forward that is more localized, more flexible, more enduring and less socially and environmentally damaging but also is in closer accord with ideas of personal meaning.

126

Figure 10.1
Multitasking
talking on the phone, selecting music tracks and walking down the street

Beyond the triple bottom line

Sustainability is commonly expressed in terms of the triple bottom line, which refers to the interdependent economic, environmental and social factors associated with human activities.[1] Some have suggested that a fourth element is needed, but there seems little agreement about what this should be; it often appears to be determined by the particular roles of those suggesting it. Some, among them local governments, have proposed a quadruple bottom line that includes 'culture',[2,3] others identify the missing ingredient as 'governance',[4,5] and still others suggest 'culture/ethics'.[6] Although these options might add a useful focus for certain sectors, none are especially valuable in advancing a more personally compelling understanding of sustainability, nor do they address the relationship between our activities and more profound notions of human purpose and fulfilment. Indeed, all these propositions can be subsumed within the *triple* bottom line. Aspects of governance, culture and ethics are related to social relationships and the development and well-being of communities and therefore can be included in the social and/or economic considerations of sustainability. What is missing from the triple bottom line is explicit recognition that human beings are not only gregarious creatures, but also individuals. Further still, we are individuals who are meaning-seekers.[7]

To ensure that our activities are both relevant to us as individuals and substantive, we must include an additional element in our conception of sustainability that recognizes the importance of this inner, more profound characteristic.[8] To this end, it has been suggested that the fourth ingredient should be spirituality,[9] and it is certainly true that this term conveys an expansive range of understandings and practices that are intimately related to meaning and the individual. However, for some, this term may be problematic because of its close associations with the soul, the sacred and religion. For this reason, and recognizing the importance of substantive values in linking sustainability with the individual, the fourth element of a quadruple bottom line for sustainability proposed here is 'personal meaning' – a term acknowledging that sustainability has to be relevant and meaningful to the individual person, as well as socially responsible. It is a term that is broad enough to include a wide range of understandings and practices that different people find meaningful and enriching. This is *not* to say that any and all understandings and activities will be meaningful; the emphasis is on those that are congruent with deeper values[10] and those more profound, meaning-seeking aspects of our humanity. Through advertising and marketing, we are constantly urged toward self-indulgence and pleasure-seeking but, for millennia, self-discipline, contemplation and virtue have all been essential aspects of the meaningful life and substantive notions of human happiness. It is also important to note the connection between personal meaning and the other elements of sustainability. For example, deteriorating ecosystems have been linked to a degradation of these deeper understandings of meaning as well as cultural identity and a variety of other factors related to the well-being of the individual.[11]

127

It is this notion of personal meaning that I would like to explore here in relation to the design and use of electronic goods. By considering how this factor might inform the priorities of design, it becomes apparent that a remarkable synergy can be reached among economic imperatives, environmental responsibilities, social concerns and substantive matters of personal meaning.

The banality of a shallow blindness

It was mentioned above that people often use electronic products in conjunction with other activities, such as listening to music on headphones and typing on a laptop computer while sipping coffee as one travels on a train. When we engage in these kinds of activities, we not only cut ourselves off from our immediate environment but also divide our attention; our mind flits from one thing to another in a rather superficial, unreflective manner. It might be said that we do not allow ourselves the opportunity to be fully cognizant of our surroundings and other people, we do not fully appreciate the music or the taste of the coffee, and we do not fully concentrate on the activity in which we are engaged on the laptop computer.

Findings from neuroscience research indicate that when two tasks are performed simultaneously, we devote fewer resources to each one, and distractions can affect how information is learned, resulting in the information being less useful in the future. Although it has been conjectured that the brain can adapt, balancing multitasking with extended periods of concentration, there is little evidence to show that this capacity to balance is actually possible.[12] The effects of multitasking on concentration have been acknowledged for many years, for example, in areas such as driving, where mobile phone use can significantly increase the risk of accidents.[13,14] Studies also indicate that information overload and multitasking can adversely affect our ability to be empathetic, ethically responsive, compassionate and tolerant and to develop emotional stability – all traits that, traditionally, have been associated with the term 'wisdom'. Our capacity for empathy, to be inspired or to be ethically concerned has been linked to the slower acting parts of the brain that require time to reflect on the information received, and it is these parts that appear to be circumvented when we engage in multiple activities simultaneously. Prolonged periods of multitasking via technological products have also been linked to an increase in anxiety and depression and a reduction in attention, intellectual ability and workplace productivity.[15–17] In addition, research into mobile phone use among young people aged 18–25 indicates that many are using their phones for several hours a day. They become upset if their calls and messages are not answered, often neglect important activities, become distanced from friends and family, and can experience problems in developing social relationships. They also feel the need to be constantly connected, becoming distressed and anxious if they do not have access to their phone.[18]

An associated concern, related to the drive to expand the development and use of services enabled by digital technologies,[19] is that these technologies offer only a filtered and unsubstantive version of reality. Despite offering 'connection', they have the effect of separating us from a direct interaction with, and awareness of, our world, which serves to add to our 'blindness'.[20] This separating effect also applies to our interactions with other people. Caller identification allows us to choose with whom we talk, and email enables us to control when and with whom we communicate; this control increases the distance between ourselves and the other – whether a friend or a stranger.[21] Text-based communications, bereft as they are of tone of voice, facial expression and other subtle forms of nonverbal communication, can also lead to misinterpretations and misjudgements.

Of course, the various concerns associated with technological goods cannot be addressed solely by product design. The modes of behaviour that such goods enable are partly a function of how they are conceived and designed and partly a function of personal choice. Nevertheless, the knowledge and creative skills of the designer can play an important role in envisioning a different path – one that is not only more environmentally benign, socially responsible and economically equitable but also, potentially, more personally meaningful to users of these products. However, on the whole, the profession is not facing up to these issues. One critic has suggested that industrial design has been reduced to toying with the surfaces of technological products and has failed to live up to its responsibilities.[22] Another suggests that making 'stuff' and the creativity related to making new 'stuff' represent the past paradigm.[23] Thus, if industrial design is to address these considerable challenges, it needs to be reinvigorated through a new sense of purpose.

129

New directions and the role of speculative design

To confront these issues, we must find ways to renew the profession by developing agendas and propositions that envision what is desirable, meaningful and sustainable; the responsibility to do so lies partly with those in the profession itself and partly with the academic institutions that educate and train its future participants. Design in academia has the opportunity to focus on fundamental, conceptual design in ways that are often more difficult to justify in corporate culture. Design at universities has the capacity and freedom to critique current approaches, examine their insufficiencies and explore new possibilities in ways that are removed from the day-to-day priorities of design consultancy (see Figure 10.2), and, in view of the urgent requirement for alternative, more benign ways forward, it has an obligation to do so.

For the contribution of design to be worthwhile and meaningful, it cannot simply produce difference and novelty as a way of stimulating sales. Such a role diminishes the discipline to a mere tool of capitalism and denies its responsibility and potential to contribute to the common good; and as we have seen, some have argued that this is just what has happened to industrial design. In developing

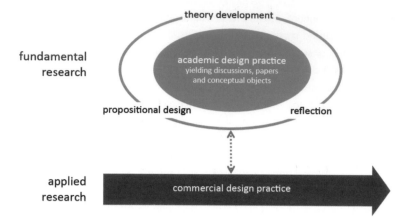

theory development

fundamental
research

academic design practice
yielding discussions, papers
and conceptual objects

propositional design

reflection

applied
research

commercial design practice

Figure 10.2
Fundamental design research in academia

a more responsible, revitalized path for design, its outcomes not only have to offer some pragmatic benefit or usefulness, which in the case of contemporary electronic products is predominantly based on the work of scientists and technologists, but must also be conceptually in accord with sustainability and facilitate forms of use that are responsible and considered.

It is important to appreciate that the role of speculative design work within academia is not to develop potentially viable 'solutions' that can be tested or measured against some predetermined, pragmatic criteria. Rather, its purpose is to probe and challenge our assumptions and to explore other, imaginative avenues that appear to be worthwhile. The objective of this kind of work is not necessarily to convince but to raise questions by exploring new design directions based on sound reasoning, which can be informed by emerging research in other fields. Such creativity-based research is driven by envisioning new possibilities, and differs in emphasis and purpose from reactive problem-solving.[24] Although this kind of work represents a particular opportunity for design within academia, some companies, such as Philips in the Netherlands, also dedicate resources to speculative inquiry, developing creative 'design probes' that explore new directions and challenge assumptions.[25,26]

Sustainability, production and product meaning

Let us now consider some of the principal inadequacies of our current approaches, especially those linked to sustainability, production and the nature of the product. This survey will allow us to identify new priorities for industrial design, and these priorities can, in turn, provide a basis for conceptual exploration:

Sustainability: Activities that aim to conform to the principles of sustainability must take into account the interrelated elements of the triple bottom line or, as has been argued here, the quadruple bottom line. The notion of sustainability requires us to explore avenues by which its various elements are addressed *concurrently*

130

and in ways that are mutually reifying. Unfortunately, we are a long way from this perspective. If they are considered at all, it is more common to address the damaging consequences of our endeavours as separate issues that require discrete actions. We try to offset the negative effects from one activity by engaging in another, which is entirely removed from the problem and its cause. For instance, one London-based organization offers people the opportunity to offset the negative environmental effects of using an iPod by planting a tree in New Zealand.[27] These kinds of initiatives can be a convenient substitute for carefully examining and reforming one's own practices.

Production: If we are to focus on the heart of the problem, the issues that arise from our specific activities have to be critiqued in relation to the priorities of sustainability and dealt with directly. In recent years, for example, mobile phone use has grown enormously all over the world, with tens of millions of units being manufactured and shipped each year. Although their compact size offers portability and a convenient means of staying in touch, their relationship to sustainability raises many concerns, not least in the ways in which they are produced. A brief outline of the main concerns will suffice in this context. For example, in terms of the economic considerations, manufacturers of these devices accrue significant annual profits.[28] Such profits are possible because first, in the manufacturing plants, employees are frequently expected to work excessive hours for low wages, with few basic rights.[29] Second, the environmental consequences of their production, shipping, use and disposal are not included in the accounting but are designated 'externalities'. Moreover, even where legislation exists to prevent companies 'externalizing' factors that have damaging environmental and social consequences,[30] illegal practices often result in toxic electronic waste being dumped in poorer countries.[31]

The product: If we consider the nature of the product itself, further concerns can be raised. Even though many different companies manufacture mobile phones, these products all reflect a similar set of design priorities; conceptually, there is little to choose between them. They are all compact, fairly robust devices that are easy to use and convenient to carry on one's person, and they all offer a host of functions in addition to being able to make and receive calls. On the face of it, these product features seem logical, reasonable and desirable, but these seemingly universally embedded notions of 'mobile phone' need to be examined in relation to the quadruple bottom line. This will allow us to develop a reformed set of priorities and establish a basis for exploring an alternative way forward.

When we decide to buy a mobile phone, we are faced with hundreds of different models. Prices vary considerably between the simplest phones and those offering a greater number of functions, and some can be tailored to one's personal requirements by downloading applications from the internet. However, in all cases the physical product is a small, hand-held device that is a discrete, fixed manifestation of a particular stage of technological development. We can choose between a touch screen and a keypad, and between a keypad on the

131

front of the phone and a slide or flip design feature, and we can choose from a variety of colours, but such differences are relatively trivial. We are also aware that, whichever phone we select, within a few years it will be outmoded and of little monetary or functional value. At this point, it will probably be discarded and replaced with a more up-to-date model, which will be another fixed entity that represents a slightly more advanced stage of technological development. In addition, when we purchase such a product, we need have little understanding of the technology on which it is based, where it comes from or the effects of its manufacture, use and disposal.

While the intricacies of digital technologies are highly complex and may well be beyond the interest of most people, it *is* possible to design electronic goods in ways that allow our decisions to be more closely associated with their consequences and that help foster a more enduring and meaningful notion of material culture. For instance, we currently cannot purchase a phone that will last for many years, that allows us to update the hardware as technology advances, and that could be considered an heirloom object that has the potential to be transgenerational in its appeal and its usefulness. We cannot select a phone that is capable of being incrementally modified in terms of its parts as our needs change, or that we can update aesthetically from locally made, culturally relevant components. And we cannot choose among phones that are conceptually diverse in terms of how their functional benefits are manifested. These various possibilities, none of which are available, could yield a more enduring interpretation of electronic products, increased opportunities for understanding and personal control of one's material goods, and greater levels of attachment. As we will see, such possibilities could also substantially reduce electronic waste and pollution and their associated consequences because individual components could be exchanged and upgraded – rather than whole products being discarded and replaced.

132

In terms of their use, the kinds of phones currently available facilitate forms of interaction that can contribute to problems associated with information overload and multitasking. The very design priorities that emphasize convenience also facilitate impulsive, unreflective use patterns that interrupt thoughts and tasks. For example, many phones include a variety of electronic games and internet functions that provide endless opportunities for distraction and, as discussed above, constantly browsing websites and checking for messages or emails can lead to addiction-like behaviours.

This survey offers clear illustrations of how our current conceptions of electronic goods – and perhaps the mobile phone in particular – support production practices that, although highly profitable, are associated with considerable environmental consequences, social inequity, ethically questionable employment regimes and massive amounts of toxic electronic waste that is often dumped, sometimes illegally, in politically or economically powerless regions. Moreover, the patterns of use of such products are associated with an erosion of empathy and ethical concern, as well as compulsive behaviours that have been linked to a variety of psychological disorders.

Although market competitiveness is a critical factor in defining the physical characteristics of a product, when manufacturers all compete by producing essentially the same kinds of goods, there is little market distinctiveness and few opportunities for people to select products that potentially represent a more positive way forward. Despite significant public awareness of the negative environmental and social consequences of consumerism, people are not being offered choices that emerge from a more meaningful and sustainable ethos. The characteristics and conventions of a production/consumption system that leads to damaging practices and harmful effects, and products that foster unreflective use patterns, are also those that restrict genuine choice. For significant change to occur, therefore, new kinds of product designs are needed, along with new kinds of enterprise models – models that not only allow for greater participation in the development and definition of products but also, potentially, contribute to community cohesion and capacity[37] and increase personal influence and product understanding.

New design values for the quadruple bottom line

To tackle these various shortcomings, design and production need to develop ways forward that are capable of taking full advantage of the opportunities made possible by technological advance while attending to the social, environmental and economic requirements of sustainability and to more substantive questions of personal meaning and fulfilment. To address these interrelated factors, design priorities are required that allow electronic products to:

- **Evolve continuously** as technology progresses, tastes change and new possibilities are developed, thereby benefiting from scientific advance and new forms of visual expression.
- **Accommodate change** in the form of new hardware components whose future volumetric requirements are both unknown and unpredictable; thus enabling incremental change through replacement of individual components, rather than whole product disposal and replacement. This would help reduce environmental burdens.
- **Be maintained, repaired and upgraded locally**. This would have positive impacts on localization, sustainability and the development of a more lasting, relevant and personally meaningful material culture.
- **Foster more considered, less distracting use patterns**. Electronic products whose design enables a focused mode of use, with fewer diversions and interruptions, would create genuine choice and more meaningful forms of engagement. The benefits of the digital economy would thus be in closer accord with enduring understandings of personal meaning and fulfilment.

133

- **Internalize impacts** through new enterprise models in which considerations related to sustainability are core to the activities. For example, business models that include product repair and upgrade services lead to meaningful, enduring and mutually beneficial relationships between producers and the people who use their products. Distributed forms of innovation, production, remanufacture and recycling create local employment and locally relevant solutions, and they draw on a wealth of imaginative possibilities while resulting in more environmentally benign and more equitable service-oriented solutions. Moreover, these electronic products could be conceived as reliable, long-lasting tools – basic workhorses whose hardware can be intermittently upgraded and supplemented with software and services provided via standard interfaces.

These design priorities emerge from a consideration of electronic products in relation to sustainability and meaning. However, they are congruent with the findings of an independent study that drew on the views of four consultative panels – 'futures', 'design', 'clients' and 'policy-makers'.[33]

The conceptual design of a mobile phone

For illustrative purposes, alternative concepts for a mobile phone have been developed that explore and encapsulate the implications of the criteria listed above. These propositions, while not intended to be viable products for the market, represent how these general criteria might be translated into physical artefacts. Their purpose is to indicate potential directions for electronic goods that respond to sustainability critiques and to the detrimental effects of multitasking and unreflective, often addiction-like use patterns. However, the concepts presented here also fully recognize the importance of scientific and technological advances and their part in improving our material culture and living standards.

To conform to the requirements outlined, the product has to be designed in a manner that enables its constituent elements to be incrementally changed over time, for purposes of repair or upgrading. Developing such a design requires a shift in how we think about the product. We have to move away from seeing it as a fixed commodity that is locked in a particular timeframe and therefore subject to obsolescence. Instead, we must begin to conceive of it as an object in a continual state of flux – as an ever-present but ever-changing, provisional product. When we think of a product as a fixed entity, we see the current product as the latest version. Earlier versions came before, and more advanced ones will be available in the future. This conception is fundamentally unsustainable because the earlier models usually end up in landfills,[34] and future versions require new resources and energy, with all the environmental consequences their extraction, processing and shipping entail. In contrast, when we regard a product as a continually evolving entity that is always with us, individual parts can be exchanged and upgraded to take advantage of new technological developments, with major reductions in waste, pollution and resource use.

Significantly, because technology is in a continual state of development, it is not possible to predict exactly what the upgrade components will be – the technologies they will employ or their size and shape. Thus, rather than creating a rigid enclosure to contain the various parts, it becomes necessary to develop solutions in which the parts are more loosely connected. As the product changes and evolves over its extended useful life, more advanced parts can be substituted. This type of evolution also suggests that any form of encasement should be flexible enough to accommodate these changing forms and sizes of components.

In the first concept developed here, the Pouch Phone (Figure 10.3), a simple fabric wrap contains the separate components of a mobile phone (Figure 10.4). This design allows the product to be incrementally upgraded as technology advances, and the flexible wrap does not constrain the inclusion of new components that may be volumetrically dissimilar to those that went before. In this disassembled state it is not a mobile phone but simply a collection of parts. Thus, it would not interrupt or intrude upon the owner's thoughts or current activities; incoming calls would simply be transferred to a message service.

Figure 10.3
'Pouch Phone' – concept

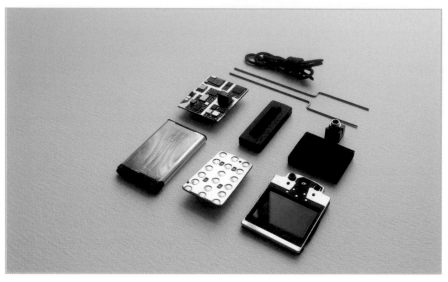

Figure 10.4
Separate components of the 'Pouch Phone' concept

The phone can be quickly assembled to create a functional arrangement in order to make a call, send a text or review stored messages – when these activities can be given dedicated attention (Figure 10.5). Although this takes only a short time, it does require a conscious decision to use the phone. When assembled, the user can attend to messages and calls as a *focused activity* (Figure 10.6). When these tasks are complete, the parts are again stored in the wrap. Thus, through its essential design as an object, this concept offers a form of use that eliminates unwanted disruptions to ongoing activities. It does not disturb face-to-face conversations or ring unexpectedly in a meeting or at a theatre performance. It also reduces the potential for impulsive use because the small amount of effort required to assemble the phone may be enough to create pause, to consider the necessity of making a call at a particular time, compared to continuing one's current activity. Thus, in this concept, the requirement for assembly prioritizes considered use over convenience and mitigates unreflective use patterns.

The Pouch Phone concept (Figure 10.7a) represents one way of encapsulating priorities of continual upgrade and considered use. However, the same principles can be expressed in very different ways. The Wallet Phone concept (Figure 10.7b) can also be incrementally upgraded but does not require assembly. It imposes somewhat tighter volumetric restrictions on component upgrades than the Pouch Phone but allows for rather more convenient use. The Pocket Phone concept (Figure 10.7c) is similar to a regular mobile phone, but with the advantage that individual components can be upgraded over time. Thus, these concepts offer a range of meaningful choices that encourage varying degrees of considered use and they offer product-service solutions in which selected parts manufacturing and component upgrades can be provided at the local level.

Figure 10.5
'Pouch Phone' – assembled for use

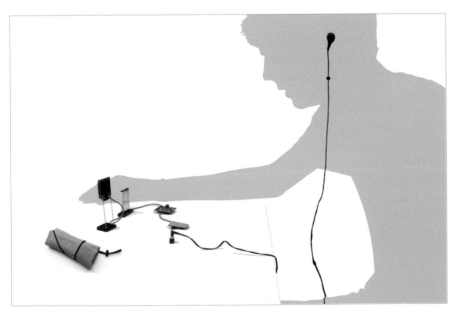

Figure 10.6
'Pouch Phone' in use – focused attention

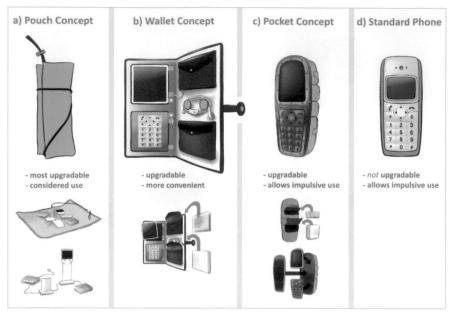

Figure 10.7
Meaningful choice – concepts offer varying degrees of upgradability and considered use

138   Such concepts have considerable environmental benefits. For example, if we consider nine incremental stages of product upgrade over a period of years, Pouch Phone A can be transformed into Pouch Phone J, with minimum waste (Figure 10.8). Rather than discarding nine full mobile phones over the same time period, users exchange only those parts required to upgrade the product. Through these stages, a number of individual parts (for example, screen, circuit board, battery and keyboard) will need replacement, either because of wear or because they become technologically outmoded. As individual components, they could be more readily recycled than complete products. In the illustrated example, this design results in obsolete components equivalent to about one and a half to two mobile phones (Figure 10.9). This represents an estimated 80 per cent reduction in electronic waste, assuming that, with conventional designs, nine complete mobile phones would be discarded in the same period to gain the equivalent technological benefits. When we consider that 400 million mobile phones are discarded each year,[35] such a design concept could contribute to major reductions in the disposal of mixed, toxic materials – equivalent to about 320 million phones per year.

In terms of environmental and social gains, the benefits over conventional models are considerable. Through incremental component change via local services, it becomes possible to reduce energy use and waste while creating local employment opportunities. This type of incremental upgrading, in conjunction with a more service-based business model, has already been explored in other sectors.

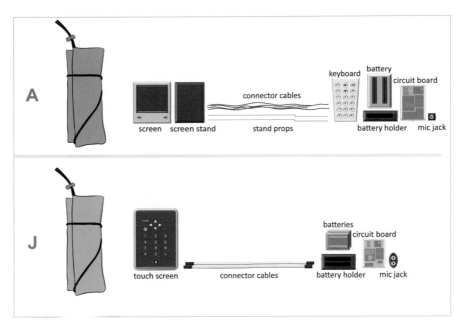

Figure 10.8
Nine stages of incremental upgrading transform Phone A to Phone J

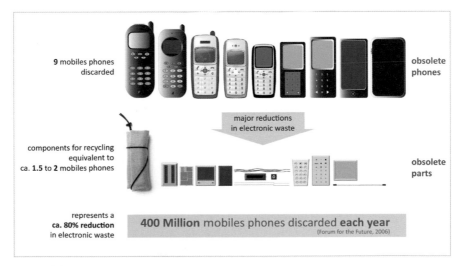

Figure 10.9
Environmental benefits of an incrementally upgradable phone concept, compared to disposal and replacement of regular mobile phones

In principle, the Pouch Phone concept is not unlike the approach developed by Interface Incorporated, the world's largest manufacturer of modular floor coverings. In the 1990s, the company redirected its vision to align its business more closely with the principles of sustainability. Instead of manufacturing and selling conventional carpets, the company produces modular carpets, elements of which can be selectively changed via extended service provision, and each aspect of the company has been scrutinized to comply with the highest standards of sustainability.[36]

When purchasing an ever-present, upgradable phone, people would have the knowledge that they are acquiring a product that will endure over an extended period of time, which can take advantage of new technologies as they become available and that can be maintained and reconstituted via locally available services. While the electronic components would still be mass-produced, other parts could be made locally. For example, the carrying pouch and screen stand could be made from a variety of locally available materials and, potentially, more complex components and tailored circuit boards could be produced using rapid prototyping and small-scale assembly technologies. Thus, such a concept is conducive to the development of local enterprises and to the integration of local and mass-produced forms of production. It also offers opportunities for products to reflect indigenous skills and cultural preferences, thereby contributing to a sense of cultural identity. In addition, the product would become a more enduring element of a person's material possessions, giving a sense that it is something worth caring for. Conceptually, it would no longer be a fixed – and therefore transient – acquisition offering only temporary benefit until a more advanced model arrives on the market. Finally, through the visibility of its constituent parts, its mode of use and its accompanying service provision, a greater sense of understanding of the object could develop, affording people an enriched experience of what the product is as a thing.

Although such concepts might not suit everyone's needs, they do illustrate an alternative path for the development of electronic goods that appears to fulfil many requirements of sustainability while encouraging forms of use that are more closely aligned with focused attention and understandings of personal meaning.

All these concepts enable practical tasks to be performed. Their constituent components result from scientific inquiry and rationalistic application, which represent important, but today predominant, aspects of our thinking. The Pouch Phone concept in particular stores these components in a disassembled state within an organic, flexible wrap. This represents a hiatus in the prevalent logic that would see these elements arranged in ready-to-use, rigid enclosures. Such encasements offer convenience, but also facilitate impulsive use, prevent adaptation, anchor products in time and guarantee their premature obsolescence. Questioning the importance of convenience allows room for another mode of thinking and an additional way of appreciating scientific advance and the ever-progressing ingenuity of humanity. It brings attention to the fact that the individual components will be continually replaced and upgraded, that this product evolution can be accommodated and, even though the elements within the pouch may regularly and incrementally change, the product itself will remain a constant. The concept also requires focused attention – a conscious decision must be made to dedicate time to it and a kind of ritual must be repeated each time it is used. The components must be unpacked, arranged in an order and connected together in a particular way. Convenience is replaced by a more reflective process that helps foster a 'focal practice' of product engagement[37] and helps steer one away from impulsive and potentially addictive use patterns.

As we have seen, the use of contemporary electronic devices can become compulsive and stoke the flames of ego – to be connected is to exist, to be relevant. All the major philosophical traditions have long taught that the path to wisdom and happiness depends on letting go of ego through selflessness and consideration of others. The detrimental consequences of electronic products can be considered in these terms, from potentially harmful use patterns to exploitative working practices in their manufacture to the dumping of toxic e-waste in poor countries. All these practices are antithetical to substantive values. The concepts presented here suggest a different relationship with technological goods by proposing a direction that is not only more compatible with the principles of sustainability but also facilitates a more considered use – one that is in accord with notions of inner meaning.

141

11

Temporal Objects

design, change
and sustainability

most of our troubles stem from attachment to
things that we mistakenly see as permanent

Dalai Lama XIV

When we create things we draw on the materials of the Earth. In the process, we unavoidably alter and in some way diminish the natural world. To build a road, we dig up vegetation and soil that may have been centuries in the making. We blast and crush rock and exploit hydrocarbons that were formed over millions of years. And we pave over land that once provided habitats, absorbed rainfall and was part of the ever-changing cycles of nature. Such industrious human activities have long been so commonplace that they are done without compunction. Indeed, our language reveals how we tend to regard the natural environment – we speak of its constituents as 'resources' and sources of 'supply' that are there to 'exploit'.

Today, we are beginning to realize that nature is fragile, precious and not inexhaustible. Yet, the attitudes that brought us to this place remain prevalent, and modifying our behaviours can seem onerously slow. Even though we have an overabundance of information about the global implications of our collective activities, vested interests and disagreements between nations have time and again resulted in procrastination and inaction.[1,2] And measures and programmes that aim to offset the effects of our activities, while they might assuage guilt, are often ineffective or even counterproductive;[3] one prominent climate scientist has even likened carbon trading to selling indulgences.[4]

Change towards more sustainable ways of living, if it is to be effective, has to occur at the level of our ordinary individual acts. Sustainability cannot be externally imposed through a one-size-fits-all approach. In conjunction with international agreements and regulation, progress depends on growing a culture of sustainability. Effecting meaningful and significant change at this everyday level requires a new sensitivity and the development of fresh perspectives. Whatever our role in society, there is a need to reflect upon our activities and, where necessary, develop new practices. Such changes can yield many benefits for individuals and communities, quite apart from any potential long-term contributions to the well-being of the natural environment.

In exploring these ideas and their implications for product design, this chapter focuses on the development of a series of functional objects that combine unprocessed natural materials with technological parts and mass-produced components with locally made elements. Thus, a number of themes from earlier discussions are brought together and, in doing so, the propositional objects highlight how locale and the concept of evolving permanence can influence the nature and aesthetics of technological objects. Here, these considerations are brought to bear in the design of simple *electrical* objects; subsequent chapters will look at how they can affect the design of *electronic* objects.

Traditionally, the designer's area of concern has been restricted to the product itself. However, the product exists within a wider system of production, consumption and disposal. To make this system less damaging, we have to change each interrelated element in ways that represent new understandings and different priorities. This is difficult to do because the system is large, multifaceted and complex and has its own inertia, making it cumbersome and unresponsive to change. The system may be problematic but at least it is known and to this point in our history it has 'worked', particularly in terms of creating economic wealth and material benefits for many. Change, on the other hand, is uncertain, risky and uncomfortable. We can try to change the system from the top down by responding to the problems it creates, but without a clear idea of what we are trying to achieve, top-down systemic changes will tend to remain incremental, reflexive, disparate and reluctant. This kind of reactive problem solving is quite different from creating new visions of how we might live and developing more positive ways forward.[5]

An alternative is to address the issues from the bottom up – to look at how products can emerge from, and be aligned with, new sensibilities – and then to develop a system that supports their effective production. Potentially, through many such bottom-up approaches and their cumulative effects, our larger, globalized production systems, which are proving so damaging and so intractable, can become transformed.

In this approach, designing, understood as a creative, integrated and iterative process of *thinking-and-doing*, becomes a key element of broader strategic change. The conceptual object or prototype becomes a tangible expression not just of functionality and aesthetics but also of strategic ideas that can illuminate and help steer systemic reform and renewal. This more expansive notion of designing, which some refer to as *design thinking*, is becoming an important aspect of contemporary design and a valuable driver of change.[6] *Design thinking*, however, is a problematic term because it fails to convey the essential *thinking-and-doing* nature of the creative process. Indeed, there are design critics who refute the whole notion of *design thinking* as a distinct category;[7] *thinking-and-doing* is a more accurate description of the iterative designing process.

Design and technology

To design a functional object, two main categories of components have to be considered. Firstly, there are the technological components that deliver the primary functional requirement. Secondly, there are those elements that enable that technology to be presented in a manner that is usable and desirable. For the moment, let us consider these two sets of elements separately so that we might more clearly identify the distinct contribution of the product designer.

In the case of a domestic lamp, for example, the technology that delivers the primary function will be some kind of electric light source. This could be an incandescent bulb, a halogen, a compact fluorescent or an array of light-emitting diodes (LEDs). As scientific research progresses, the particular and preferred technologies will continually change. Be that as it may, it is important to recognize that these technologies are not developed by product designers but by scientists and technologists. The product designer makes use of them and in some cases might even be able to influence their development, but they are based on scientific research that generally falls outside the product designer's range of expertise.

In addition, a product includes elements that enable the functionality to be presented in a manner suited to its purpose and its anticipated context. A floor lamp generally requires some kind of stem to raise the light to an appropriate height, a base to stabilize the stem and a shade around the light source to prevent glare. These elements have both a functional and an aesthetic role and they transform a technology into a useful and attractive object. Ensuring that the whole can be manufactured and delivered in an economically viable manner transforms a functional object into a marketable product. The form and arrangement of these additional functional-aesthetic elements, which will be referred to here as the *design components*, together with the effective incorporation of the *technological components*, is the responsibility of the product designer.

This distinction between the contributions of the technologist and those of the designer is intimately linked to the useful life of a product. Both the technological and the design components will eventually become outmoded, but this will occur at different rates. For example, the incandescent light bulb, first marketed in 1879

145

by Thomas Edison, lasted for about 130 years, until it started to be phased out in the first decade of the 21st century in favour of the more energy efficient compact fluorescent bulb.[8] During these 130 years, aesthetics in home decor changed many, many times – ranging from the decorative styles of later 19th century Arts and Crafts and Art Nouveau, through the abstract, rationalistic aesthetics of early 20th century Modernist movements of De Stijl and the Bauhaus to the decorative surfaces of 1980s Memphis and the whimsical styles of Droog at the beginning of the 21st century. Hence, for products such as lighting, the rate of aesthetic change is often far higher than the rate of technological change. In other cases, such as computers and mobile communication and music products, the reverse may be true, at least until technological development reaches a point where it becomes relatively stable.

It becomes clear that, when the technology on which the product depends is in a rapid state of advancement, a primary driver for product replacement will be scientific progress and improved technological capability. In such cases, the designer's contribution in ameliorating the impacts of product change will be limited, unless that contribution is able to incorporate more systemic mass-production/service changes, such as design for modularity and incremental upgrading, as explored in Chapter 10. However, when the technology is relatively stable and replacement is likely to be for aesthetic reasons, the designer can play a more significant role in ensuring that the product is designed in a manner that can be considered 'sustainable' through bottom-up change.

146

Design and change

For a product to be sustainable, those factors that can directly or indirectly affect socio-economic equity and the natural environment must be carefully considered. One way to do this might be to create products that are long-lasting, while utilizing materials and manufacturing methods that reduce environmental burdens, and by ensuring their production offers good quality employment. However, designing technology-based products to last can create conflicts with the priorities of sustainability. For instance, our financial system demands brisk product turnover and continual product replacement to ensure a buoyant economy and to create and maintain jobs. In addition, even when the technology is relatively stable, designing products to last fails to acknowledge the relatively rapid changes that occur in aesthetics and taste. And products designed to last may eventually become less energy efficient compared with more recent versions. If robust, built-to-last products are discarded anyway, in preference for ones with more up-to-date technologies or styles, then this approach to *design for sustainability* can be counterproductive.

Another approach is to accept that technologies and product preferences continually change – and to design accordingly. *Designing for change* requires an entirely different strategy, one that more fully recognizes that products are temporary accumulations of materials that will eventually be discarded and replaced. This is not only a much more realistic way of looking at products but it also brings into focus the environmental and socio-economic factors related to our activities. Firstly, there is a range of environmental considerations associated with the design and specification of components, their manufacture and their post-use implications. Creating products from a perspective that accepts the inevitability of change can help ensure that responsible, informed design specifications are developed. Secondly, a design process that acknowledges change can contribute to a system in which socio-economic development is characterized by the creation and continuation of rewarding employment opportunities; it implies an interdependent and continuous process of production, servicing and re-manufacture. Hence, the emphasis of such a system is on product maintenance and upgrading at the local level. This differs in focus from conventional definitions of product-service systems, which seek to fulfil user needs via marketable product-service combinations.[9] However, it is consistent with approaches in which product-service combinations are part of a larger strategy involving infrastructure change and system innovation.[10]

When designing products for change, the decisions made by the designer become especially critical. Every element added to the product, over and above those essential technological components that deliver the functionality, will have a range of environmental repercussions related to materials acquisition, energy use, shipping and eventual disposal. Each additional manufacturing stage represents more energy use, waste and pollution – each time materials are processed and combined to form product components they become increasingly complex and further removed from their natural state, making their recycling or disposal more problematic.

147

Therefore, the designer has to consider how products can be developed so as to be environmentally and socio-economically responsible even though they are in a continuous process of change. And as I have pointed out in earlier chapters, an essential ingredient of such a scenario is localization and 'site here to sell here' approaches.[11] Within such a scenario, the designer would be obliged to use local materials wherever possible, while recognizing that sophisticated technological components may have to be mass-produced elsewhere. Emphasis on local markets and use of local materials reduces the need for shipping and packaging, and an integrated batch-production/servicing/re-manufacture approach would offer a diverse range of local enterprise opportunities. Such a direction recognizes the importance of combining localization with mass-production. It is also in accord with developments in design for modularity and product upgrading, and contributes to product-service scenarios that allow functional goods to be maintained and adapted over time.

The implications of this kind of approach to product design are many. They suggest a quite different way forward from the globalized mass-production methods that are currently dominant and which, on the whole, create a one-way system of cradle-to-grave resource acquisition, production, consumption and disposal. The concepts presented here combine locally appropriate design with:

- cradle-to-cradle approaches;[12]
- product-service systems and creative communities;[13]
- enterprise models that recognize the diversity and heterogeneity of people's material needs;[14] and
- the tremendous potential of distributed forms of creativity and innovation.[15]

Design for change

Although it has little prominence within contemporary globalized production systems, localization *contextualizes* products by allowing them to benefit from a diversity of initiatives and innovations that are relevant to place[16] within a notion of 'multi local distributed economies'.[17]

Here, the vehicle for engaging in a design process for localization is a series of simple lamps for domestic use. Such objects require technological components to provide the light and design components to enable the light to be presented in a suitable form. If we briefly consider how such products are typically designed within our current mass-production system, this will allow us to better understand how the examples developed here for sustainability and change differ from conventional approaches.

When a floor lamp is designed to be mass-produced for international markets, the designer will make assumptions about materials and processes that are appropriate to that context and these will guide the design development. For example, the lamp shown in Figure 11.1 comprises a translucent glass shade, a cast-iron base encased in pressed and anodized aluminium and a stem of anodized aluminium, and it has a variety of fixtures and fittings. These, together with the electrical components are flat-packed for shipping to the market destination. Producing such a product entails a series of energy-intensive processes that include materials extraction, transportation and refinement followed by a variety of manufacturing stages that mould and shape the materials into components and sub-assemblies. Typically, the various parts of the lamp will be encased in layers of packaging so that it arrives to the customer in pristine condition.

In developing such a product, the designer can be located virtually anywhere in the world. The design, and each of its component parts, can be specified via a series of visualizations using a design and styling software package. And these specifications can be readily delivered to a manufacturer that might be on another continent. In manufacturing such a product, materials will often have their origins in many different countries. Such practices have become the common currency of design for mass-production.

Let us now consider a design process that adheres to the factors discussed earlier, including localization and design for change. Such a process requires an understanding of context and place, a knowledge of local materials and skills, and an awareness of the potential impacts of production on both the environment and

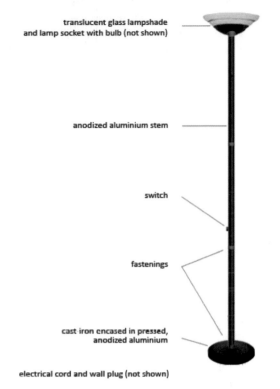

translucent glass lampshade
and lamp socket with bulb (not shown)

anodized aluminium stem

switch

fastenings

cast iron encased in pressed,
anodized aluminium

electrical cord and wall plug (not shown)

149

Figure 11.1
Rendering of a 'typical' mass-produced floor lamp

socio-economic development.[18] In the following concepts, these design criteria
were tightly constrained so as to explore the potential of the approach. In fact, for
those additional functional-aesthetic elements that are the particular concern of
the product designer, these constraints were taken to something of an extreme:

- **The aim** was to develop a concept for a floor lamp that would be
  functionally effective, aesthetically attractive and appropriate for
  domestic use. The concept also had to be adaptable to change while
  remaining in continual use.
- **The technological components** were minimized and restricted to off-the-
  shelf parts obtainable from any local hardware store.
- **The design components** – the following conditions were applied to the
  functional-aesthetic elements defined by the designer:
  - the components were minimized and restricted to materials that
    were completely natural and local, or
  - if not currently available locally, could be made so if such a
    design were to be batch manufactured. While the term 'local'

has no strict geographical boundary, for the purposes of this exercise, it was assumed to be the area that lay within a few miles of the design studio.

- fasteners were also restricted to natural materials and temporary or semi-permanent connections, which would facilitate disassembly.
- processes: in converting the raw materials into product components, processing had to be either non-existent or kept to an absolute minimum.

These tight constraints help ensure that detrimental environmental impacts associated with those functional-aesthetic elements that fall within the scope and particular decision-making of the product designer are minimal or absent altogether.

Bamboo & Stone I: In this floor lamp concept (Figure 11.2) the technological components comprise a compact fluorescent light bulb, a lamp socket, an in-line switch, a wall plug and electrical cable. These are all off-the-shelf, mass-produced electrical parts that are a) suited to a broad range of applications, b) widely available, and c) readily replaceable.

In defining the additional, non-technological elements, materials were selected that could be found as locally as possible to the design studio. Materials were chosen that were not simply *available* locally – rather, the aim was to use materials that occurred naturally or could be readily made locally. Critically, and in contrast to the design for mass-production process described earlier, the process here was not one of designing the lamp with preconceived notions of materials and manufacturing stages in mind. Instead, observations were made of the immediate vicinity while contemplating the kinds of elements that might be used in the lamp. In addition, all processing was kept to a minimum, which not only reduced energy use and waste, but also ensured that the materials remained in, or close to, their raw unadulterated state; this would allow them to be eventually returned to the natural environment without causing harm. Hence, through observation and a heightened awareness of locale and its naturally occurring elements, creative decisions become more sensitive to context and to what a place can yield without injury.

The design components comprise:

- The lamp stem: a variety of bamboo plants were found to be growing in the vicinity of the studio. Bamboo is a prolific, fast-growing plant that would provide an appropriate and attractive means of creating the lamp's stem and it is a completely natural and renewable material. A length of black bamboo was selected, which was simply pruned from the living plant and trimmed, leaving a few branch stubs in place on which to hang the electrical cable.

150

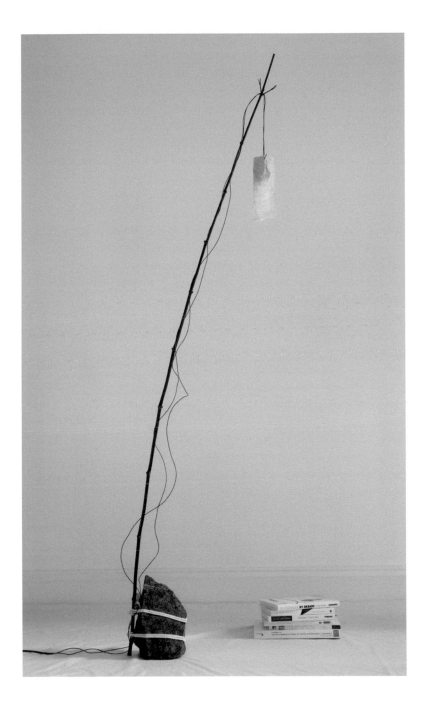

Figure 11.2
'Bamboo & Stone I'
*A floor lamp. Raw stone, unprocessed bamboo,
rawhide, handmade paper, compact fluorescent lamp
and off-the-shelf electrical parts*

- The lamp base: considering the heavy base needed to stabilize the stem, the simplest solution would be a raw stone of suitable size and form. Large natural stones in the immediate locale were inspected and one was chosen that suited the purpose. A small piece of felt made from recycled fabric was attached to the underside of the rock to protect wooden flooring. The inclusion of a specially selected stone in a mass-produced design would be entirely impractical. However, creating a local design for batch production and local use allows the incorporation of such elements. The natural differences between such unrefined components mean that each product possesses its own particular characteristics. This creates aesthetic diversity even within the same design concept, fostering heterogeneity in material artefacts that is related to place; this contrasts markedly with the sweeping homogeneity that characterizes so many contemporary 'global' products. Moreover, if the designs are for local markets, then delivery of such products to their place of use is unproblematic and requires little or no packaging.

- The connection of stem to base: a fastening was sought that would not damage the stone or require significant amounts of energy to administer. Drilling a hole in the stone to accept the bamboo stem was therefore ruled out. A rigid tie would be a suitable solution and it was decided to use un-tanned hide thongs (rawhide) for this purpose. This natural material is soaked in water before use until it is soft and pliable. It is then tied in place and as it dries it shrinks and hardens to form a tight, rigid connection. Locally produced rawhide was unavailable. However, if the product were to be batch manufactured, this material could be readily produced from a variety of local stock-raising activities. When applying this solution to the floor lamp design, a small length of green bamboo was inserted between the rock and the stem to ensure the latter stood at the desired angle. This was a simple way of overcoming the uneven surface qualities and erratic angles presented by the raw stone.

- The lampshade: this was fashioned from a piece of crumpled, rough-torn handmade paper. A pristine, smooth shade would be delicate and easily marred, so this deliberate wrinkling and tearing of the paper enhances its aesthetic durability. It was simply rolled into a cylinder and held in place with two slivers of bamboo.

In keeping with the earlier discussion, because the rates of change of the technological components will differ from those of the other elements, the lamp has been designed so that these two sets of components have only a loose connection, allowing them to be easily separated for purposes of repair, upgrading and change. The technological components are simply draped over the stem, with no permanent fixings and, because they are standard, off-the-shelf parts, they can be easily replaced when the need arises. All the other elements are completely natural, and processing has been kept to a minimum.

Bamboo & Stone II: The second example is a table light, Figure 11.3. Here, the light source is a small light emitting diode (LED), which has a relatively long useful life and consumes very little energy. However, light output from a single LED is considerably less than a typical compact fluorescent or incandescent bulb. While this constrains its practical application, the concept still serves to demonstrate the design principles at a different scale and using an alternative lighting technology. The non-electrical components are again bamboo, raw stone and handmade paper, but instead of rawhide, a natural rubber band was used to connect the stem to the stone.

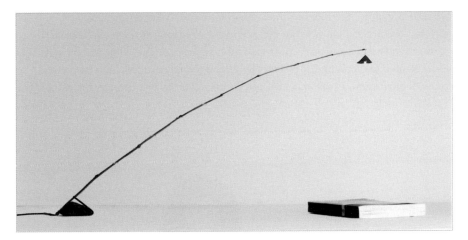

153

Figure 11.3
'Bamboo & Stone II'
A table light. Raw stone, unprocessed bamboo, natural rubber, handmade paper, LED lamp and off-the-shelf electrical parts

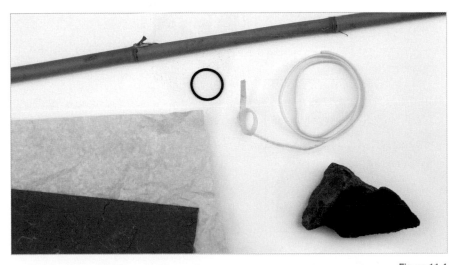

Figure 11.4
Natural, minimally processed materials for design components

In both examples, the use and processing of materials to create the non-electrical parts are kept to an absolute minimum, Figure 11.4. As a consequence, these elements can eventually be returned to the natural environment or recycled with no detrimental effect. In both cases, the aim was to create an elegant design by employing the least means possible. Almost all the materials were sourced locally; the exceptions being the rawhide thongs in the first example, which potentially could be produced locally, and the natural rubber band used in the second example. If such concepts were to be batch-produced at the local level, the most suitable fastening materials from the immediate vicinity could be sourced.

Box Sconce: When the above lamps are no longer required and the un-processed, natural components have been returned to the environment or recycled, we are still left with the technological elements. As these are electrical parts created for general use, rather than for a specific product, they can be very easily re-used in a completely different lighting design that, again, can be created for local production. An example of such a concept is the Box Sconce, the essential

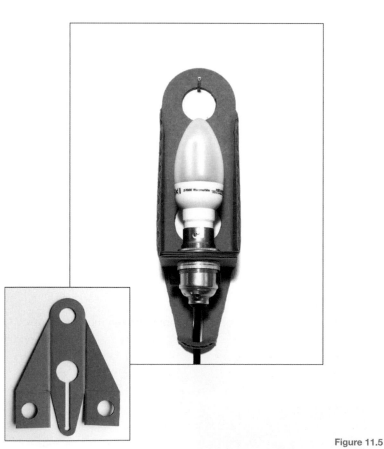

Figure 11.5
'Box Sconce'
re-used cardboard, compact fluorescent lamp and
off-the-shelf electrical parts

Figure 11.6
'Box Sconce'
with old straw hat

Figure 11.7
'Box Sconce'
with paper scroll

component for which is a simple cut-out of re-used, corrugated cardboard; this is folded along score lines and fitted with the electrical parts formerly used in the floor lamp design, Figure 11.5. It is then hung on a nail and covered, as in Box Sconce with hat, Figure 11.6, or enveloped in paper, as in Box Sconce with paper scroll, Figure 11.7.

Reflections

In developing these concepts, an attempt has been made to combine the technological with the natural, the mass-produced with the local and the simple with the sophisticated. This can be a difficult marriage of conflicting priorities and contrasting materials. However, the value of these kinds of objects lies not so much in what they do or how they look, but in what they represent. This type of critical design employs the process of creating speculative propositions to question assumptions about the nature of functional goods.[19] Such objects represent attempts to transform issues of concern into tangible things and, in the process, their implications are explored and encapsulated. The primary purpose of this kind of design work is to examine issues, challenge conventions and contribute to new ways of thinking about and developing material culture. In this sense, it is concerned with strategic directions and systemic change. While it yields specific artefacts, conventional design priorities – such as functionality, ergonomics or market segment – are not necessarily significant factors. Instead, the object of design, which could be a lamp, chair, telephone or any other kind of product, is principally a vehicle for exploring and expressing ideas about other issues.

In the concepts presented here, the issues of concern include ideas about sustainability and design for change, and the interdependent worlds of local context and distant, globalized mass-production. The 'local' suggests familiarity, small-scale, adaptability and sensitivity to place. The 'global', in terms of production capability, offers precision, standardization and sophisticated, complex processes and materials; it is also removed, unfamiliar and, too often, its effects are highly damaging. We tend to pay a high price, environmentally and socially, as we move from the local to the global, but there can also be considerable gains in terms of material benefits and economic standards. While industrialization and international trade have transformed and improved lifestyles in all kinds of ways, as we increasingly comprehend their detrimental effects it becomes important to develop new, rather different ways forward. These must not only acknowledge the advantages of technological progress and globalized production, but also afford greater prominence to the potential environmental and social gains that can evolve from localization and context specific solutions.[20] The concepts presented

156   here represent a bringing together of local and global modes of manufacture to develop more sustainable ways forward; they attempt to show a direction that can benefit and flourish from drawing on and integrating both. Of course, the precise nature of such an integration will be a continuous negotiation spanning local, regional, national and international scales of activity that encompass materials-sourcing, production methods, supply chains and product distribution, use and maintenance. However, the propositions developed here explore an approach for incorporating 'the local' in everyday consumer products and indicate the potential implications for design and product aesthetics.

It is also important to point out that the process of designing is not used to simply illustrate previously developed ideas. If the *thinking-and-doing* design process is to contribute to our understandings, it has to be creative, not merely illustrative. In the explorations carried out here, the process began with an idea to design a floor lamp, and to use this as a way of probing issues about design, change and sustainability. At the start of the exercise, no assumptions were made about materials-use or form, these emerged from observing the local environment. Through an iterative process of selection, trial and error, and sketching, the design took shape (Figure 11.8). In the process, forms emerged that depended on and were characterized by locally available materials. Completion of the floor lamp Bamboo & Stone I naturally led to the idea of trying the same principles at a different scale. In the second object, Bamboo & Stone II, lightness of touch was further accentuated. Slightly different materials (natural rubber) and a

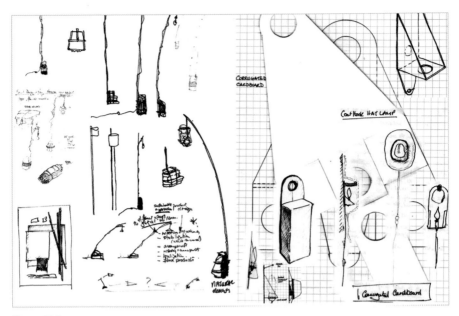

Figure 11.8
Development sketches and study model

different lighting technology (LED) were used that were more suited to the smaller scale, and the low voltage technology allowed the use of bare wires rather than plastic coated wires, which helps reduce materials, eases recycling and maintains aesthetic lightness. Reflecting on these two objects in the context of the main thesis, i.e., aesthetic change with technological constancy, led to the idea of using the same electrical components in a completely different – but equally 'light' and 'sustainable' manner, which yielded the cardboard bracket that forms the basis of the Box Sconce concept, with lampshades made from a re-used straw hat or a paper scroll.

Hence, the process was one of discovery, which took unpredictable turns and directions. Each step is sparked by what went before, which is how the creative process develops. However, while such a process involves chance, it is based on more than serendipity. Chance connections and relationships occur to the designer within an immersive process in which the 'doing' of design takes place in conjunction with thinking about and researching issues of concern. This symbiotic process of *thinking-and-doing* enables the *thinking about issues of concern* to inform the 'doing', and the *doing and reflecting on the processes and outcomes of doing* to inform one's understanding of the issues and their design implications. Lastly, these explorations are not concerned with design as a process of problem solving. Here, design is viewed as a positive, creative process of exploring opportunities and developing desirable and responsible ways forward. This represents a significant philosophical shift away from commonly accepted notions of the purpose and value of design.

Evolving an integrated production system

The direction described above can minimize resource use and waste while recognizing the important benefits of technological advance. This is shown in Table 11.1, which indicates the potential providence of each of the temporal objects' components. Waste from consumer products can be drastically reduced by adopting a design approach that facilitates: re-use of components in subsequent designs; the benign return of components to the environment through use of completely natural, no- or low-processed materials; and/or ease of recycling by ensuring the components are made from minimally processed, single type materials.

Table 11.2 demonstrates product transitions over time. Starting with the Bamboo & Stone I floor lamp (column 1), this object undergoes a *maintenance* transition (column 2) in which the paper shade is replaced. The next transition is a *design* update to a Box Sconce (column 3) in which the *design components* are replaced, but all the technological parts are re-used. The final transition is a *technology* update based on a change to LED components (column 4). At each

Table 11.1 'Sustainable' characteristics of temporal object concepts

TEMPORAL OBJECT	Technological Components	Future Potential of Technological Components	Design Components	Future Potential of Design Components
FLOOR LAMP Bamboo & Stone 1	Off-the-shelf electrical parts	Readily re-usable in another design	Unprocessed natural materials: stone, bamboo, hide	Return to natural environment with no detrimental effect
			Handmade paper	Recycle
TABLE LAMP Bamboo & Stone 2	Off-the-shelf electrical parts	Readily re-usable in another design	Unprocessed natural materials: stone, bamboo.	Return to natural environment with no detrimental effect
			Natural rubber band	Re-use in another application or recycle
			Handmade paper	Recycle
WALL LAMP 'Box Sconce'	Off-the-shelf electrical parts	Readily re-usable in another design	Re-used cardboard	Recycle
			Handmade paper	Recycle
			Re-used straw hat	Re-use in original application

stage, the added and discarded components are indicated. These transitions result in a total of nine components being discarded. Three of these – stone, bamboo and rawhide, are natural, unprocessed materials that can be returned to the environment with no ill effect, three are paper-based that can be recycled and three are general-use electrical components that can be easily re-used. By comparison, discarding three complete lighting products over the same period, such as the example in Figure 11.1 which contains 10 major parts, would result in approximately 30 assembled parts being sent to landfill. Thus, the concepts presented here result in an approximately 70 per cent reduction in discarded components and, potentially, close to 100 per cent reduction in parts that would normally be sent to landfill.

A system that integrates mass-production with complementary local production and services would mean significant change in our notions of business enterprise. It suggests a shift away from the mass-production and global distribution of complete products, and greater emphasis on mass-produced parts and modular formats that allow components to be used and re-used in locally or regionally

Table 11.2 Temporal objects – product transitions over time

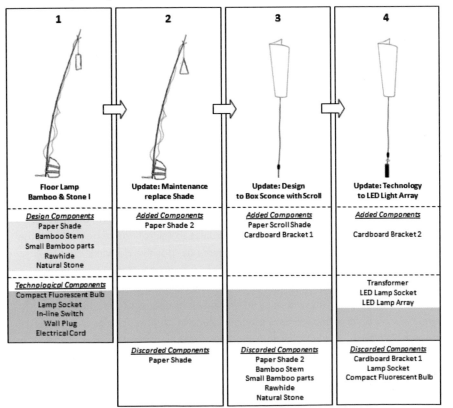

1	2	3	4
Floor Lamp **Bamboo & Stone I**	**Update: Maintenance** **replace Shade**	**Update: Design** **to Box Sconce with Scroll**	**Update: Technology** **to LED Light Array**
Design Components Paper Shade Bamboo Stem Small Bamboo parts Rawhide Natural Stone	*Added Components* Paper Shade 2	*Added Components* Paper Scroll Shade Cardboard Bracket 1	*Added Components* Cardboard Bracket 2
Technological Components Compact Fluorescent Bulb Lamp Socket In-line Switch Wall Plug Electrical Cord			Transformer LED Lamp Socket LED Lamp Array
	Discarded Components Paper Shade	*Discarded Components* Paper Shade 2 Bamboo Stem Small Bamboo parts Rawhide Natural Stone	*Discarded Components* Cardboard Bracket 1 Lamp Socket Compact Fluorescent Bulb

defined applications. It also suggests a production-service relationship in which effective supply chains are developed between large scale component producers and local scale enterprises. Such systemic change is consistent with research in ecological economics[21] as well as emergent research that addresses the environmental and social concerns of sustainability through, for example, concepts of post-materialism,[22] and use of design as a mechanism for significant social and technical change.[23]

Perhaps more importantly, such a system more explicitly recognizes the transitory nature of material culture and suggests a way forward in which:

- care for the environment becomes innate. Natural materials extracted from the vicinity would be used and re-used prudently because to do otherwise would be to degrade one's own local surroundings;
- creative, productive work becomes more strongly connected to community, culture and identity while simultaneously recognizing the value of larger-scale, 'global' contributions. This would help foster practices that would be significant to those involved. And, of course, a sense of significance can give meaning and joy to our endeavours.[24,25]

Such a system would support an ethos of responsible use, in which the discarding of materials would be seen as inefficient, harmful and wasteful. Moreover, local manufacturing and services would allow people to better understand the nature of their material products, where they come from, how they are made, their repercussions and how they can be adapted and re-adapted to meet changing needs.

This direction is consistent with democratized forms of design and innovation. The availability of suitable off-the-shelf parts is equivalent to what Von Hippel calls 'toolkits' – produced by manufacturers to enable non-specialists to create custom products that meet their needs.[26] A responsible integration of global and local means that the benefits of both scales can be drawn upon for delivering context-appropriate, sustainable solutions. In doing so, they would help overcome the homogeneity and cultural erosion that occurs from globalized, one-size-fits all solutions.[27,28] While such a direction might conflict with prevailing business forces, it is in accord with socially and environmentally responsible developments – from service systems and community initiatives to microfinance banking. Hamel refers to such organizations and social systems as 'positive deviants' and sees them as key elements of the future of business management and of strategic change.[29] In working towards such change, international corporations would benefit from the creativity and cultural diversity that occurs at the grass-roots level, which could inform context-specific solutions in other locales. Moreover, greater acknowledgement of localization can actually strengthen the economy[30] while ensuring that production practices comply with endemic employment and environmental legislation. Hence, such practices begin to *internalize* many of the socio-economic and environmental ramifications of manufacturing. Finally,

160

an economy based on multifarious, locally appropriate production and service enterprises linked to a supply of technologically sophisticated components would be intrinsically diverse and therefore more robust than the rather homogenous, globalized, product manufacturing approaches that are so prevalent today; such mono-cultures tend to be inherently vulnerable and unstable.

Therefore, in all respects, it seems that 'temporal objects' capable of continual adaptation via an integrated, responsible local-global system – exemplified here through a variety of simple lighting concepts – can be judged sustainable. However, the question remains as to whether it is possible to apply such approaches to the huge variety of short-lived products that are dependent on rapidly advancing technologies and which have become so essential to modern lifestyles and modern economies. Tackling *that* question will be the subject of the next chapter.

161

12
Meaning in the Mundane
aesthetics, technology and spiritual values

A small circle is quite as infinite as a large circle;
but though it is quite as infinite, it is not so large.

G. K. Chesterton

It is through our design decisions that our philosophies of economics and ethics
and our spiritual values find expression in the aesthetics of the mundane. Within
these decisions are found our attitudes to the natural environment, each other
and ourselves. Yet, because these attitudes are so commonplace and wrapped in
convention, it is difficult to actually see them for what they are or to imagine that
they could be otherwise. To bring them into a little sharper focus, it is useful to
step beyond our own milieu and look at examples from other cultures, historical
periods and design routes. By appreciating viewpoints and values from other
contexts – and how they lead to quite different kinds of outcomes – we can begin
to see our own actions in a new light.

In this chapter, I discuss a number of precedents, each of which illustrates
how substantive values and depth of meaning can affect the creation of tangible
artefacts. Reflecting on these precedents allows us to enlarge our understanding
of products, especially in terms of their non-instrumental factors. These ideas
are then further explored through the creative design process, with particular

reference to electronic devices. This leads to a series of functional objects that were informed by tacit understandings and aesthetic contemplation and which synthesize instrumental and non-instrumental, expressive factors. Moreover, in developing these propositional objects there is a recognition that, with microchip-based functionality, physical form is no longer closely bonded to product function.

From these explorations it becomes clear that the aesthetic expression of an electronic object can be linked to broader and deeper concerns – and in ways that remain largely unrecognized in contemporary mass-production. These connections are becoming increasingly important not only because the production of such devices is so problematic in terms of sustainability but also because, as we saw in Chapter 10, the nature of their use, which is linked to their design, is in danger of eroding our ethical and spiritual selves.[1]

Beyond words

Wittgenstein once asserted that there are propositions in ethics, aesthetics and metaphysics that lie beyond the realm of the sayable.[2] Many traditional perspectives[3,4] also acknowledge tacit ways of knowing, which can be perceived internally, felt and recognized but cannot be adequately described or expressed in words.[5] Such understandings are essential ingredients of practice-based, creative disciplines such as design and are therefore critical for developing discipline-appropriate approaches to contemporary concerns.

164

Creative activities demand deep immersion in process. These concentrated forms of engagement have been referred to as focal practices[6] or flow[7] and they are akin to spiritual exercises that cultivate single-pointed attention,[8] and 'at-one-ment'.[9] Accomplishment rests on the development and refinement of practice, perhaps over many years, the outcomes of which will be works that offer some kind of aesthetic expression. Within such practice, many decisions and actions are made intuitively, via discriminating judgements that are based in contemplation of the emerging aesthetic of the work. Moreover, the aesthetic experience of the developing work will be a product of the sensory experience of its intrinsic properties combined with contemplation of it as a thing of significance and value; that is, as a thing considered worthy of attention within a particular culture.[10] Such aesthetic judgements are made with reference to an overall, but not necessarily entirely explicit, intention and grounded in a broader contextual understanding. This may result in a completed work that, in terms of its aesthetic qualities, fulfils the intention of the practitioner, even if he or she is unable to explain why this is so because, as noted, certain aspects of our understandings lie beyond the realm of the sayable. The ability to articulate one's reasons for making a particular creative decision is an entirely different matter from one's ability to make that decision – any lack of capacity in the first has no bearing on one's proficiency in the second.

Functional objects, aesthetics and spiritual well-being

When a functional object is judged to have aesthetic merit, this ascribes to it some degree of intrinsic value, irrespective of how it works or what it does. It also has value because of the practical benefit it affords. Both these factors contribute to one's judgement of it as a thing. In addition, as we saw in Chapter 4, there are 'extrinsic' factors, including environmental and social impacts, which can also influence our judgement.

These various factors are interdependent. The aesthetic experience of an object is due, in part, to the materials and manufacturing processes employed in its production, both of which have ethical and environmental dimensions. Furthermore, ethical understandings not only pertain to societal well-being but also to an individual's sense of spiritual well-being, which is associated with the affirmation of life in relationship to self, community and environment, as well as with one's sense of the transcendent.[11] Consequently, our knowledge of the effects of an object's production, use and disposal on the natural environment, on others and on ourselves, and recognition of how these aspects are manifested in the product's appearance, will influence how we actually 'see' it.

Hence, a series of relationships emerge that connect visual appearance – which plays a major role in our judgement of an object – with social, ethical and environmental factors and with substantive values and spiritual well-being. And while there may be no logically necessary connection between spirituality and ethics, or between spirituality and conceptions of what constitutes a worthwhile, meaningful and good life, it is the case that spiritual traditions have, for centuries, served as productive paths for addressing questions of human happiness and virtue.[12] Indeed, as I discuss below, certain traditions draw strong connections between outer actions, aesthetics, ethics and spiritual well-being.

Naturally, to develop new forms of goods that represent new sensibilities, we will have to depart from current norms. To do this, we must question and perhaps set aside some of the terms we commonly use to describe the purpose of design, in order to foster new perspectives. Design is usually framed in terms of problems and solutions. However, in today's context these 'solutions', in the form of mass-produced products, have become associated with serious harm and unfulfilling routes to happiness.[13] If we believe we are developing 'solutions' to predefined 'problems', then the aim will be to design fully resolved outcomes that are complete and immutable. Obviously, such notions are untenable because advances in science and technology quickly render such products obsolete. Nevertheless, this terminology remains prevalent, and it locks design within an outmoded ontological frame.

Instead, we can express design, both as process and outcome, in terms that suggest a quite different sensibility. If we understand design as a continual process of exploring and probing possibilities, then we begin to see its discrete outcomes not as 'solutions' but as temporary, tangible manifestations of ideas that offer only fleeting benefit. By thinking of design outcomes in such terms, we

165

place them within a larger frame of reference — one in which passing benefit is seen against longer-term environmental degradation and social deprivation, as well as against personal notions of meaning and fulfilment. Within such a context of understanding, we can start to conceive of functional objects not simply as utilitarian 'solutions' encased in the fragile attractiveness and social cachet of newness, but as more holistic expressions of human meaning in a continually evolving field of understanding.

Design precedents

Despite technical advances in manufacturing, today's microchip-based goods are produced according to a rationale that remains firmly anchored in blinkered and outmoded industrial practices. The obdurate conventions of these, now globalized, approaches prioritize short-term quantitative growth over longer-term, sustainable strategies. To pursue more constructive, not to say wiser, directions, it is useful to look beyond this predominant industrial context. While many examples could be cited, four have been selected which embody aspects of the human condition that are generally ill-represented in contemporary technological objects.

A Zuni stone fetish carving from the American Southwest and the *Wabi Sabi* aesthetic of Japan exemplify approaches to material culture that are rooted in spiritual sensibilities and relationships with the natural world. A water dam, built in northwest England during the Industrial Revolution, is an example of technology and engineering that finds harmony with nature *in situ*. Lastly, objects from Andrea Branzi's collection Grandi Legni exemplify a contemporary approach that transcends conventional architectural and design boundaries. Consideration of these examples and the ideas and values they embody provide a stimulating basis from which to explore more judicious directions for the design of technology-based goods.

Zuni fetish carving: The bear fetish carving from the Zuni tribe in the American Southwest (Figure 12.1) is a modern example of an ancient object type that expresses values and ideas far removed from today's utilitarian, electronic devices. For certain indigenous peoples of North America, these kinds of objects symbolize mysteries observable in nature. They represent animal or other spirits and are used to invoke the wisdom or protection of those spirits and to affect the course of events.[14]

In modern, economically-developed cultures, such beliefs are often dismissed as superstition. However, they represent long-standing ideas within complex mythological and religious traditions that historically aimed at keeping a balanced outlook and harmony among the different facets of nature. To do this, the society's stories and laws emphasized cooperation, moral behaviour and respect for ancestors. A key element of this worldview was the interrelatedness of all things.[15] We see in this example parallels with the contemporary issue of sustainability, especially its central theme of keeping the world in good order to maintain

Figure 12.1
Zuni bear fetish carving, New Mexico, USA

human well-being. It also has strong resonances with Lovelock's Gaia Hypothesis, which emphasizes the interconnectedness of the whole system of animate and inanimate elements in the natural world. Indeed Lovelock's notion of an intuitive understanding of the finite nature of Gaia seems remarkably similar to these traditional understandings.[16] Zuni fetish carvings represent an outward acknowledgement and expression of these ideas. Different elements, such as arrowheads, stones and shells, make up the medicine bundles, which are secured to the carvings with sinew. These refer to different aspects of daily life, such as hunting, sickness, the weather or the harvest, and belief in the power of the fetish to affect events gives the object meaning. However, traditionally, a critical aspect of their 'use' was that the object itself and the spirit it represents were not held responsible if a desired outcome was not forthcoming. Instead, fault was attributed to the behaviour of the object's owner. In this way, the fetish served as a tangible reminder of appropriate behaviour, moral values and ways of living considered to be honourable and true. Hence, the onus was on the bearer – the object itself did not directly or 'magically' perform.[17] Other traditional cultures ascribe similar meanings to objects.[18,19]

167

Wabi sabi: The Japanese aesthetic philosophy of *wabi sabi* represents an attempt within the tradition of Zen Buddhism to express a love of life alongside an acknowledgement of its fragility and transience. It is founded on principles of humility, simplicity, restraint, naturalness, imperfection and the inevitability of impermanence. It draws on perception rather than rationalistic understandings and recognizes that all things are in a constant state of flux. *Wabi sabi* expresses the ephemeral, melancholy beauty of existence – that brief period between the birth and the passing of a thing, be it a flower, an object or a human life.[20,21] This sense of transience is epitomized in the 12th century poem *Hojoki* when it speaks of the ever-changing skyline of the city. While the city and the crowd remain, the individual buildings come and go, along with the faces in the crowd.[22] Acknowledging this inherent flux inevitably brings with it a sense of poignancy because we simultaneously recognize the vitality and the fleetingness of the present moment.

Figure 12.2
Wabi sabi aesthetic, sake cup by Tomio Morimoto, Tanba Hyogo, Japan

Koren suggests that the characteristics of *wabi sabi* are virtually the polar opposites of those of post-war modernism. The latter, distinguished by its minimalist perfection, still dominates much of the landscape of consumer goods and contemporary architecture. It is an aesthetic that expresses the cool, precise rationalism of technological progress through pure geometric forms and synthetic materials – an aesthetic of clarity, reductionism and control. In contrast, objects that embody the *wabi sabi* aesthetic tend to be characterized by a lack of artifice, rough textures, a faded, imperfect elegance and asymmetry but, unlike Zuni fetish carvings, they have no symbolic connotations. Rather than being homogenous and mass-produced, such objects are earthy, variegated and individual – as shown in the ceramic cup from Tanba Hyogo, Japan (Figure 12.2). *Wabi sabi* implies an intuitive sensibility that is firmly located in the present and, in stark contrast to today's widely-accepted supposition, it assumes there is no such thing as progress. The use of natural materials and organic shapes allows decay and corrosion to be absorbed without detracting from the overall aesthetic; indeed, deterioration tends to add to the object's expression. This aesthetic also suggests a broadening of sensory appreciation rather than a reduction, as it comfortably accommodates ambiguity and impermanence. However, unlike most contemporary approaches, function and utility are not of primary importance.[23]

These aesthetic characteristics are not merely a preferred style – one fashion among many – but are the outward expression of a comprehensive approach that includes metaphysical understandings, spirituality, well-being and ethical behaviour. *Wabi sabi* is rooted in observation of nature, and the idea that all things are transient.[24] It emphasizes an intuitive, direct communion with the nature of things as they are at this moment and attests to the import of the fleeting, ever-changing present. Appreciating the nature of ordinary, mundane things in this way does not mesh with a system of efficiency, measurement and targets. At such moments of absorption there is a sense of transcendence that lies beyond words, in which the mundane and the spiritual are of equal importance – no distinction is made.[25] Therefore, while *wabi sabi* is not necessarily concerned with explicitly spiritual objects, this aesthetic philosophy recognizes the importance of spiritual values in the creation and the nature of material things. It draws strong connections between outer actions, aesthetic expression, ethics and inner meaning.

The Japanese tea ceremony is a manifestation of this aesthetic philosophy, both in its forms of visual expression and in the specific actions it encompasses. The tea ceremony has been perceived as a spiritual culture, a discipline with a strong moral geometry and one in which the ordinary items of everyday life are appreciated. It simultaneously expresses – through aesthetic sensibility, ethics and spirituality – a profound perspective about humanity and nature that is grounded in notions of harmony, respect, purity and tranquillity. [26]

In developing less damaging approaches to contemporary product design and production, the implications of *wabi sabi* are significant. Accepting the constantly changing nature of existence, both of living things and human-made artefacts, highlights the importance of process over product. Acknowledging that artefacts are, and can be designed to be, in a state of continual flux reveals the limiting nature of terms such as 'definition', 'completion' and 'solution', terms that represent a cessation of change.[27] Furthermore, stressing process over product implies a certain humility. It suggests that a definitive, lasting solution is not actually attainable. Instead, human-made artefacts are considered to be in a continual state of becoming – with elements corroding, being damaged or outmoded, and being replaced, renewed or in some other way altered.

169

Abbeystead dam: In contrast to the previous examples, Abbeystead dam is an artefact of an industrial age, built on strict engineering principles. Despite its utilitarian basis, however, its use of materials, type of construction and scale, as well as the sensitivity given to its siting, all go to show that even large, highly pragmatic projects can be executed in ways that are sympathetic to and respectful of nature.

Abbeystead dam (Figures 12.3–12.5) is located on the River Wyre in an area known as the Forest of Bowland in the heart of rural Lancashire. It was constructed in 1855, at the height of the Industrial Revolution, and later enlarged to supply water to the factories further downstream.[28] It is an example of a human-made artefact that has been inserted into the natural environment – it is bonded to it and dependent upon it. It can be appreciated not merely for its practical purpose but also for its accumulating texture and ever-changing existence as a thing. It is being continually scoured by flowing water, ice and the elements. Its surfaces alter – discolouring, eroding, accruing woodland detritus and budding growths in the interstices, becoming encrusted with evaporites and lichens, and cushioned with mosses. Its enduring form has enabled it to absorb these accretions of time and acquire the patina of age, yielding an artefact both functional and beautiful.

Figure 12.3
Shaded vale under Abbeystead dam, Forest of Bowland

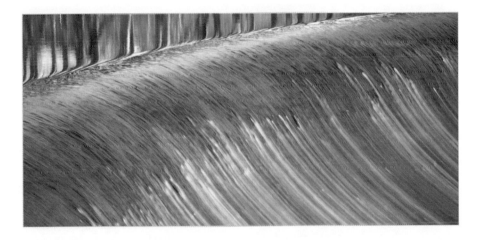

Figure 12.4
Upper overflow
Abbeystead dam

Figure 12.5
Lower overflow with overhanging leaves - Abbeystead dam

Encountering Abbeystead dam one is struck by its mottled, melancholy grace. Its evolving appearance is inseparable from its utility and both connect us to the two important but often conflicting considerations I spoke of in Chapter 1. On the one hand, this rural construction silently speaks of industry and empire – the cotton mills and smoke stacks of Manchester, the 'Hard Times' of Dickens.[29] On the other, it conjures the romantic counterpoint of the Lakeland poets. In this spot, both exist together, forming a whole that is indivisible.

Hence, Abbeystead dam is an example of an artefact that is unified with locale. In the fullness of its present utility and aesthetic, it creates a particular character of place that is replete with evocations, ideas, history and culture. The unavoidable, pragmatic needs of our physical humanity – expressed through creative endeavour in the form of a rationalized, technological construction – find harmony with the natural environment. While there is necessarily a change in that environment, we cannot avoid the fact that human needs inevitably demand intrusion into and alteration of nature. Here, however, it is done with empathy for place and in a way that, in many respects, enhances the natural environment – creating new kinds of habitats, in the form of a lake and wetlands, for fish, waterfowl and plant life. The Abbeystead reservoir might not be a spiritual place in the way we normally think about spirituality and its associations with religious meanings. However, as in the *wabi sabi* philosophy, the mundane and the spiritual exist together through a harmonious integration of utility, beauty and empathy with nature.

173

Architect Christopher Day suggests that four levels of place are essential to the creation of a harmonious built environment: physical substance, time continuum or flow, mood and essence or inspiration. Thinking of place in such terms acknowledges that our world is more than simply material; it is also living, being populated by sentient animals and by human beings who can be inspired and stimulated by ideals.[30] All these elements are manifest in Abbeystead dam.

Grandi Legni

Italian designer Andrea Branzi's collection Grandi Legni comprises a series of large, enigmatic objects that are not easily classified – two examples are shown in Figures 12.6 and 12.7. Somewhere between architecture and furniture, they are constructed from old timber beams, larch wood cabinets, metal brackets and even a bird cage. They have an archaic, mythological character and are evocative of ancient, forgotten truths that lie beyond the veil of memory and recorded history.

Essentially, and surprising as it may seem, these pieces are a response to the capabilities offered by micro-chip technologies. However, Branzi is not seeking reconciliation between the virtual and the material, but rather a somewhat distanced complementarity. In a time when digital utility has rendered material functionality largely impotent and its design theories irrelevant, Branzi sees the conventions of design as being outmoded and having no substance because

Figure 12.6
'Grandi Legni GL 01'
by Andrea Branzi. Old beams, wrought iron, larch wood cabinets.
L300 x W18 x H205. Reproduced with permission; photo by Rui Teixeira, 2010

Figure 12.7
'Grandi Legni GL 02'
by Andrea Branzi. Old beams with larch wood cabinets.
L320 x W28 x H270. Reproduced with permission; photo by Rui Teixeira, 2010

they lack sacredness. Consequently, design practice endlessly repeats variations on a theme – regurgitating forms that fail to respond to the seismic changes brought about by the new technologies.[31] The virtual environments and digitized functionalities enabled by these technologies have liberated physical objects from the constraints of utility, enabling them to address more substantive matters. Physical design becomes a mediation between the mundane and the meaningful – a conduit for retrievals and expressions of histories, myths and human spirituality. Freed from prosaic function, design can address those very things that virtualization lacks – the real and the tangible, scale and weight, the textured and tactile, the patinas of age, weathering and corrosion, connection to Earth and the indefinable bond between the ever-decaying corporeal and the spiritual. Through the unique, unrepeatable qualities of concrete materiality and natural elements, Branzi attempts to draw connections between the physical world and deeper, sacred aspects of our humanity.

A substantive basis for design

Zuni fetishes, the *wabi sabi* aesthetic, Abbeystead dam and Branzi's Grandi Legni stem from different cultures and time periods. While each emphasizes particular aspects of material culture, collectively they suggest a strong direction for addressing contemporary concerns through design.

Insights and reflections drawn from such examples can inform and help steer product design. Clearly, considerations of environmental care, social justice and ethical responsibility must become intrinsic systemic elements rather than optional add-ons that are too easily and too frequently avoided. But perhaps even more importantly, as a foundational change that prefigures but is linked to these concerns, we must find ways of imbuing design with more profound notions of meaning in order to restore and reflect a sense of our full humanness in our material culture.

Converting these ideas into defined axioms, objectives or criteria is less important than absorbing their tenor and spirit and allowing them to inform the design development during the creative process itself. This is why it is so important to recognize that, in practice-based disciplines such as design, the process itself is vital to the formation and expression of new understandings and directions.

175

Propositional objects

Design explorations were conducted concurrently with the theoretical ideas and the examination of the above precedents – some of the preparatory sketches are shown in Figure 12.8. The resulting objects are only tangentially associated with specific points and conclusions from the precedents, but intimately associated with and, it is hoped, reflective of, their overall nature and disposition. The approach is, therefore, one of synthesis rather than analysis, which is not only entirely appropriate for a design-centred inquiry (see Table 7.1), but is also consistent with the aesthetic philosophy of *wabi sabi*.[32]

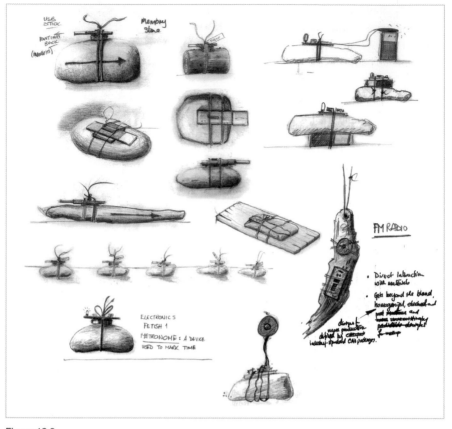

Figure 12.8
Propositional designs
development sketches

The propositional objects have a somewhat different focus from the precedents in that they address issues of sustainability and meaning related specifically to electronic products; and unlike the Grandi Legni pieces of Branzi, they incorporate these technologies. Through creative practice, the aim was to find locally achievable, harmonious aesthetic relationships between mass-produced electronics and unique, minimally-processed or entirely natural elements – not by seeking an integration but through a loosely attached juxtaposition. This results in an aesthetic synthesis characterized by a visual separation between the local and the mass-produced, the natural and the artificial. This separation acknowledges the divisions that exist between these very different types of components, including those of production scale, process and impact. It also allows for their physical separation after use – for benign return of the natural elements to the local environment and for re-use or re-processing of the mass-produced elements.

Such an approach addresses a number of critical aspects in the development of a meaningful material culture, which implies both incremental improvement and radical change. It acknowledges the necessity, transience and impact of mass-produced components in delivering functionality, while recognizing that the useful life of these components can be prolonged through design for disassembly and reuse, and impacts can be reduced through incremental improvement in manufacturing practices. And, as has been discussed in earlier chapters, the approach recognizes the potential benefits of localization. However, important as these are, they are not enough. Beyond these prosaic gains, the character of our material culture must reflect new sensibilities and new relationships with nature, locale and people. In these propositions, an attempt has been made to embody such ideas through the selection of materials – especially the natural elements – and through the overall aesthetic compositions. The inclusion of stones and wood found on the shoreline or the forest floor not only represents a less invasive ethos, it also makes each object unique – no two pebbles are ever the same. As Branzi points out, this imbues each object with a quality akin to sacredness, which technology can never reproduce or impart.[33]

This takes us a step further towards an understanding of material culture in which objects are meaningful in ways that surpass functionality, important as that may be. As discussed in the previous chapter, the design approach assumes an entirely different system for production, resulting in the emergence of a new vernacular that combines mass-produced and locally sourced elements. In other words, the material culture would become an embedded, meaningful element of the culture as a whole. These propositional objects, therefore, attend to different levels of meaning. They address the most fundamental notion of meaning, our physiological needs, by minimizing damage to the natural environment. They address ethical understandings of meaning by contributing to a system in which livelihood and living conditions are intrinsic considerations. And they help foster a cultural sense of identity and belonging, even sacredness, that contributes to spiritual well-being, which is, in part, associated with the affirmation of life in relation to self, community and environment.

However, these propositional objects are not presented as alternative design 'solutions' to contemporary mass-produced products; it would be both inappropriate and counterproductive to do so. Culturally meaningful objects cannot simply be created independent of context, as mass-producible, universal solutions for consumer culture. Instead these objects are indicative of a potential direction, one that must emerge over time and evolve locally to meet local needs and preferences. Functional objects will then be able to reflect meanings pertinent to a particular culture or individual. Hence, the propositional designs presented here can be understood as intimations of how such objects might be manifested. Functional electronic objects begin to throw off the shackles of anonymity, aesthetic perfection and unrepairable novelty – the damaging, unsustainable and ultimately unfulfilling priorities of an outmoded era.

177

The particular function of these propositional objects is of only secondary importance, the main concerns being aesthetic synthesis and, consistent with the previous examples, a broadening of sensory appreciation and object meaning:

- 'Tempo I' (Figure 12.9) is a metronome with adjustable speed flashing lights (LEDs). In this object, the natural and the mass-produced are, literally and figuratively, bound together to create a synthesized whole. The electronics are combined with local Sunderland Point stone and an organic hemp binding.
- 'Tempo II' (Figure 12.10) is also a metronome – with adjustable sound and lights. Circuitry, battery and climbing cord are attached to forest floor wood from the Trough of Bowland.
- 'Lagan Bell' (Figure 12.11) is a wireless electronic bell with speaker circuitry mounted on Cumbria driftwood. The bell-push is bound to a Bowland river stone with hemp cord. Shot silk elements attest to the silk industry that was once a prominent feature of the local economy.
- 'Wireless' (Figure 12.12) is a small am/fm radio, which combines electronics with Cumbria coast pebbles and shot silk.

These objects are included as indicators of a potential direction and for aesthetic contemplation. They are concrete visualizations of the ideas discussed earlier and, as such, they offer layers of expression and resolution that go beyond verbal description. Words inevitably give prominence to rational arguments and concepts, but there are deeper aspects, variously referred to as non-rational, a-rational, or supra-rational, that yield knowledge but require a different form of comprehension.[34,35]

Conclusions

Contemporary electronic goods can be adapted to individual needs in terms of their software and applications, but their essential manufacturing construct remains firmly in an outmoded industrial age. Within this system sustainability can be addressed only through incremental changes. In contrast, the propositional designs presented here are suggestive of a more radical change. One in which the nature of the functional object becomes intimate to place – in terms of its materials, manufacture, aesthetics and essential qualities as a thing. Such a direction demands a letting go of ego along with externally imposed notions of style so as to allow 'place' to inform and become part of the object's character. In addition, the functional elements – whether harmless or damaging – can be made visible and explicit, rather than hidden within often arbitrarily styled casings. Furthermore, these propositions are very much concerned with the present context – not the past or the future. Such present-oriented design has to be ephemeral, partly because technology is always moving on and partly because today's concerns and sensibilities will not be those of tomorrow; tomorrow will have its own expressions for its own time.

In a more localized, continually changing material culture, the object can be tailored to cultural and individual requirements. As long as its production, use and after-use are not damaging, and parts that cannot be readily returned to the natural environment can be re-used, the object need not last forever. To conceive of technological goods in such terms allows for a lightness of touch that is lacking in the more considered, consequential world of mass-production. It offers space for artistic and cultural expression to pervade material goods and to reflect and express contemporary sensibilities. In so doing, there is an opportunity not only to reinvigorate design, for it to become truer to the creative imagination that lies at its heart, but also to imbue mundane, functional goods with meaning, thereby contributing to cultural and spiritual well-being.

Figure 12.9
'Tempo I'
Metronome with adjustable speed LEDs. Electronics,
Sunderland Point stone, hemp cord

Figure 12.10
'Tempo II'
Metronome with adjustable sound and LEDs. Electronics,
climbing cord, forest floor wood from the Trough of Bowland, Lancashire

Figure 12.11
'Lagan Bell'
Wireless reception bell.
Electronics, Cumbria coast
driftwood, Bowland river stone,
hemp cord, shot silk

Figure 12.12
'Wireless'
AM/FM radio. Electronics,
Cumbria coast pebbles,
shot silk, cords (various materials)

13

Wordless Questions
the physical, the virtual and the meaningful

It is never wise to neglect the heart's reasons
which reason knows nothing of.

Eric Hobsbawm

In this chapter objects are developed that encompass time, memory and enduring
meaning – *functionally* through technology and *aesthetically* through allusion. The
resulting propositions are conceived as aged fragments – vestiges that incorporate
digital devices, yet are somehow old and familiar – evoking impressions and
prompting deeper stirrings. Again, these objects are not products but simply
questions in form; silent queries that invite pause for reflection and ask if our
present course might be otherwise.

Exploring these issues through design raises questions concerning the
possibilities and conflicts posed by digitized functionality and the creation of its
requisite materiality. It is hardly enough for the nature and form of this materiality
to be compliant with social and environmental accountability – though that would
be a considerable improvement over current practices. Surely there are higher
principles and more inspiring aims for our efforts than mere compliance and
accountability? Potentially, we can create a material culture that embodies and
expresses another dimension of life, one that reaches beyond the day to day.

Striving to do so can only deepen our understanding of design for sustainability – giving it a foundation that touches the heart as well as the head.

In the following propositions, an attempt has been made to take a few steps down this road. As in any such design-based investigation, these objects embody but one stage and one series of incarnations in a continuing process of inquiry and emergence. A discussion of the theoretical underpinnings that, as in previous chapters was developed reciprocally along with the design explorations, yields an emerging clarity of intention and a crystallization of direction.

Progress and meaning

Progress is generally understood to mean continual human development through technological and material advances within a free-market, growth-based economic system. But let us be clear, this notion of progress is not a verifiable truth but an ideology, and a highly destructive ideology to boot; one that Eagleton has called 'a bright-eyed superstition'.[1]

Although vigorously promoted, this version of progress ultimately offers only an impoverished, prosaic view of human aspiration. Despite this, relatively recent developments in digital technologies have given it a significant boost – heralding a host of new consumer products and creating countless economic and manufacturing opportunities. The rationalized, systematic mass-production of these products is creating wealth, jobs and all kinds of material possibilities. Yet, the longer-term ramifications continue to accumulate and deeper questions concerning the role of material culture within a more comprehensive understanding of human purpose are assiduously avoided.

The ideology of progress, no matter how coherent and rigorous the intellectual reasoning, has always been attended by a conviction that there is more to life than the benefits of material development and the market economy. Historically, this critique has centred firstly, on arguments against excessive rationalism, and secondly, on the premise that an over-reliance on reason has the effect of devaluing other important aspects of being human, such as experience, intuition and spirituality. In opposition to materialism, it has also been contended that competitive individualism and the dehumanization of the market adversely affect community well-being, cooperation and the social order, all of which are regarded as essential elements of life[2] and, it may be argued, of sustainability.

Rationalized mass-production systems have been creating huge wealth, at least for some, and offering material improvements for many since the Industrial Revolution of 18th and 19th century England. Invariably, these systems have also been dogged by environmental degradation and pollution, as well as social deprivation and inequity – and this continues to be the case. As we have seen, the antithesis of instrumental reason and its more brutish effects is epitomized by Wordsworth and Coleridge, who emphasized intuition, speculative modes of thinking, the virtues of rural life and the beauty of nature. This Romantic perspective was both pastoral and spiritual.[3] It sought to recognize and express spiritual values and a sense of holistic awareness that intuitive apprehension can reveal, but which resist quantitative measurement, systematic analysis and verifiable proof.[4]

Poets, artists and mystics have long attempted to express these aspects of our humanity, this sense of the unity of all things, which has been variously referred to as non-dualism, the All, the Real or the Absolute. To develop a more comprehensive, inclusive approach to design, it becomes important to recognize this vital aspect of human understanding, even though any attempts to articulate it through creative design will always be limited and inadequate. However, this is no reason to ignore it – to do so diminishes the nature and quality of our everyday material culture and aesthetic experiences. Its lack of prominence in our thinking, including the ways in which we perceive and frame the role of design, only serves to reinforce a conception of the discipline that stresses instrumental priorities. Such priorities are, of course, important, but they represent only a partial picture.

In recent times, with the expansion of global markets, free trade and consumerism, such critiques have attained a new sense of urgency. Concerns have widened to encompass social and economic inequities between nations, acute environmental and health implications, and consequences for individual well-being. These concerns are accompanied by a growing awareness of the inadequacies of homogenous 'solutions' that ignore local knowledge and are insensitive to culture and context.[5]

187

Design, meaning and sustainability

In Chapter 10, I proposed a quadruple bottom line for sustainability that included *personal meaning*. I chose this term in preference to *spirituality* partly to include broader substantive values (see below), and partly because the traditional link between spirituality and religion[6–9] merges the inner search for meaning with explanatory interpretations, which for many are no longer credible.[10,11]

Today, the traditional bond between religion and spirituality is beginning to loosen. As would be expected, this is especially so in societies where atheist and secular viewpoints are common. Modern secular understandings of spirituality are not dependent on belief in a deity, but rather meaning and sources of values have to be found in the process of living in the world.[12] Contemporary, progressive definitions of spirituality tend to be broader in their reach and can be applied to both religious and non-religious forms.[13]

With or without religious associations, *personal meaning* refers to a wide range of experiences and practices that, collectively, are considered important aspects of human well-being.[14] They include *substantive values* and *matters of ultimate concern* which, together with *practical values*, encompass our ways of acting in the world, ethical behaviours related to our social interactions and personal inner development (see Figure 13.1).

everyday needs	substantive values	+ ultimate concern
practical meaning	ethical meaning	spiritual meaning
health + wellbeing	one's moral compass (personal)	inner search (sense of purpose)
economic needs (food, shelter, clothing, etc.)	relationship to others (social)	outer actions (others, the world)
care for environment (for healthy living)		
basic needs	social needs	higher needs

Figure 13.1 *Personal meaning: substantive values and ultimate concern*

- **Substantive values**: These are the values that have proved to be critical to individuals and societies over the centuries. They include the ethical values and wisdom teachings developed during the axial age, ca. 500 BCE, common to Greek philosophy, the Abrahamic religions, Buddhism, Taoism and Confucian philosophy. They embrace an ethics of justice, peace, compassion and charity, which have been essential to the development of culture and community. And they embrace ideas of communion, truth, self-knowledge and the human capacity to rise above one's own concerns and to reach out to others.[15] Some add to these the ethics of the Modern age, developed from the Enlightenment, which include democracy, freedom of thought, civil liberties, separation of church and state, and human rights.[16,17] This latter group, however, tends to represent particular ways of interpreting and expressing ethical values, rather than adding anything fundamentally new.

- **Matters of ultimate concern**: The term *personal meaning* also recognizes a deeper aspect of our humanity that lies beyond ethics and wisdom – but has long been seen as reciprocally related to them – and is sometimes referred to as ultimate value[18] or matters of ultimate concern.[19] It is associated with the mystery of *being* itself, but not necessarily with religion or faith. This subjective facet of personal meaning can take us beyond the ego and self-oriented preoccupations. It has been characterized by simplicity, unity and silence. While it is inclusive of reason it goes beyond it, though it is not irrational. It is described as self-evident – *being* itself in the fullness of reality.[20]

These understandings of personal meaning are closely related to human creativity and resourcefulness,[21–23] and to the environmental, ethical and economic considerations of sustainability (Figure 13.2). Their contribution to the creation

188

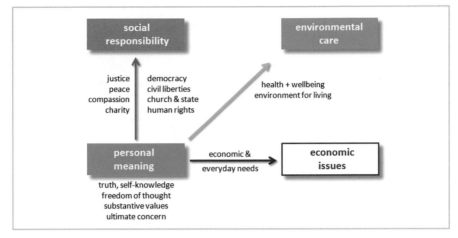

Figure 13.2
Relationship of personal meaning to other elements in a quadruple bottom line

of a more sustainable and meaningful material culture is shown in Figure 13.3. In this 'quadruple bottom line' the critical, interrelated elements of personal meaning, social responsibility and environmental care all help shape the definition of our material culture. Economic considerations play a somewhat different role – serving as an important, pragmatic 'lubricant' that enables the interrelationships among the other elements to be negotiated and realized.

189

It is also important to recognize that these more profound dimensions of personal meaning are *experiential* in nature. They have more to do with practice than with theory, more to do with perceiving than with thinking.[24,25] This is also true of the creative process, critical aspects of which include aesthetic sensitivity, understanding relationships, and awareness of material qualities. Synthesis through an intense engagement in practice, together with a recognition of the ethical implications of creative decisions, links the design process with contemporary, multidimensional understandings of personal meaning.[26] Greater acknowledgement of this link and its implications would enable the outcomes of our creative endeavours to support, rather than undermine, our spiritual selves. Given the values and concerns by which they are characterized, they will also take us in a direction that adheres more closely to sustainable principles. In turn, our material productions are likely to become worthier and nobler expressions of human capability and human dignity – qualifiers that are difficult to apply to our current system in which, according to some estimates, 97 per cent of the energy and material resources used to produce goods are wasted.[27]

In drawing together these relationships between substantive values, matters of ultimate concern and creative activities, it is evident that the triple bottom line of sustainability is ultimately inadequate in its implied aspiration. It only partially addresses these more fundamental notions of what it means to be human; notions that are essential to our own, and therefore the world's, vitality and flourishing continuance.

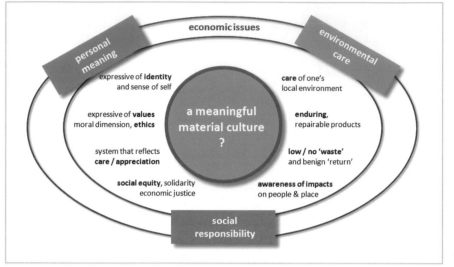

Figure 13.3
The quadruple bottom line – personal, social, environmental, economic

Design values and intentions

The foregoing provides a basis for a more mature and responsible conception
of design, one that reaches beyond conventional, narrowly framed notions of
industrial design, and also beyond contemporary conceptions of craft.

Industrial design is usually defined as a professional service that aims to
enhance the effectiveness of product function, appearance and value for users
and manufacturers.[28] More comprehensive descriptions tend to be couched in
quasi-scientific language that conveys an impression of efficiency and precision.
They emphasize optimization, data analysis and specification, and designate
people as 'users' or 'consumers'. A particular characteristic of industrial
design is the separation of the definition of an object from the process of its
making.[29] Today, industrial design is part of a globalized production system
in which prime motivators are profit maximization and the self-interest of the
corporation, and where, too often, moral concerns are neither recognized nor
acted upon.[30] Within this system, industrial design has become a key ingredient
in encouraging consumerism. Its contributions, which include the deliberate
designing of functional or perceived obsolescence, help stimulate ever-more
sales of increasingly short-lived products.[31,32] As a result, mass-produced material
culture has become, to all intents and purposes, disposable and consequently
massively wasteful, exploitative and damaging. Such narrowly framed motivations
and values are antithetical to any comprehensive interpretation of sustainability.
They also represent a corrosive influence on those values and ideas considered
important to spiritual development and individual well-being, which, in practical
terms, are always about compassion for others and overcoming inequity and
injustice.

In contrast to industrial design, descriptions of contemporary craft tend to be more poetic, with references to beauty, tactility, materials and the qualities and care of making. Craft is concerned with creating one-off objects that exhibit refined skills and which may or may not be functional.[33] While some practitioners employ modern technologies,[34] craft is usually based in traditional methods and skills and tacit knowledge. It is sometimes seen as an antidote to mass-production, where the time and skill invested in the production of an artefact is part of its value.[35] Collections of functional objects at the Crafts Council in London include ceramics and glass, furniture, metalwork and jewellery, musical instruments and books. However, there is generally little representation of objects that incorporate the many electronic and communication technologies used everyday around the world and few examples of technology-based artefacts in general.[36] Hence, contemporary craft is often closer to painting and sculpture than to product design – being concerned with creating beautifully made, desirable, collectable objects that are the result of skilled artisanship.[37]

These contemporary understandings of industrial design and craft are instructive. They reveal the divergent paths taken to design and produce our material culture in the years spanning the late 19th and early 20th centuries. Today, common, everyday objects on which we depend are mass-produced, relatively inexpensive, and frequently unrepairable and expendable. Consequently, in the longer term, they are valueless, meaningless waste. In contrast, craft products are comparatively rare, expensive objects often regarded as *objets d'art*. The detrimental characteristics of the former and the relatively marginal place of the latter mean that, in and of themselves, neither represents a feasible way forward for design. Instead, the creation of more sustainable, more meaningful products needs to draw on elements of both. Such products will have to incorporate the functional advantages offered by modern technologies coupled with those elements associated with craft – sensitivity to materials, place, skills and care – that can help instil objects with meaning and lasting value. It will also need to recognize that these two worlds of ubiquitous mass-produced technologies and unique, handmade crafts not only offer complementary attributes but also yield disparities and conflicts. Highly valued, long-lasting craft objects do not necessarily merge comfortably with mechanically produced, technology-based objects that are valued primarily for their short-lived utilitarian benefit. Clashes and incompatibilities arise in aesthetic experience and in interpretation, meaning and implication. As we have seen in preceding chapters, the relatively low costs of modern technological devices are associated with corporate practices that externalize ethical and environmental issues that would otherwise encroach on profitability. Therefore, many contemporary technological devices result from business practices that are inherently at odds with sustainability. They are also at odds with the respect for materials, artisanship, tradition and place that characterize craft practices. These differences and contradictions demand careful consideration and present particular design challenges.

191

The artefacts included here explore some of these issues. They combine mass-produced technologies with one-off, locally made or hand-crafted elements. In doing so, they represent an attempt to take into account factors associated with sustainability as well as substantive values and profound understandings. These propositions can be seen as questions in form – that ask us to reflect on how modern, transient, digital technologies might be reconciled with environmental and social concerns and with deeper notions of human meaning.

Form follows meaning

The propositional objects all incorporate some kind of contemporary data storage device – a technological memory for keeping documents, images or other information. They also draw on a variety of archetypal object-forms and elements that have traditionally been associated with spiritual practices; these include icons, prayer beads, images, texts and amulets. Found elements and re-used materials and objects come together with new technological devices and locally-acquired, hand-crafted parts fashioned from natural materials adjoin mass-produced parts made from synthetic materials. In this way, localized craft is combined with globalized mass-production, natural materials and traditional forms with digital technologies, and short-lived functionality with enduring meaning. Form becomes delinked from function. Its role is expressive – of substantive values – or evocative – of profound understandings; instrumental functionality being held within the digital realm.

The objects are presented, with respect to their figure numbers, in the order they were created, which helps convey something of the emergence and development of the ideas. Four of the designs are wall-mounted pieces:

- 'Memoria Humanus' (Figure 13.4) comprises a USB flash memory stick mounted on Cumbria driftwood. The surface bears a graffito outline of the human form (Figure 13.4a) and is finished in abraded acrylic. Old labels dangle loosely from its front edge.
- 'iKon' (Figure 13.8) incorporates a hard-drive set in Trough of Bowland oak inscribed with a partial circle and cross, and the alchemical symbol for the element earth (Figure 13.8a). It has a pendant of silk, hemp and glass bead.
- 'Codex Morte' (Figure 13.9) holds a series of memory cards wrapped in silk and secured with hemp cord (Figure 13.9a). Created from a panel of weathered plywood, a modern material that belies its seemingly archaic provenance, it features a series of hand-chiselled 'memory niches'. Sayings from an ancient codex are inscribed into its surface, below which is a graffito figure (Figure 13.9b). Remnants of a chaplet, made from natural seeds, hangs from its lower edge.
- 'Commemoro' (Figure 13.10) bears a single memory card wrapped in silk and bound to a holly switch with hemp cord. A series of three such 'memory sticks' and a detail are also shown (Figures 13.10a and 13.10b).

Three of the above pieces include images or inscriptions associated with spiritual meaning and are made from re-used, decayed wood. The exception being the 'Commemoro' design, made from freshly cut holly. However, in all cases, the visual qualities and wall-mounted form mean that, potentially, the objects could remain in 'use' and be of aesthetic or contemplative value even after their technological components have become outdated. In the case of 'Codex Morte', the niches are not fitted to the exact size of the memory cards so could be used to hold different memory devices or other artefacts entirely. However, if the objects are no longer wanted once their technological components have become outmoded, the wooden elements can be disposed of without ill effect, and the raw technological parts, free as they are from any plastic enclosures, can be more readily reprocessed than similar, encased products.

Two of the objects are designed to be portable:

- 'Memento Credo' (Figure 13.5) is a chain or pendant that combines a USB memory stick with a variety of other elements to create a kind of technologically functional amulet. A crucifix juxtaposed with stone, bone, wood and coin is suggestive of orthodoxy mixed with relics of other beliefs. When the technology becomes ineffective or is superseded, the USB stick can either be retained for aesthetic effect or simply detached. The adhesive cotton tape surrounding it can be readily removed, yielding the basic, unenclosed circuitry for reprocessing.

- 'Memoria Porto' (Figure 13.6) is a small hard drive with a cover **193** fashioned from hand-knitted hemp and a patchwork of linen and silk. The cover has no explicit reference to spiritual ideas but, rather, is indicative of coarse homespun. It can be separated from the hard drive within to reveal the essential circuitry. The natural materials of the cover and the raw circuitry can be easily recycled.

The remaining object addresses the issues in a rather different way:

- 'Memoria Capsula' (Figure 13.7 and 13.7a) employs a re-used wooden box as the protective casing for a hard-drive. Natural azuki beans are used to keep the hard-drive in place. The precise size and shape of a future replacement hard-drive cannot be predicted, but the relatively large box allows for a range of potential devices to be accommodated, and the small beans provide a flexible 'packing' that, within the dimensional limitations of the box, is capable of securing a variety of sizes and shapes. Alternatively, the beans can be discarded and the box used for a different purpose entirely. Here, re-use of locally available artefacts and natural materials yields an enduring, adaptable object that is both practical and indicative of a considered, restrained and environmentally respectful notion of material culture.

In all these propositional objects there is an acknowledgement that the technological components will be of only fleeting usefulness. In some cases, these

Figure 13.4
'Memoria Humanus'
Cumbria driftwood, re-used clothing labels on linen, USB memory stick

Figure 13.4a
'Memoria Humanus' *detail*
graffito and acrylic figure

Figure 13.5
'Memento Credo'
*wood, stones, coin, crucifix,
cotton tape, leather, silk,
brass wire, chain, USB
memory stick*

Figure 13.6
'Memoria Porto'
*hand-knitted hemp,
linen, silk, cord, 80GB
hard drive*

Figure 13.7
'Memoria Capsula'
*re-used toolbox, clothing label,
brass lock, silk, cotton thread,
azuki beans,160GB hard drive*

Figure 13.7a 'Memoria Capsula' *interior detail*

Figure 13.8
'iKon'
*Bowland oak , linen,
hemp, glass,
160GB hard drive*

Figure 13.8a
'iKon' *detail,*
alchemical symbol
for the element earth

Figure 13.9
'Codex Morte'
Lune estuary driftwood with graffiti, silk, hemp cord, seed beads,
six 2GB memory cards

Figure 13.9a
'Codex Morte' *detail,*
hand-chiselled memory niches,
2GB memory cards, silk, hemp cord

Figure 13.9b
'Codex Morte' *detail,*
graffito and
acrylic figure

Figure 13.10
'Commemoro'
*holly switch, silk,
hemp cord, paper,
2GB memory card*

Figure 13.10a
'Commemoro'
series

Figure 13.10b
'Commemoro'
detail

components can remain in place and the object can continue to fulfil a decorative or contemplative role. In all cases, the raw technological parts can be readily separated for reprocessing – leaving behind a variety of artefacts for adaptation to new uses, benign return to the natural environment, or recycling.

The objects also respond to the challenges of sustainability through their product qualities. Their use of natural materials means that they can be readily maintained, and they possess tactile qualities and textures that are often considered aesthetically pleasing. More importantly, there is a recognition of cultural heritage, time, aging and decay through the choice of materials, surface treatments and the use and adaptation of old, even archaic, forms. These objects are 'born antique';[38] their materials are used and worn, their surfaces scoured and their forms familiar. Their characteristics and imagery include:

- a primitive outline of the human figure;
- an ancient religious inscription;
- medieval alchemical symbolism;
- a talisman – of Christian and other symbols;
- an old locked box that, perhaps, holds secrets;
- greenwood sticks – reminiscent of divining, archery or bodging; and
- a knitted and patchwork covering, representative of domestic pursuits.

None of these are associated with rationalized mass-production and the dominance of modern instrumentalism. Instead, they are expressive of tradition, myth, folk beliefs and local crafts. They are products of, and can stimulate, the human imagination, and they call to mind a-rational or supra-rational intuitive ways of knowing. As such they are indicative of the retrievals that are needed if we are to endow our material culture with qualities that not only serve our utilitarian needs but also touch the heart. It is these kinds of product qualities that are so sorely needed if we are to restore a more holistic, inspiring and balanced approach to our endeavours – to counter the devastating effects of an over-rationalized, technocentric and ever-accelerating version of 'progress'. Such forms maintain fidelity with the past while embracing the new and their earthy countenance is a tangible reminder of our environmental dependency. They convey a sense of continuity and change and these qualities help avoid premature perceived obsolescence – a fate commonly associated with more fashionable products. Furthermore, improvisation and the imprecision of the handmade are embraced in defining the aesthetic qualities of the artefacts. These can contribute to an improved sense of empathy with the object and greater product understanding – especially compared to the meticulously considered uniformity and high-precision façades of mass-production where, for many, methods and materials remain a mystery.

Perhaps of particular importance, the forms of these objects are not dictated by the function of the technologies they incorporate. Their purpose is as much about aesthetic experience and reflection as about the requisites of functional necessity.

The result is a new kind of hybrid object that merges old and new, reason and intuition, global and local, and where form follows meaning.

Proximate objects

The creation of these objects represents an attempt to aesthetically unify the handmade with the mass-produced, and traditional materials and forms with new technologies. Even though, on one level, the resulting objects might be judged to have achieved this aim, on another these two facets remain distinct and separate. Traditional and contemporary processes, forms and materials are brought into proximity – arranged together to create an aesthetic whole, yet they remain apart – existing in and representing different worlds and different aspects of the human condition. As such, they ask us to consider these two sides of our nature and they raise questions about how and if they can be further reconciled – the systematic rationalism of industry and utility alongside forms of creative expression used to convey more profound notions of human fulfilment.

These enduring questions and dichotomies are not simply academic – for some of the most forward-looking, successful companies they help shape the nature of day to day activities. For example, a prominent business leader in one of the world's most pioneering international corporations, Uday Chaturvedi, draws on his spiritual heritage to inform the essential qualities of his leadership. He cites the Hindu word *maya* as a summary of the challenges; in Hindu philosophy *maya* refers to how the transitory, sense-world of manifest phenomena obscures and conceals the spiritual and the unity of all things. Bringing this into his managerial decision-making, he sees the provision of good quality jobs and caring for the environment not as costs to be cut or externalized but as valuable investments for the future.[39]

The propositional objects here ask us to ponder these issues and to develop new directions for defining and producing functional objects that, in practical terms, ensure quality of work, economic and social equity, and environmental care. Only by pursuing such directions can the discipline of design, and our material culture, become more sustainable, more just and more meaningful expressions of human endeavour.

205

14

Epilogue

do you know that the pleasure which you get when you find something
lost is greater than the joy of possessing it?

Idries Shah

Over the past half century, economically developed, consumer-based societies
have tended to become increasingly secular and values have become more
and more relative. In Western countries, beliefs are now a matter of individual
choice where virtually anything goes providing it does not harm others. While
many see this as a positive development, others argue that it hardly makes for a
coherent sense of society or community in which there is a common, tacitly agreed
foundation of motivating principles and values. Nevertheless, such societies 'work'
after a fashion and in the short term because they are pragmatic – we simply have
to maintain a minimum level of acceptable behaviour and, most importantly, we
must keep on consuming.[1] In this way, according to the rhetoric of the times, we
can sustain or improve our material standards of living and, by implication, this
offers us a better quality of life and makes us happier.

Such societies are indifferent to, or even discouraging of, spiritual commitment
and traditions – especially in the public realm. They are also inclined to promote
a life that is numbingly mundane, encouraging us to think seriously about our

choice of washing powder or the thinness of our mobile phone. Deeper beliefs about meaning, values and purpose are tolerated in a spirit of liberal acceptance as long as they are restricted to the private domain, which effectively neutralizes them and makes them virtually irrelevant to public discourse. Consequently, the dominant themes within these societies are practical activities that a) enable governance, which with the departure of distinctive political stances has become increasingly managerial in style, and b) facilitate continued economic growth, which in practice means consumption.

Contrary to the pervasive assertions of the capitalist marketplace, the only effective way to address sustainability and to develop a material culture that is congruent with deeper notions of human meaning is to *decrease* consumption. This means reducing the number of goods we purchase, which means rethinking our modes of creating wealth and of ensuring well-being. Such a shift in direction requires a fundamental change in our economic system – away from the growth and 'progress' model that we have taken for granted for decades. This is not to say that progress *per se* is undesirable, but its present, predominantly technological form – so tightly bound as it is to consumerism – needs to be reassessed against measures of true progress that include serious commitment to reducing socio-economic inequities and environmental destruction. Naturally, to achieve this we must place greater value on activities that are commensurate with understandings of ethical responsibility and environmental stewardship – activities that contribute to a sense of fellowship and to focused engagement, which can give our lives a deeper sense of meaning and purpose.

It is no coincidence that such endeavours generally require little in the way of consumption, but they do demand personal investment of time and effort. Playing a musical instrument, reading a book, volunteering, being with family and friends or going for a hike all require our time and dedicated attention. By contrast, the quick and easy solutions offered by consumerism always demand a purchase, but their effects are scarcely as fulfilling, enduring or personally engaging. Moreover, they rarely nourish a deeper sense of personal understanding or awareness and they are seldom environmentally benign. Nevertheless we are constantly told that prepackaged, technology-based solutions are better, not because they necessarily are better but because they are the driver, the essential fuel, of the progress and growth system that is contemporary capitalism.

Reducing consumption, especially among the richer nations, would not only have enormous environmental benefits, it would also require that we give greater consideration to the fewer possessions we do purchase. In this way, a smaller number of enduring material goods would become more highly valued, and potentially more meaningful to us, than a host of transient, often trivial, purchases.

The development of such a scenario requires that we conceive of our material goods, and especially those that rely on rapidly advancing technologies, in terms that include more than instrumental reason and rationalism.

Beyond reason

Many environmental scientists agree that human activities are causing changes in the Earth's climate that could have devastating effects. Despite the weight of evidence behind these forecasts, there is much scepticism about their veracity. This is, in part, stoked by a global corporate system whose short-term self-interests trump all else; environmentalists have been painted anti-capitalist, promoters of apocalyptic ideas and eccentric antagonists of modern, technological civil society.[2] Yet, even those who fundamentally disagree with the defenders of globalized capitalism may be inclined to resist the warnings of the scientific community – not simply because confidence in such warnings is sometimes undermined by questionable practices,[3,4] but also because the history of civilization has been filled with such warnings. As far back as the 6th century, Gregory the Great opined that the world was growing old and hastening to its end.[5]

However, the basis of such scepticism may be more systemic and grounded in the inadequacy of reason itself. Eagleton has pointed out that, even though we cannot do without the faculty of reason, we must go deeper than reason to tap into that which is most fundamental to us – an interior depth that both encompasses and transcends reason.[6] Critical aspects of human understanding that do not fit comfortably or wholly within the facts and premises on which reason depends span such things as aesthetic sensitivity; tacit knowledge; intuition; spontaneous ideas, creativity and imagination; faith and fidelity to cultural tradition; and compassion and love. Hence, despite the evidence-based research and rational arguments, it seems that reason alone is not enough to convince us of a change in priorities and direction. And it is certainly not enough for the creation of a material culture that is in accord with substantive values and resonant with the deeper self. Indeed, it is the narrowly framed rationalism behind the production of so many of today's products that is exacerbating environmental change and social inequity, and nurturing discontent. Reason alone cannot provide the basis for a more meaningful material culture. As Virgil, the voice of reason, is given to say in the *Divine Comedy*, 'if you too wish to make the climb, a spirit worthier than I must take you'.[7]

Objects, environment and meaning

For centuries, across very different kinds of societies, the main path for developing substantive values and a sense of ultimate meaning in one's life has been religious practice. Today, however, many people living in economically developed, consumer-based societies have little to do with the traditional religions of their culture. Despite this disillusion with, or outright rejection of, institutionalized religion there remains for many a spiritual hunger. This is to be expected because, with or without religion, we remain meaning-seeking beings.

This creates a crisis of meaning in contemporary secular societies. The absence of suitable communal forms of meaning-seeking practices that resonate with contemporary sensibilities has encouraged on the one hand the development of individualistic, and hence atomizing, pick-and-mix forms of quasi-spiritual practice. These often combine consumerism with self-help and attractive elements from various religious traditions. On the other hand, the yearning to fill the 'meaning' gap is sought through cultural consumerism. This can range from attending blockbuster exhibitions at major art galleries and museums to cultural tourism, where hundreds of thousands of people annually descend on the cities of culture, tombs of the pharaohs or last remaining natural places. Here, art and nature become interwoven with consumerism. And while great art and natural places can move us and inspire us because they have a spiritual dimension, they are no substitute for true inner development – the examined life. But, as we have seen, such self-reflection or 'inner work' is continually frustrated by the distractions offered by consumer culture.

The perennial but irresolvable questions that inspire the artist, the poet and the composer can perhaps also inspire the designer who wishes to help create a material culture that is congruent with, and thence alludes to, the truly meaningful and the transcendent in our day to day mundane acts of practical utility. This is not an easy task because, unlike pure art, design must combine deeper meaning and aesthetics with functionality and economic viability. Nevertheless, it becomes clear from the foregoing that developing such a material culture implies creating utilitarian artefacts in ways that contribute positively to human welfare and do not violate the natural environment. Both of these conditions are important aspects of all the major meaning-seeking traditions. Approaches that conform to these conditions can lead to artefacts that possess intrinsic value. In addition, as we saw in the previous chapter, it is possible to imbue functional objects with symbolic references that more directly link day to day activities with deeper notions of meaning. Such references can serve as reminders or touchstones within the busy-ness of the everyday and contribute to the development of a material environment that is a more comprehensive expression of our full humanity.

Hence, there are avenues for design that can embrace profound understandings and – whether inherent or more explicitly symbolic – can transcend the gross deficiencies of narrowly defined, rationalized approaches. By taking on these creative challenges we have the opportunity to fundamentally reform and revitalize the discipline. In doing so, we will be discovering the true spirit of design.

Notes

1 Introduction

[1] Blake, W. (1804) *Milton: A Poem*, Preface: 26.

2 Sambo's Stones – sustainability and meaningful objects

An earlier version of this chapter appeared in the Design and Culture Journal, vol 2, no 1, pp45–62 (copyright 2010). With kind permission of Berg Publishers, an imprint of A&C Black Publishers Ltd.

[1] Grantham, P. (2004) *Sambo's Grave, Sunderland Point*, available at www.grantham.karoo.net/paul/graves/sambo.htm, accessed 20 September 2010.

[2] Ashworth, E. (2005) *Sunderland Point and Samboo's Grave*, available at www.timetravel-britain.com/05/July/sunderland.shtml, accessed 20 September 2010.

[3] Cunliffe, H. (2004) *The Story of Sunderland Point – From the Early Days to Modern Times*, R.W. Atkinson, Sunderland Point, Lancashire, pp5–12.

[4] Calais, E. (2007) 'Samboo's Grave', in *From a Slow Carriage*, Road Works Publ, Lancaster, p57.

[5] Hague, W. (2007) *William Wilberforce: The Life of the Great Anti-Slave Trade Campaigner*, HarperCollins, London, pp159–160.

[6] Aymes, T. (2008) *Holikey-Provence* website, www.holikey.fr, accessed 28 August 2008.

[7] La Provence (2008) *L'histoire: Il invente les 'clés USB provençales'*, 8 August 2008, available at www.laprovence.com/articles/2008/08/08/534738-Region-en-direct-L-histoire-il-invente-les-cles-USB-provencales.php, accessed 27 August 2008.

[8] Robinson, B. H. (2009) 'E-waste: An assessment of global production and environmental impacts', *Science of the Total Environment*, 408, Elsevier, pp183–191.

[9] Borgmann, A. (1984) *Technology and the Character of Contemporary Life: A Philosophical Inquiry*, University of Chicago Press, Chicago, p41.

[10] NetRegs (2010) *Waste Electrical and Electronic Equipment (WEEE)*, available at www.netregs.gov.uk/netregs/topics/WEEE/default.aspx, accessed 20 September 2010.

[11] Smith, D. (2006) 'Blair: Britain's "sorrow" for shame of slave trade', *The Observer*, 26 November 2006, available at www.guardian.co.uk/politics/2006/nov/26/race.immigrationpolicy, accessed 20 September 2010.

[12] Tozer, J. (2006) 'Kneeling in chains, the dramatic apology from slave trader descendant', *Daily Mail*, 21 June 2006, available at www.dailymail.co.uk/news/article-391860/Kneeling-chains-dramatic-apology-slave-trader-descendant.html, accessed 20 September 2010.

[13] Curtis, G. and Mackay, M.(2007) 'London mayor issues apology for slave trade', *Christian Today*, 23 March 2007, available at www.christiantoday.com/article/mayor.of.london.urges.blair.to.formally.aplogise.for.uks.role.in.slave.trade/10069.htm, accessed 20 September 2010.

212

3 Following Will-o'-the-Wisps and Chasing Ghosts – re-directing design through practice-based research

An earlier version of this chapter appeared under a slightly different title in the Design Journal, vol 11, no 1, pp51–64 (copyright 2008). With kind permission of Berg Publishers, an imprint of A&C Black Publishers Ltd.

[1] Woodham, J. M. (1997) *Twentieth Century Design*, Oxford University Press, Oxford pp65–67.

[2] Tarnas, R. (1991) *The Passion of the Western Mind: Understanding the Ideas that have Shaped Our Worldview*, Harmony Books, New York, p398.

[3] Spencer, L. (1998) 'Postmodernism, modernity and the tradition of dissent', in S. Sim (ed) *The Icon Critical Dictionary of Postmodern Thought*, Icon Books, Cambridge, p161.

[4] Thackara, J. (2005) *In the Bubble: Designing in a Complex World*, MIT Press, Cambridge, MA, pp1–8.

[5] Fuad-Luke, A. (2004) *Slow Design*, Section 2.2, Slow Theory, available at www.slowdesign.org, accessed 8 May 2007.

[6] Hawken, P., Lovins, A. and Lovins, L. H. (1999) *Natural Capitalism*, Little, Brown & Co, New York, pp2–3.

[7] Hardstaff, P. (2007) Interview, BBC Radio 4, *Today Programme*, 27 January 2007. An interview concerning the relocation of the Burberry clothing factory from the UK to China in which Hardstaff, head of policy at the World Development Movement, suggested that government policies encourage companies to move from place to place to seek the lowest labour and environmental standards.

[8] Walker, S. (2006) *Sustainable by Design: Explorations in Theory and Practice*, Earthscan/James & James Science Publishers, London, pp114–119.

[9] Hobsbawm, E. J. (1968) *Industry and Empire*, Penguin Books, London, pp58–78.

[10] Frayling has referred to this type of research as 'research into design', his other categorizations differ somewhat from the designations I use here, see: Frayling, C. (1993/4) *Research in Art and Design*, Royal College of Art Research Papers, Royal College of Art, London, vol 1, no 1.

[11] Sparke, P. (2004) *An Introduction to Design and Culture: 1900 to the Present*, second edition, Routledge, London.

[12] Dormer, P. (1993) *Design Since 1945*, Thames & Hudson, London.

[13] Heskett, J. (1986) *Industrial Design*, Thames & Hudson, London.

[14] Verbeek, P-P., (2005) *What Things Do: Philosophical Reflections on Technology, Agency and Design*, Penn State University Press, Philadelphia.

[15] Buchanan, R. and Margolin, V. (eds) (1995) *Discovering Design: Explorations in Design Studies*, University of Chicago Press, Chicago.

[16] Margolin, V. (2002) *The Politics of the Artificial: Essays on Design and Design Studies*, University of Chicago Press, Chicago.

[17] Cross, N. (2006) *Designerly Ways of Knowing*, Springer, New York.

[18] Hannah, G. G. (2002) *Elements of Design*, Princeton Architectural Press, New York.

[19] Visocky O'Grady, J. and Visocky O'Grady, K. (2006) *A Designer's Research Manual*, paperback edition 2009, Rockport Publ. Ltd., Beverly, MA.

[20] Thackara, J. (2006) *Design and the Growth of Knowledge* (Afterword), Faculty of Industrial Design Engineering, Delft University of Technology, Netherlands, available at http://studiolab.io.tudelft.nl/static/gems/symposium/screenversie72dpi.pdf, accessed 10 May 2006.

[21] Grayling, A. C. (2001) *The Meaning of Things*, Orion Books, London, p149.

[22] Waters, L. (2004) *Enemies of Promise*, Prickly Paradigm Press, Chicago, pp9, 68.

[23] Waters, L. (2004) *Enemies of Promise*, Prickly Paradigm Press, Chicago, p73

[24] Grayling, A. C. (2006) *The Form of Things*, Weidenfeld & Nicholson, London, p143.

[25] Dunne, A. and Gaver, W. W. (1997) *The Pillow: Artist-Designers in the Digital Age*, CHI97 Electronic Publishing, available at http://acm.org/sigchi/chi97/proceedings/short-talk/wwg.htm, accessed 10 May 2007.

[26] van der Lugt, R. and Stappers, P. J. (2006) *Design and the Growth of Knowledge* (Introduction), Faculty of Industrial Design Engineering, Delft University of Technology, Netherlands, available at http://studiolab.io.tudelft.nl/static/gems/symposium/screenversie72dpi.pdf, accessed 10 May 2006.

27 Seago, A. and Dunne, A. (1999) 'New methodologies in art and design research: The object as discourse', *Design Issues*, vol 15, no 2, pp11–17.
28 van der Lugt, R. and Stappers, P. J. (2006) *Design and the Growth of Knowledge* (Introduction), Faculty of Industrial Design Engineering, Delft University of Technology, Netherlands, available at http://studiolab.io.tudelft.nl/static/gems/symposium/screenversie72dpi.pdf, accessed 10 May 2006.

4 After Taste – the power and prejudice of product appearance

An earlier version of this chapter appeared in the Design Journal, vol 12, no 1, pp25–40 (copyright 2009). With kind permission of Berg Publishers, an imprint of A&C Black Publishers Ltd.

1 Sparke, P. (1995) *As Long as it's Pink – The Sexual Politics of Taste*, HarperCollins, London, p1.
2 *Dictionary of Quotations* (1998) Wordsworth Reference Series, Wordsworth Editions Ltd, Ware, Herts, p326.
3 Hughes, R. (1987) 'Gentlemen of New South Wales', *The Fatal Shore*, Collins Harvill, London, pp342–343.
4 Carey, J. (2005) *What Good Are The Arts?*, Faber & Faber, London, p54.
5 O'Doherty, B. (1986) *Inside the White Cube: The Ideology of the Gallery Space*, Lapis Press, Santa Monica, p76.
6 Hughes, R. (2006) *Things I Didn't Know, A Memoir*, Alfred Knopf, New York, p31.
7 Scruton, R. (1999) 'Kitsch and the modern predicament', *City Journal*, vol 9, no 1, available at www.city-journal.org/html/9_1_urbanities_kitsch_and_the.html, accessed 24 September 2010.
8 Muelder Eaton, M. (2001) *Merit: Aesthetic and Ethical*, Oxford University Press, Oxford, p51.
9 Dormer, P. (1997) *The Culture of Craft: Status and Future*, Manchester University Press, Manchester, p142.
10 Sawyer, C. A. (2001) *All in a Day's Work*, Automotive Design and Production Field Guide to Automotive Technology, available at www.autofieldguide.com/articles/030101.html, accessed 24 September 2010.
11 Bakhtiar, L. (1976) *SUFI – Expression of the Mystical Quest* (Part 3: Architecture and Music), Thames & Hudson, London, pp106–107.
12 Muelder Eaton, M. (2001) *Merit: Aesthetic and Ethical*, Oxford University Press, Oxford, p131.
13 MacMillan, J. (2007) 'I wish you God – among the arts, music offers the most sustained challenge to the secular consensus. It asserts the heart's deepest truths and sharpens our sense of the real', *The Tablet*, 24 February 2007, p27.
14 MAMAC (2006) *Robert Rauschenberg: On and Off the Wall* (exhibition catalogue), Musée d'Art moderne et d'Art contemporain, Nice, France, pp50–51.
15 Martin, C. (2006) *A Glimpse of Heaven*, Foreword by Cardinal Cormac Murphy-O'Connor, English Heritage, Swindon, pp8–9.

[16] Muelder Eaton, M. (2001) *Merit: Aesthetic and Ethical*, Oxford University Press, Oxford, p50.

[17] Roxyrama (2008) The Bryan Ferry and Roxy Music Archive, *Bryan Ferry Biography*, available at www.roxyrama.com/classic/biographies/bryan_ferry.shtml, accessed 24 September 2010.

[18] BBC News (2007) 'Ferry apologises for Nazi remarks', 16 April 2007, available at http://news.bbc.co.uk/go/pr/fr/-/2/hi/entertainment/6561177.stm, accessed 24 September 2010.

[19] This response was given during a Q&A session following a keynote address at an international design conference. The designer in question shall remain anonymous. It would be unfair to single out one person when the attitude is evidently systemic.

5 Extant Objects – seeing through design

An earlier version of this chapter appeared in the International Journal of Sustainable Design, vol 1, no 1, pp4–11 (copyright 2008). With kind permission of Inderscience Switzerland who retain copyright of the original papers.

[1] Chapman, J. (2005) *Emotionally Durable Design: Objects, Experience, Empathy*, Earthscan, London, p16.

[2] Elkington, J. (1998) *Cannibals with Forks: The Triple Bottom Line of 21st Century Business*, New Society Publishers, Gabriola Island, Canada.

[3] Robèrt, K. H. (2002) *The Natural Step Story – Seeding a Quiet Revolution*, New Society Publishers, Gabriola Island, Canada.

[4] McDonough, W. and Braungart, M. (2001) *Cradle to Cradle: Remaking the Way We Make Things*, Douglas & McIntyre, Vancouver.

[5] Pré (2010) *Life Cycle Tools to Improve Environmental Performance and Sustainability*, Pré Consultants, Netherlands, available at www.pre.nl, accessed 4 October 2010.

[6] Factor 10 (2009) *Factor 10 – An Introduction*, Factor 10 Institute, Canoules, France, available at www.factor10-institute.org, accessed 4 October 2010.

[7] Sparke, P. (2004) *An Introduction to Design and Culture: 1900 to the Present*, second edition, Routledge, London, p64.

[8] McCabe, H. (2005) *The Good Life: Ethics and the Pursuit of Happiness*, Continuum, London, p5.

[9] Wood, J. et al (2010) *Attainable Utopias online*, available at http://attainable-utopias.org/tiki/tiki-index.php, accessed 4 October 2010.

[10] Scharmer, C. O. (2009) *Theory U: Leading from the Future as it Emerges*, Berrett-Koehler Publishers, Inc, San Francisco, CA

[11] Manzini, E., Meroni, A. et al (2010) *Creative Communities*, Sustainable Everyday, available at www.sustainable-everyday.net/main/?page_id=19, accessed 4 October 2010.

215

[12] Woodham, J. M. (1997) *Twentieth-Century Design*, Oxford University Press, Oxford, pp145, 227–228.

[13] DeAngelis, T. (2004) 'Consumerism and its discontents', *Monitor on Psychology*, vol 35, no 6 June, available at www.apa.org/monitor/jun04/discontents.html, accessed 4 October 2010.

[14] Leonard, A. (2010) *The Story of Stuff*, Constable and Robinson Ltd, London, p314.

[15] European Commission (2004) 'EU policy-making: Counting the hidden costs', European Commission Environment Research document, 16 August 2004, available at http://ec.europa.eu/research/environment/print.cfm?file=/comm/research/environment/newsanddoc/article_1444_en.htm, accessed 4 October 2010.

[16] Scott, R. (2003) 'The high price of "free" trade', EPI Briefing Paper no 147, Economic Policy Institute, Washington, DC, 17 November 2003, available at www.epinet.org/content.cfm/briefingpapers_bp147, accessed 4 October 2010.

[17] Ades, D., Cox, N. and Hopkins, D. (1999) *Marcel Duchamp*, World of Art series, Thames & Hudson, London, p146.

[18] Rose, B. (2005) Rauschenberg – On and Off the Wall, in *Rauschenberg – On and Off the Wall – Works from the 80's and 90's*, Musée d'Art moderne et d'Art contemporain, Nice, France, pp47–73.

[19] Williams. G. (2004) 'Use it again', in R. Ramakers (ed) *Simply Droog – 10+1 years of Creating Innovation and Discussion*, Droog Publishing, Amsterdam, pp25–34.

216

6 Sermons in Stones – argument and artefact for sustainability

An earlier version of this chapter appeared in Les Ateliers de l'éthique/The Ethics Forum, vol 5, no 2, pp101–116 (creative commons licence 2010). With kind permission of The Centre de recherche en éthique de l'Université de Montréal.

[1] Waste Online (2008) Electrical and Electronic Equipment Recycling Information Sheet, at: http://www.wasteonline.org.uk/resources/informationsheets/electricalelectronic.htm, accessed 6 October 2010.

[2] CAFOD (2008) Report Highlights Workers' "Abuse", Friday 8 February 2008, at: http://www.cafod.org.uk/news_and_events/news/report_2008_02_07, accessed 6 October 2010.

[3] For example, in the UK research in the arts and humanities has had an annual research council budget of ca £75 million compared to £1556 million for research in engineering, science and technology, not including medical science (£500 million for the Engineering and Physical Sciences Research Council, £336 million for the Biotechnology and Biological Sciences Research Council, £220 million for the Natural Environment Research Council, and £500 million for the Science and Technology Facilities Council), Research Councils of the United Kingdom, www.rcuk.ac.uk, accessed 11 January 2008.

[4] For example, Korten, D. C. (2001) *When Corporations Rule the World*, second edition, Chapter 3, The Growth Illusion, Kumarian Press Inc, Bloomfield, Connecticut and Berrett-Koehler Publishers Inc, San Francisco, CA, pp43–56.

[5] Douglas, N. (2006) 'The overall sale experience', *Socialist Review*, available at www.socialistreview.org.uk/article.php?articlenumber=9706, accessed 6 October 2010.

[6] Hummer (2006) *Restore the Balance* TV commercial, available at www.youtube.com/watch?v=Z0bnXI4nTUQ, accessed 6 October 2010.

[7] Miller, V. J. (2005) *Consuming Religion*, Continuum, New York, p2.

[8] IDSA (2007) CONNECTING'07, The ICSID/IDSA World Design Congress, 17–20 October 2007, San Francisco, CA.

[9] Straubel J. B. and Hatt, B. (2007) 'Sleek and green', a presentation of the Tesla Roadster, 18 October 2007, CONNECTING'07, The ICSID/IDSA World Design Congress, 17–20 October 2007, San Francisco, CA.

[10] Tesla (2010) *Tesla Motors*, www.teslamotors.com, accessed 6 October 2010.

[11] Seymour, R. (2007) *Space Tourism*, a presentation of the Virgin Galactic space tourism project, 18 October, CONNECTING'07, The ICSID/IDSA World Design Congress, 17–20 October 2007, San Francisco, CA.

[12] Virgin Galactic (2010) *The Virgin Corporations Commercial 'Spaceline'*, description and video presentations available at www.virgingalactic.com, accessed 6 October 2010.

[13] De Graaf, J., Wann, D. and Naylor, T. H. (2001) *Affluenza: The All-Consuming Epidemic*, Berrett-Koehler Publishers, San Francisco, CA.

[14] Badke, C. and Walker, S, (2008) 'Designers anonymous', *Innovation – The Journal of the Industrial Designers*, Spring 2008, pp40–43.

[15] Tata (2008) 'Tata Motors unveils the people's car', press release, 10 January 2008, available at www.tatamotors.com/our_world/press_releases.php?ID=340&action=Pull, accessed 6 October 2010.

[16] Taylor, C. (2007) *A Secular Age*, Belknap Press, Cambridge, MA, pp716–717.

[17] Northcott, M. S. (2007) *A Moral Climate: The Ethics of Global Warming*, Darton, Longman and Todd, London, pp175–177.

[18] Ratzinger, J. (2007) *Jesus of Nazareth*, Doubleday, London, p33.

[19] Armstrong, K. (2006) *The Great Transformation*, Atlantic Books, London, pxi.

[20] Beattie, T. (2007) *The New Atheists*, Darton, Longman and Todd, London, pp132–136.

[21] Beattie, T. (2007) *The New Atheists*, Darton, Longman and Todd, London, p139.

[22] Beattie, T. (2007) *The New Atheists*, Darton, Longman and Todd, London, p133.

[23] Northcott, M. S. (2007) *A Moral Climate: The Ethics of Global Warming*, Darton, Longman and Todd, London, p186. Emphasis in original.

[24] BBC News (2007) 'Archbishop launches attack on US', BBC News, 25 November 2007, http://news.bbc.co.uk/1/hi/uk/7111686.stm, accessed 6 October 2010.

[25] De Botton, A. (2004) *Status Anxiety*, Penguin Books, London, p201.

[26] University of Cumbria (2007) 'It's not where you are, it's where you're going', banner displayed on the Lancaster campus of University of Cumbria, September 2007. University of Liverpool (2007) 'It's not where you are, it's where you want to be', advertisement in *FT Magazine*, 13/14 October 2007, p43.

[27] Chesterton, G. K. (1908) *Orthodoxy*, 2001 edition by Image Books, New York, p103.

[28] Eno, B. (2001) 'The big here and the long now', essay available at http://digitalsouls.com/2001/Brian_Eno_Big_Here.html, accessed 6 October 2010.

[29] Long Now (2008) *The Long Now Foundation*, available at www.longnow.org, accessed 6 October 2010.

[30] Steindl-Rast, D. and Lebell, S. (2002) *Music of Silence: A Sacred Journey through the Hours of the Day*, Seastone, Berkeley, CA, p7.

[31] Miró, J. (1974) *L'esperança del condemnat a mort I-III/The Hope of the Man Condemned to Death I-III*, acrylic on canvas, Fundació Joan Miró, 1974.

[32] Longfellow, H. W. (1838) A Psalm for Life, in Herbert, D. (ed.) (1981) Everyman's Book of Evergreen Verse, A Psalm of Life by Henry Wadsworth Longfellow, Dent, London, UK, pp188-189.

[33] Armstrong, K. (2006) *The Great Transformation*, Atlantic Books, London, pxi.

[34] For example, Phaedo by Plato, in Tredennick, H. and Tarrant, H. (trans) (1954) *The Last Days of Socrates* by Plato, Penguin Books, London, p125.

[35] For example, Mascaró, J. (trans) (1965) *The Upanishads*, Penguin Books, London, p61.

[36] For example, the Intergovernmental Panel on Climate Change (IPCC) suggests that in a little more than a decade, up to 250 million people in Africa will 'be exposed to increased water stress', and 'agricultural production, including access to food, in many African countries is projected to be severely compromised', with crop yields in some countries down by 50 per cent. (While errors have been found in some of its projections, the vast majority of its findings have general support from climate change experts.) *Intergovernmental Panel on Climate Change Fourth Annual Report – Climate Change 2007: Synthesis Report*, www.ipcc.ch/pdf/assessment-report/ar4/syr/ar4_syr.pdf, accessed 6 October 2010.

[37] Feng, G. F and English, J. (trans) (1989) *Tao Te Ching by Lao Tsu*, Vintage Books, New York, p48.

[38] 1 Corinthians, 7:30–31, The Holy Bible, New International Version, New Testament, Zondervan Publishing House, Grand Rapids, Michigan, 1973, p226.

[39] Thoreau, H. D. (1854) 'Walden', in *Walden and Civil Disobedience*, 1983 edition, Penguin Books, New York, p95.

[40] Schumacher, E. F. (1979) *Good Work*, Abacus, London, p27.

[41] Iyer, R. (1993) *The Essential Writing of Gandhi*, Oxford University Press, Delhi, p378.

[42] Mercedes-Benz TV, Weekly Show, 29 February 2008, promotional film for the CLC car 'Key Visual Shooting part 2', available at www.mercedes-benz.tv/index.

html?csref=mbcom_ws_mbtv0107_uk_en, accessed 31 January 2008.

43 Rolex Watches website, information about the GMT-Master II watch, available at www.rolex.com/en/#/en/xml/collection/extraordinary-watches/gmt-master/features/gold, accessed 31 January 2008.

44 Apple Store website, information about the iPod nano, available at http://store.apple.com/1-800-MY-APPLE/WebObjects/AppleStore.woa/wa/RSLID?nnmm=browse&mco=3587D037&node=home/shop_ipod/family/ipod_nano, accessed 31 January 2008.

45 'Google profits disappoint Market', BBC News Online, 1 February 2008, available at http://news.bbc.co.uk/1/hi/business/7221170.stm, accessed 6 October 2010.

46 Print advertisement for Glacéau smartwater in Vanity Fair, July 2007, p85.

47 Proud, L. (2000) Icons, A Sacred Art, Jarrold, Norwich, p8.

48 Achemeimastou-potmaianou, M. (1987) From Byzantium to El Greco: Greek frescoes and Icons, The Theology and Spirituality of the Icon by Rt Rev Dr Kallistos Ware, Greek Ministry of Culture, Athens, pp38–39.

49 Walker, S. (2006) Sustainable by Design: Explorations in Theory and Practice, Earthscan, London, pp39–51.

50 Schaff, P. (ed) (1886) Socrates and Sozomenus Ecclesiastical Histories Creator(s): Socrates Scholasticus, Christian Literature Publishing Co, New York, available at www.ccel.org/ccel/schaff/npnf202.txt, accessed 6 October 2010.

51 Schaff, P. (1889) History of the Christian Church, Volume III: Nicene and Post-Nicene Christianity. A.D. 311–600, 5th edition, Chapter 32, available at www.ccel.org/ccel/schaff/hcc3.iii.vii.v.html, accessed 6 October 2010.

52 St Paul, M. Sr (2000) Clothed with Gladness: The Story of St Clare, Our Sunday Visitor Inc, Huntington, IN, p24.

53 LeShan, L. (1974) How to Meditate, Bantam Books, New York, p67.

54 Easwaran, E. (1978) Meditation-Commonsense Directions for an Uncommon Life, 1986 edition, Penguin Books, London, p11.

219

7 Gentle Arrangements – artefacts of disciplined empathy

An earlier version of this chapter was presented at Design Connexity, 8th International Conference of the European Academy of Design, Aberdeen, 1–3 April 2009, and appeared in the proceedings.

1 The term 'disciplined sympathy' is used by Armstrong to refer to long-taught practices that can lead to spiritual transformation. Here, a modified version of this term is employed, namely 'disciplined empathy'. Whereas 'sympathy' is most commonly used in reference to other people, 'empathy' can be used in reference to people, other living creatures and even inanimate objects. It is, therefore, less anthropocentric and a more appropriate term to use in the context of design. Armstrong, K, (2006) The Great Transformation, Atlantic Books, London, p391.

2 Taylor, C. (2007) A Secular Age, Belknap Press, Cambridge, MA, p9.

[3] Thackara, J. (2005) *In the Bubble: Designing in a Complex World*, MIT Press, Cambridge, MA, pp212–213.

[4] Wood, J. (2008) *Changing the Change: A Fractal Framework for MetaDesign*, Proceedings of the Changing the Change Conference, Turin, 10–12 July 2008, available at http://emma.polimi.it/emma/showEvent.do?idEvent=23, accessed 28 July 2008.

[5] Young, R. A. (2008) *A Taxonomy of the Changing World of Design Practice: A Vision of the Changing Role of Design in Society Supported by a Taxonomy matrix Tool,* Proceedings of the Changing the Change Conference, Turin, 10–12 July 2008, available at http://emma.polimi.it/emma/showEvent.do?idEvent=23, accessed 28 July 2008.

[6] Buchanan, R. and Margolin, V. (1995) *Discovering Design: Explorations in Design Studies*, University of Chicago Press, Chicago, Section 1 essay, 'Rhetoric, Humanism and Design' by R. Buchanan, pp23–66.

[7] Buchanan, R. (1992) 'Wicked problems in design thinking', *Design Issues*, vol 8, no 2, pp5–21.

[8] Thompson, D. (2006) *Tools for Environmental Management: A Practical Introduction and Guide*, University of Calgary Press, Calgary.

[9] For example, *Measuring Progress: Sustainable Development Indicators 2010*, a National Statistics Compendium publication, Department for Environment, Food and Rural Affairs, London, available at www.defra.gov.uk/sustainable/government/progress/documents/SDI2010_001.pdf, accessed 11 October 2010.

[10] The Kyoto Protocol, which was agreed in 1997 and came into force in 2005, aimed to reduce greenhouse gases through binding emissions targets. Available at http://unfccc.int/kyoto_protocol/items/2830.php, accessed 7 October 2010.

[11] WEEE – Waste Electrical and Electronic Equipment Legislation from the European Commission – information available at http://ec.europa.eu/environment/waste/weee/index_en.htm, accessed 7 October 2010.

[12] Northcott, M. S. (2007) *A Moral Climate: The Ethics of Global Warming*, Darton, Longmann and Todd Ltd, London, pp181–182.

[13] Black, R. (2008) 'Moral appeal for UK energy saving', BBC News, 27 February 2008, available at http://news.bbc.co.uk/go/pr/fr/-/1/hi/sci/tech/7267915.stm, accessed 7 October 2010.

[14] WCED (1987) *Our Common Future,* World Commission on Environment and Development, Oxford University Press, Oxford, p43.

[15] Van der Ryn, S. and Cowan, S. (1996) *Ecological Design*, Island Press, Washington, DC, pp139–140.

[16] Korten, D. C. (2006) *The Great Turning: From Empire to Earth Community*, Kumarian Press Inc, Bloomfield, CT, and Berrett-Koehler Publishers Inc, San Francisco, CA, pp302–305.

[17] BBC (2007) 'Business call for plan on climate: Global businesses have called for a legally binding and comprehensive international deal on climate change', BBC News, 30 November 2007, available at http://news.bbc.co.uk/go/pr/fr/-/1/hi/business/7120324.stm, accessed 7 October 2010.

[18] Charlesworth, A. (2010) 'Global carbon emissions to rise 43 per cent by 2035, says US report', BusinessGreen.com, available at www.businessgreen.com/business-green/news/2263703/global-carbon-emissions-rise, accessed 7 October 2010.

[19] *Global CO$_2$ Emissions: Increase Continued in 2007*, Netherland Environmental Assessment Agency, 13 June 2008, available at www.pbl.nl/en/publications/2008/GlobalCO2emissionsthrough2007.html, accessed 7 October 2010.

[20] Kinver, M. (2008) 'EU industry sees emissions rise', BBC News, 2 April 2008, http://news.bbc.co.uk/go/pr/fr/-/2/hi/science/nature/7326834.stm, accessed 7 October 2010.

[21] Tarnas, R. (1991) *The Passion of the Western Mind: Understanding the Ideas that have Shaped Our Worldview*, Harmony Books, New York, p398.

[22] Taylor, C. (2007) *A Secular Age*, Belknap Press, Cambridge, MA, pp5, 773–774.

[23] Humphreys, C. (1949) *Zen Buddhism*, William Heinemann Ltd, London, pp6–11.

[24] Fry, T. (1995) 'Sacred design 1: A re-creational theory', in R. Buchanan and V. Margolin (eds) *Discovering Design: Explorations in Design Studies*, University of Chicago Press, Chicago, p194.

[25] Armstrong, K. (2005) *A Short History of Myth*, Canongate Books Ltd, Edinburgh, pp32–33.

[26] Hick, J. (1989) *An Interpretation of Religion: Human Responses to the Transcendent*, Yale University Press, New Haven, CT, p14.

[27] Hick, J. (1989) *An Interpretation of Religion: Human Responses to the Transcendent*, Yale University Press, New Haven, CT, pp157-8.

[28] Taylor, C. (2007) *A Secular Age*, Belknap Press, Cambridge, MA, pp5–7.

[29] Tredennick, H. and Tarrant, H. (trans) (1954) *The Last Days of Socrates by Plato*, Penguin Books, London, pp125–126.

[30] Griffith, T. (trans) (1986) *Symposium of Plato*, University of California Press, Berkeley, sections 202–208.

[31] Smart, N. and Hecht, R. D. (eds) (1982) *Sacred Texts of the World: A Universal Anthology,* MacMillan Publishers Ltd, London, p305.

[32] Lau, D. C. (1979) *Confucius – The Analects*, Penguin Books, London, iv:9; xv:24; xvi:7.

[33] Comte-Sponville, A. (2008) *The Book of Atheist Spirituality*, Bantam, London, pp2, 204.

[34] Taylor, C. (2007) *A Secular Age*, Belknap Press, Cambridge, MA, p5.

[35] Humphreys, C. (1949) *Zen Buddhism*, William Heinemann Ltd, London, pp3–4.

[36] Suzuki, D. T. (1937) *Buddhism in the Life and Thought of Japan*, Tourist Library Series No 21, quoted in C. Humphreys (1949) *Zen Buddhism*, William Heinemann Ltd, London, p3.

[37] Taylor, C. (2007) *A Secular Age*, Belknap Press, Cambridge, MA, p9.

[38] Mascaró, J. (trans) (1965) *The Upanishads*, Penguin Books, London, pp58–60.

[39] Gladwell, M. (2005) *Blink: The Power of Thinking Without Thinking*, Back Bay Books/Little, Brown and Co, New York, pp264–269.

[40] Gladwell, M. (2005) *Blink: The Power of Thinking Without Thinking*, Back Bay Books/Little, Brown and Co, New York, p16.

[41] Senge, P., Scharmer, C. O., Jaworski, J. and Flowers, B. S. (2005) *Presence: Exploring Profound Change in People, Organizations, and Society*, Nicholas Brealey Publishing, London, p14.

[42] Humphreys, C. (1949) *Zen Buddhism*, William Heinemann Ltd, London, pp11–12.

[43] Humphreys, C. (1949) *Zen Buddhism*, William Heinemann Ltd, London, p1.

[44] Beatty, L. (1939) *The Garden of the Golden Flower: The Journey to Spiritual Fulfilment*, Senate, London, pp292–293.

[45] Gröning, P. (2007) *Into Great Silence: A Film by Philip Gröning*, DVD distributed by Soda Pictures Ltd, London.

[46] Meisel, A. C. and del Mastro, M. L. (trans) (1975) *The Rule of St Benedict*, Doubleday, New York, p76.

[47] Stryk, L. (trans) (1985) *On Love and Barley: Haiku of Basho*, Penguin Books, London.

[48] 'Interview: Philip Glass on making music with no frills', *The Independent*, 29 June 2007, available at www.independent.co.uk/arts-entertainment/music/features/interview-philip-glass-on-making-music-with-no-frills-455067.html, accessed 12 October 2010. Also see liner notes of *Kundun: Music from the Original Soundtrack*, composed by Philip Glass, Nonesuch Records, 1997.

[49] For example, Chief John Snow, of the Stoney People of Alberta, Canada writes: 'Technology is not wisdom … Only wisdom can harness technology so that man can build a better world' (Snow, J. (1977) *These Mountains are our Sacred Places: The Story of the Stoney*, Samuel Stevens, Toronto, pp154–160).

[50] See Chapters 4 and 5, and also 'Light touch: Ephemeral objects for sustainability', Chapter 14 of Walker, S. (2006) *Sustainable by Design: Explorations in Theory and Practice*, Earthscan, London, pp167–183.

8 The Chimera Reified – design, meaning and the post-consumerism object

An earlier version of this chapter appeared in Design Journal, vol 13, no 1, pp3–30 (copyright 2010). With kind permission of Berg Publishers, an imprint of A&C Black Publishers Ltd.

[1] Fry, T. (2009) *Design Futuring: Sustainability, Ethics and New Practice*, Berg, Oxford, p172.

[2] Schluep, M., Hagelueken, C., Kuehr, R., Magalini, F., Maurer, C., Meskers, C., Mueller, E. and Wang, F. (2009) *Recycling: From E-Waste to Resources*, United Nations Environment Programme and United Nations University, Table 11, p41,

available at www.unep.org/PDF/PressReleases/E-Waste_publication_screen_FINALVERSION-sml.pdf, accessed 14 October 2010.

[3] Greenpeace (2008) *The E-Waste Problem*, available at www.greenpeace.org/international/campaigns/toxics/electronics/the-e-waste-problem, accessed 14 October 2010.

[4] Lansley, S. (1994) *After the Gold Rush – The Trouble with Affluence: 'Consumer Capitalism' and the Way Forward*, Century Business Books, London, p18.

[5] Verbeek, P-P. (2005) *What Things Do: Philosophical Reflections on Technology, Agency and Design*, Penn State University Press, Philadelphia, pp205–206.

[6] Walker, S. (2006) *Sustainable by Design: Explorations in Theory and Practice*, Earthscan, London, Chapter 5.

[7] Klein, N. (2000) *No Logo*, Vintage Canada, Toronto, p197.

[8] Porritt, J. (2007) *Capitalism as if the World Matters*, Earthscan, London, p224.

[9] Ralston Saul, J. (2005) *The Collapse of Globalism and the Reinvention of the World*, Viking Canada, Toronto, pp148–150.

[10] Shanshan, W. (2007) 'The grim reality of e-waste burden', *China Daily*, 30 January 2007, available at www.chinadaily.com.cn/china/2007-01/30/content_795855.htm, accessed 14 October 2010.

[11] Milmo, C. (2009) 'Dumped in Africa: Britain's toxic waste', *The Independent*, 18 February 2009, available at www.independent.co.uk/news/world/africa/dumped-in-africa-britain8217s-toxic-waste-1624869.html, accessed 20 February 2009.

[12] Walker, J. A. and Chaplin, S. (1997) *Visual Culture*, Manchester University Press, Manchester, pp165–166.

[13] Borgmann, A. (2003) *Power Failure: Christianity in the Culture of Technology*, Brazos Press, Grand Rapids, MI, p22.

[14] Dunne, A. (2005) *Hertzian Tales: Electronic Products, Aesthetic Experience, and Critical Design*, Cambridge, MA, p84.

[15] For example, Rust, C., Mottram, J. and Till, J. (2007) *AHRC Research Review: Practice-led Research in Art, Design and Architecture*, Arts and Humanities Research Council, London, p11.

[16] Borgmann, A. (2003) *Power Failure: Christianity in the Culture of Technology*, Brazos Press, Grand Rapids, MI, pp17–18.

[17] Dunne, A. and Raby, F. (2008) 'Design for debate', *Neoplasmatic Design, Architectural Design*, vol 78, no 6, available at www.dunneandraby.co.uk/content/bydandr/36/0, accessed 14 October 2010.

[18] Dunne, A. (2009) 'Interpretation, collaboration, and critique', interview with Raoul Rickenberg, *The Journal of Design + Management*, vol 3, no 1, pp22–28, available at www.dunneandraby.co.uk/content/bydandr/465/0, accessed 14 October 2010.

[19] Associated Press (2008) 'GM to close 4 factories, may drop Hummer: Automaker to curtail truck, SUV production amid soaring fuel prices', *MSNBC Online News*, 3 June 2008, available at www.msnbc.msn.com/id/24947044/, accessed 14 October 2010.

223

[20] BBC (2008) 'Speeders to pay for police chases', 1 July 2008, available at http://news.bbc.co.uk/1/hi/world/americas/7482934.stm, accessed 14 October 2010.

[21] Rohter, L. (2008) 'Rising cost of shipping drives new strategies: Oil prices help push relocation of factories closer to consumers', International Herald Tribune, 4 August 2008, pp1, 14.

[22] Balakrishnan, A. (2008) 'Rise in food prices fuels inflation', The Guardian, 12 February 2008, available at www.guardian.co.uk/business/2008/feb/12/economics.retail, accessed 14 October 2010.

[23] European Position Paper UITP (2006) 'The role of public transport to reduce Green House Gas emissions and improve energy efficiency: Position on the European Climate Change Programme and the Green Paper on Energy Efficiency', March 2006, available at www.uitp.com/eupolicy/positions/2006/03/Climate_Change_EN.pdf, accessed 14 October 2010.

[24] Batty, D. (2007) 'London councils push for plastic bag ban', The Guardian, 13 July 2007, available at www.guardian.co.uk/environment/2007/jul/13/plasticbags.supermarkets, accessed 14 October 2010.

[25] Rennie, G. (2008) 'Three-bag limit urged for garbage pickup', The Windsor Star, 7 June 2008, available at www.canada.com/windsorstar/features/soundoff/story.html?id=9f7aca82-0a14-4f46-9f8e-676379811aeae, accessed 14 October 2010.

[26] Parsons, A. W. (2007) 'Global warming: The great equaliser', Share The World's Resources (STWR) Thinktank, September 2007, available at www.stwr.org/climate-change-environment/global-warming-the-great-equaliser.html, accessed 14 October 2010.

[27] UNFCCC (2008) 'Rising industrialized countries emissions underscore urgent need for political action on climate change at Poznan meeting', press release, United Nations Framework Convention on Climate Change, 17 November 2008, available at http://unfccc.int/files/press/news_room/press_releases_and_advisories/application/pdf/081117_ghg_press_release.pdf, accessed 14 October 2010.

[28] For example, a leading manufacturer recently developed a mobile phone encased in corn-derived bioplastic, on the assumption that this would be a more eco-friendly solution. However, the special measures needed to recycle these polymers make them energy inefficient, and in landfill they can release methane, a greenhouse gas far more potent than carbon dioxide. Widespread use of corn-based plastics can also exacerbate the growing industrial demand for crops that began with biofuels, reducing the amount of land dedicated to food production, inflating prices and most acutely affecting those living in the poorest nations. Schmemann, S. (ed) (2008) 'Corn-phone' [editorial], International Herald Tribune, 21 August 2008, p6; and Vidal, J. (2008) '"Sustainable" bio-plastic can damage the environment', The Guardian, 26 April 2008, available at www.guardian.co.uk/environment/2008/apr/26/waste.pollution, accessed 6 September 2008.

[29] Davison, A. (2001) *Technology and the Contested Meanings of Sustainability*, State University of New York Press, Albany, pp15, 22.

[30] Young, R. A. (2008) 'A taxonomy of the changing world of design practice', Proceedings of the Changing the Change Conference, Turin, 10–12 July 2008, available at http://emma.polimi.it/emma/showEvent.do?idEvent=23, accessed 28 July 2008.

[31] Thackara, J. (2005) *In the Bubble: Designing in a Complex World*, MIT Press, Cambridge, MA, p18.

[32] Mathews, F. (2006) 'Beyond modernity and tradition: A third way for development', *Ethics & the Environment*, vol 11, no 2, pp85–113.

[33] Rodwell, J. (2009) 'Redeeming the land' [keynote address], *Doing Justice to the Land*, M. B. Reckitt Trust Conference, London, 24 February 2009.

[34] For example, all these attributes were singled out in the 2007 launch of the iPhone, see BBC News (2007) 'Steve Jobs launches iPhone', 9 January 2007, available at http://news.bbc.co.uk/player/nol/newsid_6240000/newsid_6246600/6246625.stm?bw=bb&mp=rm&ncws=1&nol_storyid=6246625&bbcws=1, accessed 28 July 2008.

[35] This conclusion is supported by Banham's observation that Americans, arguably the foremost exponents of such progress, tend to have a strong belief in technology, best exemplified by their propagation of domestic products. Banham, R. (1996) *A Critic Writes: Essays by Reyner Banham*, University of California Press, Berkeley, p115.

[36] Borgmann, A. (2003) *Power Failure: Christianity in the Culture of Technology*, Brazos Press, Baker Books, Grand Rapids, MI, pp8, 81.

[37] Inayatullah, S. (2009) 'Spirituality as the fourth bottom line', Queensland University of Technology, available at www.metafuture.org/Articles/spirituality_bottom_line.htm, accessed 2 July 2009.

[38] One example of layered interpretations of meaning, which greatly surpasses materialistic notions, is the *quadriga* – a traditional form of interpreting sacred texts within Judeao-Christian culture. The *quadriga* encompasses literal, allegorical, moral and anagogical or spiritual interpretations, McGrath, A. E. (ed) (2007) *A Christian Theology Reader*, third edition, Blackwell Publishing, Oxford, pp81–82.

[39] Daly, H. (2008) 'A steady state economy', Sustainable Development Commission, 24 April 2008, available at www.theoildrum.com/node/3941, accessed 8 February 2008.

[40] Verbeek, P-P. (2005) *What Things Do: Philosophical Reflections on Technology, Agency and Design*, Penn State University Press, Philadelphia, p222.

[41] Chapman, J. (2005) *Emotionally Durable Design: Objects, Experiences and Empathy*, Earthscan, London.

[42] Borgmann, A. (1984) *Technology and the Character of Contemporary Life: A Philosophical Inquiry*, University of Chicago Press, Chicago, pp41, 92.

[43] Borgmann, A. (2003) *Power Failure: Christianity in the Culture of Technology*, Brazos Press, Grand Rapids, MI, p21.

[44] Borgmann, A. (2003) *Power Failure: Christianity in the Culture of Technology*, Brazos Press, Grand Rapids, MI, p73.

[45] Verbeek, P-P. (2005) *What Things Do: Philosophical Reflections on Technology, Agency and Design*, Penn State University Press, Philadelphia, pp230–231.

[46] Verbeek, P-P. (2005) *What Things Do: Philosophical Reflections on Technology, Agency and Design*, Penn State University Press, Philadelphia, p27.

[47] Dunne, A. and Raby, F. (2008) 'Fictional functions and functional fictions', in conversation with Troika, *Digital by Design*, Thames & Hudson, London, available at www.dunneandraby.co.uk/content/bydandr/46/0, accessed 4 July 2009.

[48] Easwaran, E. (1978) *Meditation: Commonsense Directions for an Uncommon Life*, 1986 edition, Penguin Books, London, pp116–125.

9 The Spirit of Design – notes from the shakuhachi flute

An earlier version of this chapter appeared in the International Journal of Sustainable Design, vol 1, no 2, pp130–144 (copyright 2009). With kind permission of Inderscience Switzerland who retain copyright of the original papers.

[1] Norton, T. (2008) 'Cardinal wants Piero in a church', *The Tablet*, 6 December 2008, p36.

[2] Nes, S. (2004) *The Mystical Language of Icons*, Canterbury Press, Norwich, pp12, 16.

[3] Williams, R., (2008) Picture Perfect, *RA: Royal Academy of Arts Magazine*, London, no 101, Winter 2008, pp40–44.

[4] Verbeek, P-P. (2005) *What Things Do: Philosophical Reflections on Technology, Agency and Design*, Pennsylvania State University Press, Philadelphia, p206.

[5] Feenberg, A. (2002) *Transforming Technology: A Critical Theory Revised*, Oxford University Press, Oxford, pp162–190.

[6] Davison, A. (2001) *Technology and the Contested Meanings of Sustainability*, State University of New York Press, Albany, p204.

[7] Fry, T. (2009) *Design Futuring: Sustainability, Ethics and New Practice*, Berg Publishers, Oxford, pp3, 118.

[8] Malm, W. P. (2000) *Traditional Japanese Music and Musical Instruments: The New Edition*, Kodansha International, Tokyo, p171.

[9] De Ferranti, H. (2000) *Japanese Musical Instruments*, Oxford University Press, Hong Kong, p70.

[10] Bhikshu, K. (2008) *The Shakuhachi: Zen Flute*, International Buddhist Meditation Center, Los Angeles, available at www.urbandharma.org/kusala/revkus/zenflute.html, accessed 31 October 2008.

[11] Ribble, D. B. (2003) 'The shakuhachi and the ney: A comparison of two flutes from the far reaches of Asia', departmental bulletin paper, Kocho

University Repository, Kochi, Japan, available at https://ir.kochi-u.ac.jp/dspace/bitstream/10126/256/1/KJ00004267899.pdf, accessed 17 October 2010, p6.

[12] Ribble, D. B. (2003) 'The shakuhachi and the ney: A comparison of two flutes from the far reaches of Asia', departmental bulletin paper, Kocho University Repository, Kochi, Japan, available at https://ir.kochi-u.ac.jp/dspace/bitstream/10126/256/1/KJ00004267899.pdf, accessed 17 October 2010, pp6–7.

[13] De Ferranti, H. (2000) *Japanese Musical Instruments*, Oxford University Press, Hong Kong, pp70–71.

[14] Malm, W. P. (2000) *Traditional Japanese Music and Musical Instruments: The New Edition*, Kodansha International, Tokyo, p175.

[15] Sanford, J. S. (1977) 'Shakuhachi zen: The fukeshu and komuso', *Monumenta Nipponica*, vol 32, no 4, pp411–440.

[16] Casano, S. (2005) 'From fuke shuu to uduboo: The transnational flow of the shakuhachi to the West', *World of Music*, vol 47, no 3, pp17–33.

[17] Keister, J. (2003) 'The shakuhachi as a spiritual tool: A Japanese Buddhist instrument in the West', *Asian Music: The Journal of the Society of Asian Music*, vol 35, no 2, pp99–131.

[18] Master *shakuhachi* player Clive Bell points out that context can be an important consideration in how the flute is played and understood, which is particularly relevant with the *shakuhachi* now being widely played outside its traditional setting. Personal correspondence, 27 February 2010.

[19] Mayers, D. E. (1976) 'The unique shakuhachi', *Early* Music, vol 4, no 4, p467.

[20] Deaver, T. (2008) *Shaku Design*, 24 April 2008, available at http://navaching.com/shaku/hochiku.html, accessed 17 October 2010.

[21] Keister, J. (2003) 'The shakuhachi as a spiritual tool: A Japanese Buddhist instrument in the West', *Asian Music: The Journal of the Society of Asian Music*, vol 35, no 2, pp110–111

[22] Levenson, M. (2008) *Jinashikan: Natural Bore Shakuhachi*, available at www.shakuhachi.com/Q-Models-Jinashi.html, accessed 17 October 2010.

[23] Brooks, R. (2000) *Blowing Zen: Finding an Authentic Life*, H. J. Kramer Inc, Tiburon, CA, p80.

[24] Ribble, D. B. (2003) 'The shakuhachi and the ney: A comparison of two flutes from the far reaches of Asia', departmental bulletin paper, Kocho University Repository, Kochi, Japan, available at https://ir.kochi-u.ac.jp/dspace/bitstream/10126/256/1/KJ00004267899.pdf, accessed 17 October 2010, pp4–8.

[25] Chaurasia, H. (2008) website of bansuri player Hariprasad Chaurasia at www.hariprasadchaurasia.com/index.htm, accessed 17 October 2010.

[26] I have given a general description of the relationship between the quantity and nature of material possessions, and their link to spiritual ways of living in Walker,

227

S. (2006) *Sustainable by Design: Explorations in Theory and Practice*, Earthscan, London, pp61–70.

[27] Jamison, C. (2008) *Finding Happiness: Monastic Steps for a Fulfilling Life*, Weidenfeld & Nicolson, London, pp106–108.

[28] Perhaps inevitably, with its broader, international appeal, these traditional distinctions are becoming more blurred. As *shakuhachi* player Clive Bell notes, today, *hōchiku* flutes are sometimes used in concert performances, and modern, lacquered *shakuhachi* are being used in meditative practices – not least because they are easier to find and, possibly, easier to play. Personal correspondence, 27 February 2010.

[29] Keister, J. (2003) 'The shakuhachi as a spiritual tool: A Japanese Buddhist instrument in the West', *Asian Music: The Journal of the Society of Asian Music*, vol 35, no 2, pp110–111.

[30] Keister, J. (2003) 'The shakuhachi as a spiritual tool: A Japanese Buddhist instrument in the West', *Asian Music: The Journal of the Society of Asian Music*, vol 35, no 2, pp110–111.

[31] Keister, J. (2003) 'The shakuhachi as a spiritual tool: A Japanese Buddhist instrument in the West', *Asian Music: The Journal of the Society of Asian Music*, vol 35, no 2, pp105, 112.

[32] Schnee, D. (2006) 'A beginner's guide to suizen', *Canadian Musician*, vol 28, no 3, p29.

[33] Sanford, J. S. (1977) 'Shakuhachi zen: The fukeshu and komuso', *Monumenta Nipponica*, vol 32, no 4, p414.

[34] Schnee, D. (2006) 'A beginner's guide to suizen', *Canadian Musician*, vol 28, no 3.

[35] Ribble, D. B. (2003) 'The shakuhachi and the ney: A comparison of two flutes from the far reaches of Asia', departmental bulletin paper, Kocho University Repository, Kochi, Japan, available at https://ir.kochi-u.ac.jp/dspace/bitstream/10126/256/1/KJ00004267899.pdf, accessed 17 October 2010, pp5, 7.

[36] Ribble, D. B. (2003) 'The shakuhachi and the ney: A comparison of two flutes from the far reaches of Asia', departmental bulletin paper, Kocho University Repository, Kochi, Japan, available at https://ir.kochi-u.ac.jp/dspace/bitstream/10126/256/1/KJ00004267899.pdf, accessed 17 October 2010, p9.

[37] Williams, A. (trans) (2006) *Spiritual Verses – Rumi*, Penguin Books, London, pxxv.

[38] Cage, J. (1961) *Silence: Lectures and Writing by John Cage*, Wesleyan University Press, Hanover, NH, USA, pp7-8.

[39] Katz, V. (2006) 'A genteel iconoclasm', *Tate Etc*, vol 8, autumn 2006, available at www.tate.org.uk/tateetc/issue8/erasuregenteel.htm, accessed 18 October 2010.

[40] Lubbock, T. (2009) 'A right royal treat', review of Gardens and Cosmos: The Royal Paintings of Jodhpur, British Museum, 28 May–23 August 2009, especially 'The Emergence of Spirit and Matter' attributed to Shivdas, ca 1828, *The Independent*, 27 May 2009, p13.

[41] Steindl-Rast, D. and Lebell, S. (2002) *Music of Silence: A Sacred Journey through the Hours of the Day*, Seastone, Berkeley, p7.

[42] Easwaran, E. (1978) *Meditation*, Arkana, London, p140.

[43] Coltrane, J. (1966) *A Love Supreme*, Impulse IMP 11552, MCA Records.

[44] Brooks, R. (2000) *Blowing Zen: Finding an Authentic Life*, H. J. Kramer Inc., Tiburon, CA, p28.

[45] Sanford, J. S. (1977) 'Shakuhachi zen: The fukeshu and komuso', *Monumenta Nipponica*, vol 32, no 4, p422.

[46] Ribble, D. B. (2003) 'The shakuhachi and the ney: A comparison of two flutes from the far reaches of Asia', departmental bulletin paper, Kocho University Repository, Kochi, Japan, available at https://ir.kochi-u.ac.jp/dspace/bitstream/10126/256/1/KJ00004267899.pdf, accessed 17 October 2010, p7.

[47] Ribble, D. B. (2003) 'The shakuhachi and the ney: A comparison of two flutes from the far reaches of Asia', departmental bulletin paper, Kocho University Repository, Kochi, Japan, available at https://ir.kochi-u.ac.jp/dspace/bitstream/10126/256/1/KJ00004267899.pdf, accessed 17 October 2010, p10.

[48] Needleman, J. (1994) *The Indestructible Question: Essays on Nature, Spirit and the Human Paradox*, Arkana, London, pp128–130.

[49] Verbeek, P.-P. (2005) *What Things Do: Philosophical Reflections on Technology, Agency and Design*, Pennsylvania State University Press, Philadelphia, p187.

[50] Verbeek, P.-P. (2005) *What Things Do: Philosophical Reflections on Technology, Agency and Design*, Pennsylvania State University Press, Philadelphia, p188.

[51] Verbeek, P.-P. (2005) *What Things Do: Philosophical Reflections on Technology, Agency and Design*, Pennsylvania State University Press, Philadelphia, p225.

[52] Walker, S. (2006) *Sustainable by Design: Explorations in Theory and Practice*, Earthscan, London, pp39–51.

[53] Feenberg, A. (2002) *Transforming Technology: A Critical Theory Revised*, Oxford University Press, Oxford, pp13, 184.

[54] Ralston Saul, J. (2005) *The Collapse of Globalism and the reinvention of the World*, Viking Canada, Toronto, p31.

[55] Wilkinson, R. and Pickett, K. (2009) *The Spirit Level: Why More Equal Societies Almost Always Do Better*, Allen Lane, London, p263.

[56] Wilkinson, R. and Pickett, K. (2009) *The Spirit Level: Why More Equal Societies Almost Always Do Better*, Allen Lane, London, p263.

[57] Korten, D. C. (1999) *The Post-Corporate World: Life After Capitalism*, Berrett-Koehler Publishers, San Francisco, CA, and Kumarian Press, Inc. West Hartford, CT, pp66, 200.

[58] Borgmann, A. (2003) *Power Failure: Christianity in a Culture of Technology*, Brazos Press, Grand Rapids, MI, p73.

[59] Brooks, R. (2000) *Blowing Zen: Finding an Authentic Life*, H. J. Kramer Inc, Tiburon, CA, p80.

[60] For example, the extraction of oil from the mining of tar sands at Fort McMurray in Alberta, Canada is accompanied by destruction of landscapes, many of which have been important to indigenous peoples for centuries, as hunting grounds and sacred places. Operations drain three rivers for the extraction processes, and toxic tailing ponds on the landscape have affected ground water and resulted in the death of wild fowl. See CBC News, available at www.cbc.ca/technology/story/2010/09/07/oilsands-tailing-ponds-bird-deaths.html, accessed 18 October 2010; and Oil Sands Watch, Pembina Institute, available at www.pembina.org/oil-sands, accessed 18 October 2010.

[61] Borgmann, A. (2003) *Power Failure: Christianity in a Culture of Technology*, Brazos Press, Grand Rapids, MI, p73.

[62] Brooks, R. (2000) *Blowing Zen: Finding an Authentic Life*, H. J. Kramer Inc, Tiburon, CA, pp83–84, 231.

[63] Oakeshott, R. (2000) 'Jobs and fairness: The logic and experience of employee ownership', in R. Wilkinson and K. Pickett (2009) *The Spirit Level: Why More Equal Societies Almost Always Do Better*, Allen Lane, London, p250.

10 Wrapped Attention – designing products for evolving permanence and enduring meaning

An earlier version of this chapter appeared in Design Issues, vol 26, no 4, pp94–108 (copyright 2010). With kind permission of MIT Press, US.

[1] Bhamra, T. and Lofthouse, V. (2007) *Design for Sustainability: A Practical Approach*, Gower, Aldershot, p15.

[2] 'Sustainability and QBL' (2009) City of Norwood Payneham and St Peters, Australia, available at www.npsp.sa.gov.au/site/page.cfm?u=1608, accessed 20 October 2010.

[3] 'Reporting on the triple or quadruple bottom line' (2009) Creative Decisions Ltd, Auckland, New Zealand, available at www.creativedecisions.co.nz/sustainable_development/reporting.cfm#faq130995, accessed 20 October 2010.

[4] 'QBL – governance, economic, social and environment' (2007) Wingecarribee Shire Council, Moss Vale, NSW, Australia, available at www.wsc.nsw.gov.au/environment/1176/3953.html, accessed 18 September 2009.

[5] 'ToolBox 12 reference – quadruple bottom line' (2005) Department of Infrastructure and Planning, Queensland Government, Brisbane, available at www.localgovernment.qld.gov.au/docs/corporate/publications/local_govt/plan_and_deliver/toolbox_12_reference.pdf, accessed 20 October 2010.

[6] Tjolle, V. (2008) *Your Quadruple Bottom Line: Sustainable Tourism Opportunity*, SMILE Conference 2008, Guinness Storehouse, Dublin, Ireland, 27 May 2008, available at www.smileconference.com/downloads.html, accessed 20 October 2010.

[7] Armstrong, K. (2006) *The Great Transformation*, Atlantic Books, London, pxi.

[8] Senge, P. et al (2005) *Presence: Exploring Profound Change in People, Organizations and Society*, Nicholas Brealey Publishing, London, p56.

[9] Inayatullah, S. (2009) 'Spirituality as the fourth bottom line', Tamkang University, Sunshine Coast University and Queensland University of Technology, Australia, available at www.metafuture.org/Articles/spirituality_bottom_line.htm, accessed 20 October 2010.

[10] Stuart, C. (2009) *How People Make Decisions*, European Futurists Conference, Luzerne, Switzerland, 16 October 2009, available at www.european-futurists. org/wEnglisch/programm/Programm2009/programm2009.php, accessed 20 October 2010.

[11] Corvalan, C., Hales, S., McMichael, A. et al (2005) *Ecosystems and Human Well-being: Health Synthesis, A Millennium Ecosystem Assessment Report*, World Health Organization, available at www.who.int/globalchange/ecosystems/ecosys. pdf, accessed 20 October 2010, pp13, 33.

[12] Foehr, U. G. (2006) *Media Multitasking Among American Youth: Prevalence, Predictors and Pairings*, Henry J. Family Foundation, Menlo Park, CA, available at www.kff.org/entmedia/upload/7592.pdf, accessed 20 October 2010, p24.

[13] M. Ritchell (2009) 'In the car, on the mobile phone and headed for trouble', *International Herald Tribune*, 20 July 2009, p2.

[14] Dave Lamble et al (1999) 'Cognitive load and detection thresholds in car following situations: safety implications for using mobile (cellular) telephones while driving', *Accident Analysis and Prevention 31*, available at http://virtual. vtt.fi/virtual/proj6/fits/impacts/Lamble_Kauranen_Laakso_Summala_1999.pdf, accessed 20 October 2010, pp617–623.

[15] Naish, J. (2009) 'Warning: Brain overload', *The Times*, 2 June 2009, available at http://women.timesonline.co.uk/tol/life_and_style/women/the_way_we_live/ article6409208.ece, accessed 2 June 2009.

[16] Immordino-Yang, M. H. et al (2009) 'Neural correlates of admiration and compassion', *Proceedings of the National Academy of Sciences*, available at www. pnas.org/content/early/2009/04/17/0810363106.full.pdf+html, accessed 20 October 2010, pp8021–8026.

[17] Rosen, C. (2008) 'The myth of multitasking', *The New Atlantis: A Journal of Technology and Society*, spring edition, available at www.thenewatlantis.com/ docLib/20080605_TNA20Rosen.pdf, accessed 20 October 2010, pp105–110.

[18] Torrecilals, F. L. (2007) 'Four in ten young adults are mobile-phone addicts, a behaviour that can cause severe psychological disorders', *The Medical News*, 27 February 2007, available at www.news-medical.net/news/2007/02/27/22245. aspx, accessed 20 October 2010.

[19] For example, 'Digital Britain – the interim report' (2009) Department for Culture, Media and Sport and Department for Business, Enterprise and Regulatory Reform, London, www.culture.gov.uk/images/publications/digital_britain_ interimreportjan09.pdf, accessed 20 October 2010.

[20] Thackara, J. (2009) 'Design and ecology', keynote presentation, LiftFrance09 Conference, Marseille, France, 18–19 June 2009, www.liftconference.com/ person/john-thackara, accessed 20 October 2010.

[21] Borgmann, A. (2000) 'Society in the postmodern era', *The Washington Quarterly*, vol 23, no 1, available at http://muse.jhu.edu/journals/washington_quarterly/v023/23.1borgmann.html, accessed 20 October 2010, pp189–200.

[22] Borgmann, A. (2001) 'Opaque and articulate design', *International Journal of Technology and Design Education*, vol 11, pp5–11.

[23] Thackara, J. (2009) 'Design and ecology', keynote presentation, LiftFrance09 Conference, Marseille, France, 18–19 June 2009, www.liftconference.com/person/john-thackara, accessed 20 October 2010.

[24] Senge, P. et al (2008) *The Necessary Revolution: How Individuals and Organizations are Working Together to Create a Sustainable World*, Nicholas Brealey Publishing, London, p50.

[25] van Heerden, C. (2009) 'Future of lifestyle', European Futurists Conference, Luzerne, Switzerland, 15 October 2009), available at www.european-futurists.org/wEnglisch/programm/Programm2009/programm2009.php, accessed 20 October 2010.

[26] Electronic Tattoo: Philips Design Probe (2008), available at www.youtube.com/watch?v=NM1VuN5Iouc, accessed 20 October 2010.

[27] 'We love our iPods, we love our planet: Help plant a tree to offset your iPod' (2009) available at http://acornhq.net, accessed 20 October 2010.

[28] 'China heads list of mobile phone manufacturing bases' (2009) C114.net, Shanghai, 5 January 2009, www.cn-c114.net/578/a374763.html, accessed 20 October 2010.

[29] Chan, J. et al (2008) 'Silenced to deliver: Mobile phone manufacturing in China and the Philippines', SOMO and SwedWatch, Stockholm, available at www.germanwatch.org/corp/it-chph08.pdf, accessed 20 October 2010.

[30] For example, *Waste Electrical and Electronic Equipment (WEEE)* (2007) Environmental Agency, available at www.environment-agency.gov.uk/business/topics/waste/32084.aspx, accessed 20 October 2010.

[31] Clayton, J. (2009) 'MoD computers at centre of dangerous trade in the slums', *The Times*, 18 July 2009, p7.

[32] Fuad-Luke, A. (2009) *Design Activism*, Earthscan, London, p193.

[33] Willliams, A. et al (2009) 'Design 2020: An investigation into the future for the design profession', in T. Inns (ed) *Designing for the 21st Century: Research Projects*, Ashgate, Farnham.

[34] Senge, P. et al (2008) *The Necessary Revolution: How Individuals and Organizations are Working Together to Create a Sustainable World*, Nicholas Brealey Publishing, London, p16.

[35] Berry, T. and Goodman, J. (2006) *Earth Calling: The Environmental Impacts of the Mobile Telecommunications Industry*, Forum for the Future, London, available at www.forumforthefuture.org.uk/library/earth-calling, accessed 20 October 2010.

36 Interface (2008) *Toward a More Sustainable Way of Business*, Interface Incorporated, available at www.interfaceglobal.com/Sustainability.aspx, accessed 20 October 2010.

37 Borgmann, A. (2003) *Power Failure*, Brazos Press, Grand Rapids, MI, p22.

11 Temporal Objects – design, change and sustainability

An earlier version of this chapter appeared in Sustainability, vol 2, pp812–832 (copyright 2010). With kind permission of MDPI, Switzerland.

1 Webster, B. and Lewis, L. (2009) 'World leaders deal major blow to Copenhagen climate change deal', *The Times*, 16 November 2009, available at www.timesonline.co.uk/tol/news/environment/article6917564.ece, accessed 18 November 2009.

2 Fisher, A. (2009) 'Climate agreement sparks anger', *Aljazeera Online News (Europe)*, 19 December 2009, available at http://english.aljazeera.net/news/europe/2009/12/20091218224724782996.html, accessed 21 October 2010.

3 For example, Rosenthal, E. (2009) 'Paying more for flights eases guilt, not emissions', *New York Times*, 18 November 2009, available at www.nytimes.com/2009/11/18/science/earth/18offset.html?_r
=1&ref=global-home&pagewanted=print, accessed 21 October 2010.

4 Bone, J. (2009) 'Climate scientist James Hansen hopes summit will fail', *The Times*, 4 December 2009, available at www.timesonline.co.uk/tol/news/environment/article6941974.ece, accessed 4 December 2009. (Note: in the Catholic church an 'indulgence' is a remission of the temporal punishment due for committing sin; though the guilt of the sin has been forgiven through absolution, *Catholic Encyclopedia*, available at www.newadvent.org/cathen, accessed 21 October 2010.)

5 Senge. P., Smith, B., Kruschwitz, N., Laur, J. and Schley, S. (2008) *The Necessary Revolution: How Individuals and Organizations Are Working Together to Create a Sustainable World*, Nicholas Brealey Publishing, London, p51.

6 Brown, T. (2009) *Change by Design*, HarperCollins, New York, pp7, 89.

7 Woudhuysen, J. (2009) 'Keynote address', Design to Business (D2B2) Conference China, Tonji University, Beijing, China, 23–26 April 2009.

8 BBC World Service (2009) 'Old-Style light bulbs banned in EU' (2009) BBC World Service News, 1 September, available at www.bbc.co.uk/worldservice/lg/news/2009/09/090901_bulbs_nh_sl.shtml, accessed 21 October 2010.

9 Goedkoop, M. J., van Halen C. J. G., te Riele, H. R. M. and Rommens, P. J. M. (1999) *Product Service Systems, Ecological and Economic Basics*, Ministry of Housing, Spatial Planning and the Environment Communications Directorate, p18: referred to in Morelli, N. (2003) 'Product-Service systems, a perspective shift for designers: A case study: The design of a telecentre', *Design Studies*, vol 24, pp73–99. This latter paper was presented at the 2002 Common Ground Conference and is available at www.score-network.org/files//825_15.pdf, accessed 21 October 2010.

233

[10] Bhamra, T. and Lofthouse, V. (2007) *Design for Sustainability: A Practical Approach*, Gower Publishing Limited, Aldershot, pp122–123.

[11] Porritt, J. (2007) *Capitalism as if the World Matters*, Earthscan, London, p306.

[12] McDonough, W. and Braungart, M. (2002) *Cradle to Cradle*, North Point Press, New York, pp119–120.

[13] Manzini, E. (2007) 'A laboratory of ideas: Diffused creativity and new ways of doing', in A. Meroni (ed) *Creative Communities: People Inventing Sustainable Ways of Living*, Edizioni POLI, Milan, pp13–15, available at http://81.246.16.10/videos/publications/creative_communities.pdf, accessed 21 October 2010.

[14] Fuad-Luke, A. (2009) *Design Activism: Beautiful Strangeness for a Sustainable World*, Earthscan, London, pp193–194.

[15] von Hippel, E. (2005) *Democratizing Innovation*, MIT Press, Cambridge, MA, pp93, 103–104.

[16] Walker, S. (2009) 'Touchstones: Conceptual products for sustainable futures', keynote address, 5th European Futurists Conference, Luzerne, Switzerland, 15 October 2009, available at www.europeanfuturists.org/wEnglisch/programm/Programm2009/programm2009.php, accessed 21 October 2010.

[17] Manzini, E. (2007) 'The scenario of a multi-local society: Creative communities, active networks and enabling solutions', in J. Chapman and N. Gant (eds) *Designers, Visionaries and Other Stories: A Collection of Sustainable Design Essays*, Earthscan, London, pp81–86.

[18] Day, C. (2002) *Spirit and Place*, Architectural Press, London, p162.

[19] Dunne, A. and Raby. F. (2009) *Critical Design FAQ*, available at www.dunneandraby.co.uk/content/bydandr/13/0, accessed 21 October 2010.

[20] Meroni, A. (2009) *Strategic Design for Territorial Development: A Service Oriented Approach*, public lecture, Lancaster University, Lancaster, 25 November 2009.

[21] Daly, H. (2007) *Ecological Economics and Sustainable Development*, Edward Elgar Publishing, Cheltenham, pp117–124.

[22] Mathews, F. (2006) 'Beyond modernity and tradition: A third way for development', *Ethics & the Environment*, vol 11, no 2, pp85–113.

[23] Ryan, C. (2008) 'The Melbourne 2032 Project: Design-visions as a mechanism for (sustainable) paradigm change', *Proceedings of the Changing the Change Conference*, Turin, Italy, 10–12 July 2008, available at http://emma.polimi.it/emma/showEvent.do?idEvent=23, accessed on 2 March 2010.

[24] James, W. (1899) 'On a certain blindness in human beings', in G. Gunn (ed) *Pragmatism and Other Writings* (2000) Penguin Books, London, p269.

[25] Lerner, M. (1996) *The Politics of Meaning*, Addison Wesley Publishing, Reading, MA, p6.

[26] von Hippel, E. (2005) *Democratizing Innovation*, MIT Press, Cambridge, MA, p147.

[27] Senge, P., Smith, B., Kruschwitz, N., Laur, J. and Schley, S. (2008) *The Necessary Revolution: How Individuals and Organizations Are Working Together to Create a Sustainable World*, Nicholas Brealey Publishing, London, p37.

234

[28] McDonough, W. and Braungart, M. (2002) *Cradle to Cradle*, North Point Press, New York, p141.

[29] Hamel, G. (2007) *The Future of Management*, Harvard Business School Press, Boston, p187.

[30] Hawken, P. (2007) *Blessed Unrest*, Viking, New York, p157.

12 Meaning in the Mundane – aesthetics, technology and spiritual values

An earlier version of this chapter was presented at the Cumulus 2010 Conference, Tonji University, Shanghai, China, 6–10 September 2010, and appeared in proceedings.

[1] Lanier, J. (2010) *You Are Not A Gadget*, Allen Lane, London, pp20–22.

[2] Biletzki, A. and Matar, A. (2009) 'Ludwig Wittgenstein', *Stanford Encyclopedia of Philosophy*, Metaphysics Research Lab, Stanford University, available at http://plato.stanford.edu/entries/wittgenstein, accessed 14 February 2010.

[3] For example, Buddhist philosophy, see Juniper, A. (2003) *Wabi Sabi: The Japanese Art of Impermanence*, Tuttle Publishing, Boston, pix.

[4] For example, Sufism, see Williams, A. (trans) (2006) *Rumi: Spiritual Verses: The First Book of the Masnavi-ye Ma'navi*, Penguin Books, London, p8.

[5] Polanyi, M. (1966) *The Tacit Dimension*, Doubleday and Company Inc, Garden City, NY, p4.

[6] Borgmann, A. (2003) *Power Failure; Christianity in the Culture of Technology*, Brazos Press, Grand Rapids, MI, p22.

[7] Csikszentmihalyi (1990) *Flow: The Psychology of Optimal Experience*, HarperCollins, New York, pp55–56.

[8] Nhat Hanh, T. (1995) *Living Buddha, Living Christ*, Riverhead Books, New York, pp10–11.

[9] Shibayama, Z. (1970) *A Flower Does Not Talk: Zen Essays*, Charles E. Tuttle Co Inc, Tokyo, p28.

[10] Muelder Eaton, M. (2001) *Merit: Aesthetic and Ethical*, Oxford University Press, Oxford, p10.

[11] Arnold, S., Herrick, L. M., Pankratz, V. S. and Mueller, P. S. (2007) 'Spiritual well-being, emotional distress, and perception of health after a myocardial infarction', *The Internet Journal of Advanced Nursing Practice*, vol 9, no 1, available at www.ispub.com/ostia/index.php?xmlFilePath=journals/ijanp/vol9n1/health.xml, accessed 12 February 2010.

[12] Cottingham, J., (2005) *The Spiritual Dimension: Religion, Philosophy and Human Value*, Cambridge University Press, Cambridge, p140.

[13] Schor, J. (2006) 'Learning Diderot's lesson: Stopping the upward creep of desire', in T. Jackson (ed) *The Earthscan Reader in Sustainable Consumption*, Earthscan, London, pp178, 187–188.

[14] Whittle, K. (2006) *Native American Fetishes, Carvings of the Southwest*, second edition, Schiffer Publishing Ltd, Atglen, PA, p6.

[15] Whittle, K. (2006) *Native American Fetishes, Carvings of the Southwest*, second edition, Schiffer Publishing Ltd, Atglen, PA, p13.

[16] Lovelock, J. (2007) *The Revenge of Gaia: Why the Earth is Fighting Back and How We Can Still Save Humanity*, Penguin Books, London, p20.

[17] Whittle, K. (2006) *Native American Fetishes, Carvings of the Southwest*, second edition, Schiffer Publishing Ltd, Atglen, PA, p15.

[18] Bahti, M. (1999) *Spirit in Stone: A Handbook of Southwest Indian Animal Carvings and Beliefs*, Treasure Chest Books, Tucson, AZ, p19.

[19] Papanek, V. (1996) *The Green Imperative*, Thames & Hudson, New York, pp52, 234.

[20] Juniper, A. (2003) *Wabi Sabi: The Japanese Art of Impermanence*, Tuttle Publishing, Boston, ppix, 1.

[21] Koren, L. (1994) *Wabi-Sabi for Artists, Designers, Poets & Philosophers*, Stone Bridge Press, Berkeley, pp15, 18.

[22] Moriguchi, Y. and Jenkins, D. (trans) (1996) *Hojoki: Visions of a Torn World*, Stone Bridge Press, Berkeley, p32.

[23] Koren, L. (1994) *Wabi-Sabi for Artists, Designers, Poets & Philosophers*, Stone Bridge Press, Berkeley, pp25–29.

[24] Koren, L. (1994) *Wabi-Sabi for Artists, Designers, Poets & Philosophers*, Stone Bridge Press, Berkeley, pp41, 46.

[25] Okakura, K. (1906) *The Book of Tea*, 1989 edition, Kodansha International, Tokyo, pp70, 101.

[26] Sen XV, S. (1989) 'Introduction' and 'Afterword', in K. Okakura (1906) *The Book of Tea*, 1989 edition, Kodansha International, Tokyo, pp21, 139.

[27] Okakura, K. (1906) *The Book of Tea*, 1989 edition, Kodansha International, Tokyo, pp50–61.

[28] Farrer, W. and Brownbill, J. (eds) (1914) 'Townships: Over Wyresdale', *A History of the County of Lancaster: Volume 8*, pp76–79, British History Online, available at www.british-history.ac.uk/report.aspx?compid=53269, accessed 6 February 2010.

[29] Charles Dickens published his novel *Hard Times – For these Times*, better known simply as *Hard Times*, in 1854 following its serialization in Dickens' own weekly journal *Household Words* during the summer of 1854. The novel is set against the industrial backdrop of a northern England milltown of the mid-19th century and recounts the appalling living and working conditions of the industrial poor caused by the single-minded pursuit of productivity, growth and profit. It also berates the then prevalent utilitarian philosophy, which paid little heed to the human imagination and regarded people as mere cogs in an industrial system rather than as full human beings.

[30] Day, C. (2002) *Spirit and Place*, Elsevier, Amsterdam, p29.

[31] Branzi, A. (2009) *Grandi Legni*, Design Gallery Milano and Nilufar, Milan, Italy, exhibition catalogue for Grandi Legni exhibition, Galerie Alaïa, Paris, 10 December 2009–16 January 2010.

[32] Richie, D. (2007) *A Tractate on Japanese Aesthetics*, Stone Bridge Press, Berkeley, p33.

[33] Branzi, A. (2009) *Grandi Legni*, Design Gallery Milano and Nilufar, Milan, Italy, exhibition catalogue for Grandi Legni exhibition, Galerie Alaïa, Paris, 10 December 2009–16 January 2010.

[34] Otto, R. (1923) *The Idea of the Holy*, Oxford University Press, Oxford, p2.

[35] Eagleton, T. (2009) *Reason, Faith and Revolution: Reflections on the God Debate*, Yale University Press, New Haven, pp91, 121.

13 Wordless Questions – the physical, the virtual and the meaningful

[1] Eagleton, T. (2009) *Reason, Faith and Revolution: Reflections on the God Debate*, Yale University Press, New Haven, p28.

[2] Hobsbawm, E. (1962) *The Age of Revolution: Europe 1789–1848*, Abacus, London, pp297–298, 355.

[3] Brookner, A. (2000) *Romanticism and its Discontents*, Farrar, Straus and Giroux, New York, pp1, 7.

[4] Hobsbawm, E. (1962) *The Age of Revolution: Europe 1789–1848*, Abacus, London, p355.

[5] Leonard, A. (2010) *The Story of Stuff*, Constable & Robinson Ltd, London, pp73, 78–79.

[6] Comte-Sponville, A. (2008) *The Book of Atheist Spirituality*, trans N. Huston, Penguin Books, London, p140.

[7] Hill, P. C., Pargament, K. I., Hood Jr, R. W., McCullough, M. E., Swyers, J. P., Larson, D. B. and Zinnbauer, B. J. (2000) 'Conceptualizing religion and spirituality: Points of commonality, points of departure', *Journal for the Theory of Social Behaviour*, vol 30, no 1, pp51–77.

[8] Giordan, G. (2009) 'The body between religion and spirituality', *Social Compass*, vol 56, no 2, pp226–236.

[9] McGrath, A. E. (1999) *Christian Spirituality*, Blackwell Publishing, Oxford, p2.

[10] Holloway, R. (2004) *Looking in the Distance: The Human Search for Meaning*, Canongate, Edinburgh, p7.

[11] Eagleton, T. (2009) *Reason, Faith and Revolution: Reflections on the God Debate*, Yale University Press, New Haven, p7.

[12] Holloway, R. (2004) *Looking in the Distance: The Human Search for Meaning*, Canongate, Edinburgh, p31.

[13] For example, Schneiders, S. M. (2003) 'Religion vs spirituality: A contemporary conundrum', *Spiritus: A Journal of Christian Spirituality*, vol 3, no 2, pp163–185.

[14] King, U. (2009) *The Search for Spirituality: Our Global Quest for Meaning and Fulfilment*, Canterbury Press, Norwich, p3.

[15] Schneiders, S. M. (2003) 'Religion vs spirituality: A contemporary conundrum', *Spiritus: A Journal of Christian Spirituality*, vol 3, no 2, pp163–185.

[16] Comte-Sponville, A. (2008) *The Book of Atheist Spirituality*, trans N. Huston, Penguin Books, London, p27.

237

[17] Eagleton, T. (2009) *Reason, Faith and Revolution: Reflections on the God Debate*, Yale University Press, New Haven, p69.

[18] Schneiders, S. M. (2003) 'Religion vs spirituality: A contemporary conundrum', *Spiritus: A Journal of Christian Spirituality*, vol 3, no 2, pp163–185.

[19] Borgmann, A. (2003) *Power Failure: Christianity in the Culture of Technology*, Brazos Press, Grand Rapids, MI, p81.

[20] Comte-Sponville, A. (2008) *The Book of Atheist Spirituality*, trans N. Huston, Penguin Books, London, p160.

[21] King, U. (2009) *The Search for Spirituality: Our Global Quest for Meaning and Fulfilment*, Canterbury Press, Norwich, p3.

[22] Lynch, G. (2007) *The New Spirituality: An Introduction to Progressive Belief in the Twenty-first Century*, I. B. Tauris, London, p35.

[23] Porritt, J. (2007) *Capitalism as if the World Matters*, Earthscan, London, p169.

[24] Schneiders, S. M. (2003) 'Religion vs spirituality: A contemporary conundrum', *Spiritus: A Journal of Christian Spirituality*, vol 3, no 2, pp163–185.

[25] Cottingham, J. (2005) *The Spiritual Dimension: Religion, Philosophy and Human Value*, Cambridge University Press, Cambridge, pp3–4.

[26] Hill, P. C., Pargament, K. I., Hood Jr, R. W., McCullough, M. E., Swyers, J. P., Larson, D. B. and Zinnbauer, B. J. (2000) 'Conceptualizing religion and spirituality: Points of commonality, points of departure', *Journal for the Theory of Social Behaviour*, vol 30, no 1, pp51–77.

[27] Leonard, A. (2010) *The Story of Stuff*, Constable & Robinson Ltd, London, pp237–238.

[28] IDSA (2010) Industrial Designers Society of America, available at www.idsa.org, accessed 8 June 2010.

[29] Heskett, J. (1980) *Industrial Design*, Thames & Hudson, London, p11.

[30] Bakan, J. (2004) *The Corporation: The Pathological Pursuit of Profit and Power*, Constable, London, pp28, 60, 84.

[31] Leonard, A. (2010) *The Story of Stuff*, Constable & Robinson Ltd, London, pp237–238.

[32] Dormer, P. (1993) *Design Since 1945*, Thames & Hudson, London, p69.

[33] Greenlees, R. (2010) Crafts Council Director, quoted at *What is Craft?*, Victoria and Albert Museum, London, available at www.vam.ac.uk/collections/contemporary/crafts/what_is_craft/index.html, accessed 8 June 2010.

[34] Wallace, J. (2010) 'Emotionally charged: A practice-centred enquiry of digital jewellery and personal emotional significance', PhD thesis, available at www.digitaljewellery.com, accessed 12 July 2010.

[35] Roux, C. (2010) *Crafts Magazine*, quoted at *What is Craft?*, Victoria and Albert Museum, London, available at www.vam.ac.uk/collections/contemporary/crafts/what_is_craft/index.html, accessed 8 June 2010.

[36] Crafts Council (2010) *Collections and Exhibitions*, Crafts Council, London, available at www.craftscouncil.org.uk/collection-and-exhibitions, accessed 8 June 2010.

37 Abrahams, C. (2008) quoted in *Craft Matters*, Crafts Council, London, available at www.craftscouncil.org.uk/files/about-us/CraftMatters.pdf, accessed 8 June 2010.

38 Branzi, A. (2009) *Grandi Legni*, Design Gallery Milano and Nilufar, Milan, Italy, exhibition catalogue for Grandi Legni exhibition, Galerie Alaïa, Paris, 10 December 2009–16 January 2010.

39 Chaturvedi, U. (2010) managing director, Corus Strip Products UK, Tata Group, personal discussion 18 June 2010, and *Business Weekly* interview, BBC World Service, London, broadcast 7 May 2010.

14 Epilogue

1 Eagleton, T. (2009) *Reason, Faith and Revolution: Reflections on the God Debate*, Yale University Press, New Haven, pp143, 146.

2 Gray, J. (2009) *Gray's Anatomy: Selected Writing*, Penguin Books, London, pp307–310.

3 *The Disclosure of Climate Data from the Climatic Research Unit at the University of East Anglia*, House of Commons Science and Technology Committee, Her Majesty's Stationery Office, London, 31 March 2010, available at www.publications.parliament.uk/pa/cm200910/cmselect/cmsctech/387/387i.pdf, accessed 30 October 2010.

4 Leake, J. and Hastings, C. (2010) 'World misled over Himalayan glacier meltdown' [referring to errors in the International Panel on Climate Change (IPCC) 2007 report], *The Sunday Times*, 17 January 2010, available at www.timesonline.co.uk/tol/news/environment/article6991177.ece, accessed 20 January 2010.

5 Weber, E. (1999) *Apocalypses: Prophecies, Cults and Millennial Beliefs Throughout the Ages*, Random House, London, p48.

6 Eagleton, T. (2009) *Reason, Faith and Revolution: Reflections on the God Debate*, Yale University Press, New Haven, pp109, 139.

7 Musa, M. (trans) (1995) 'The Divine Comedy: Inferno, Canto I: 121-122', in *The Portable Dante*, Penguin Books, London, p8.

239

Sources of quotations at the beginning of each chapter

Ch.

1	John Milton	*Paradise Lost*, 1667
2	John Ruskin	*The Two Paths*, 1859
3	Evelyn Waugh	*Brideshead Revisited*, 1945
4	William Wordsworth	*Lines Written a Few Miles above Tintern Abbey*, 1798
5	Rainer Maria Rilke	*Letters to Clara*, 1907
6	William Shakespeare	*As You Like It*, 1623
7	Charles Taylor	*A Secular Age*, 2007
8	Roland Barthes	*Mythologies*, 1957
9	Robert Louis Stevenson	*The Lantern Bearers*, 1888

10   Ovid   *Metamorphoses, 1st century*
11   Dalai Lama XIV   *How to see yourself as you really are, 2007*
12   G. K. Chesterton   *Orthodoxy, 1908*
13   Eric Hobsbawm   *The Age of Revolution, 1962*
14   Idries Shah   *Caravan of Dreams, 1968*

Bibliography

Achemeimastou-potmaianou, M. (1987) *From Byzantium to El Greco: Greek frescoes and Icons*, The Theology and Spirituality of the Icon by Rt. Rev. Dr. Kallistos Ware, Greek Ministry of Culture, Athens, Greece.

Ades, D., N. Cox and D. Hopkins (1999) *Marcel Duchamp*, 'World of Art' series, Thames & Hudson, London, UK.

Armstrong, K. (2005) *A Short History of Myth*, Canongate Books Ltd, Edinburgh, UK.

Armstrong, K. (2006) *The Great Transformation*, Atlantic Books, London, UK.

Bahti, M. (1999) *Spirit in Stone: A Handbook of Southwest Indian Animal Carvings and Beliefs*, Treasure Chest Books, Tucson, AZ, USA.

Bakan, J. (2004) *The Corporation: The Pathological Pursuit of Profit and Power*, Constable, London, UK.

Bakhtiar, L. (1976) *SUFI: Expression of the Mystical Quest* (Part 3: Architecture and Music), Thames & Hudson, London, UK.

Beattie, T. (2007) *The New Atheists*, Darton, Longman and Todd, London, UK.

Beatty, L. (1939) *The Garden of the Golden Flower: The Journey to Spiritual Fulfilment*, Senate, Random House, London, UK.

Bhamra, T. and Lofthouse, V. (2007) *Design for Sustainability: A Practical Approach*, Gower, Aldershot, UK.

Borgmann, A. (1984) *Technology and the Character of Contemporary Life: A Philosophical Inquiry*, University of Chicago Press, Chicago, IL, USA.

Borgmann, A. (2003) *Power Failure: Christianity in the Culture of Technology*, Brazos Press, Baker Books, Grand Rapids, MI, USA.

Branzi, A. (2009) *Grandi Legni*, Design Gallery Milano and Nilufar, Milan, Italy, exhibition catalogue for 'Grandi Legni' exhibition, Galerie Alaïa, Paris, France.

Brookner, A. (2000) *Romanticism and its Discontents*, Farrar, Straus and Giroux, New York, NY, USA.

Brooks, R. (2000) *Blowing Zen: Finding an Authentic Life*, H. J. Kramer Inc, Tiburon, CA, USA.

Brown, T. (2009) *Change by Design*, HarperCollins, New York, NY, USA.

Buchanan, R. and Margolin, V. (eds) (1995) *Discovering Design: Explorations in Design Studies*, University of Chicago Press, Chicago, IL, USA.

Cage, J. (1961) *Silence: Lectures and Writing by John Cage*, Wesleyan University Press, Hanover, NH, USA.

Calais, E. (2007) Samboo's Grave, in *From a Slow Carriage*, Road Works Publ, Lancaster, UK, 2007.

Carey, J. (2005) *What Good Are The Arts*, Faber and Faber, London, UK.

Chapman, J. (2005) *Emotionally Durable Design: Objects, Experiences and Empathy*, Earthscan, London, UK.

Chesterton, G. K. (1908) *Orthodoxy*, 2001 edition by Image Books, Random House, New York, NY, USA.

Comte-Sponville, A. (2008) *The Book of Atheist Spirituality*, Bantam, Random House, London.

Cottingham, J., (2005) *The Spiritual Dimension: Religion, Philosophy and Human Value*, Cambridge University Press, Cambridge, UK.

Cross, N. (2006) *Designerly Ways of Knowing*, Springer, New York, NY, USA.

Csikszentmihalyi (1990) *Flow: The Psychology of Optimal Experience*, HarperCollins, New York, NY, USA.

Cunliffe, H. (2004) *The Story of Sunderland Point: From the Early Days to Modern Times*, R.W. Atkinson, Sunderland Point, Lancashire, UK.

Daly, H. (2007) *Ecological Economics and Sustainable Development*, Edward Elgar Publishing, Cheltenham, UK.

Davison, A. (2001) *Technology and the Contested Meanings of Sustainability*, State University of New York Press, Albany, NY, USA.

Day, C. (2002) *Spirit and Place*, Architectural Press, London, UK.

De Botton, A. (2004) *Status Anxiety*, Penguin Books, London, UK.

De Ferranti, H. (2000) *Japanese Musical Instruments*, Oxford University Press (China) Ltd, Hong Kong.

De Graaf, J., Wann, D. and Naylor, T. H. (2001) *Affluenza: The All Consuming Epidemic*, Berrett-Koehler Publishers Inc, San Francisco, CA, USA.

Dictionary of Quotations (1998) Wordsworth Reference Series, Wordsworth Editions Ltd, Ware, Herts, UK.

Dormer, P. (1993) *Design since 1945*, Thames & Hudson, London, UK.

Dormer, P. (1997) *The Culture of Craft: Status and Future*, Manchester University Press, Manchester, UK.

Dunne, A. (2005) *Hertzian Tales: Electronic Products, Aesthetic Experience, and Critical Design*, Cambridge, MA, USA.

Eagleton, T. (2009) *Reason, Faith and Revolution: Reflections on the God Debate*, Yale University Press, New Haven, CT, USA.

Easwaran, E. (1978) *Meditation: Commonsense Directions for an Uncommon Life*, Arkana, Penguin Books edition (1986), London, UK.

Elkington, J. (1998) *Cannibals with Forks: The Triple Bottom Line of 21st Century Business*, New Society Publishers, Gabriola Island, BC, Canada.

Feenberg, A. (2002) *Transforming Technology: A Critical Theory Revised*, Oxford University Press, Oxford, UK.

Feng, G. F and English, J. (trans) (1989) *Tao Te Ching, by Lao Tsu*, Vintage Books, Random House, New York, NY, USA.

Fry, T. (2009) *Design Futuring: Sustainability, Ethics and New Practice*, Berg, Oxford, UK.

Fuad-Luke, A. (2009) *Design Activism*, Earthscan, London, UK.

Gladwell, M. (2005) *Blink: The Power of Thinking Without Thinking*, Back Bay Books/Little, Brown and Co, New York, NY, USA.

Gray, J. (2009) *Gray's Anatomy: Selected Writing*, Penguin Books, London, UK.

Grayling, A. C. (2001) *The Meaning of Things*, Orion Books, London, UK.

Grayling, A. C. (2006) *The Form of Things*, Weidenfeld & Nicholson, London, UK.

Griffith, T. (trans) (1986) *Symposium of Plato*, University of California Press, Berkeley, CA, USA.

Hague, W. (2007) *William Wilberforce: The Life of the Great Anti-Slave Trade Campaigner*, HarperCollins, London, UK.

Hamel, G. (2007) *The Future of Management*, Harvard Business School Press, Boston, MA, USA.

Hannah, G. G. (2002) *Elements of Design*, Princeton Architectural Press, New York, NY, USA.

Hawken, P., Lovins, A. and Lovins, L. H. (1999) *Natural Capitalism*, Little, Brown & Co, New York, NY, USA.

Hawken, P. (2007) *Blessed Unrest*, Viking, Penguin Group, New York, NY, USA.

Herbert, D. ed (1981) *Everyman's Book of Evergreen Verse*, Dent, London, UK.

Heskett, J. (1986) *Industrial Design*, Thames & Hudson, London, UK.

Hick, J. (1989) *An Interpretation of Religion: Human Responses to the Transcendent*, Yale University Press, New Haven, CT, USA.

Hobsbawm, E. (1962) *The Age of Revolution: Europe 1789-1848*, Abacus, London, UK.

Hobsbawm, E. J. (1968) *Industry and Empire*, Penguin Books, London, UK.

Holloway, R. (2004) *Looking in the Distance: The Human Search for Meaning*, Canongate, Edinburgh, UK.

243

Hughes, R. (1987) *The Fatal Shore*, Collins Harvill, London, UK.

Hughes, R. (2006) *Things I Didn't Know: A Memoir*, Alfred Knopf, New York, NY, USA.

Humphreys, C. (1949) *Zen Buddhism*, William Heinemann Ltd, London, UK.

Iyer, R. (1993) *The Essential Writing of Gandhi,* Oxford University Press, Delhi, India.

Jackson, T. ed (2006) The Earthscan Reader in Sustainable Consumption, Earthscan, London, UK.

James, W. (1899) *Pragmatism and Other Writings*, Gunn, G. (ed), Penguin Books, London, UK, 2000.

Jamison, C. (2008) *Finding Happiness: Monastic Steps for a Fulfilling Life*, Weidenfeld & Nicolson, London, UK.

Juniper, A. (2003) *Wabi Sabi: the Japanese Art of Impermanence*, Tuttle Publishing, Boston, MA, USA.

King, U. (2009) *The Search for Spirituality: Our Global Quest for Meaning and Fulfilment*, Canterbury Press, Norwich, UK.

Klein, N. (2000) *No Logo,* Vintage Canada, Random House, Toronto, ON, Canada.

Koren, L. (1994) *Wabi-Sabi for Artists, Designers, Poets & Philosophers*, Stone Bridge Press, Berkeley, CA, USA.

Korten, D. C. (1999) *The Post-Corporate World: Life After Capitalism*, Berrett-Koehler Publishers, San Francisco, CA and Kumarian Press Inc, West Hartford, CT, USA.

Korten, D. C. (2001) *When Corporations Rule the World*, second edition, Kumarian Press Inc, Bloomfield, Connecticut and Berrett-Koehler Publishers Inc, San Francisco, CA, USA.

Korten, D. C. (2006) *The Great Turning: From Empire to Earth Community*, co-published by Kumarian Press Inc, Bloomfield, CT and Berrett-Koehler Publishers Inc, San Francisco, CA, USA.

Lanier, J. (2010) *You Are Not A Gadget*, London, UK: Allen Lane, Penguin Group, London, UK.

Lansley, S. (1994) *After the Gold Rush: The Trouble with Affluence: 'Consumer Capitalism' and the Way Forward*, Century Business Books, Random House, London, UK.

Lau, D. C. (1979) *Confucius: The Analects*, Penguin Books, London, UK.

Leonard, A. (2010) *The Story of Stuff*, Constable and Robinson Ltd, London, UK.

Lerner, M. (1996) *The Politics of Meaning*, Addison Wesley Publishing, Reading, MA, USA.

LeShan, L. (1974) *How to Meditate*, Bantam Books, New York, NY, USA.

Lovelock, J. (2007) *The Revenge of Gaia: Why the Earth is Fighting Back and How We Can Still Save Humanity*, Penguin Books, London, UK.

Lynch, G. (2007) *The New Spirituality: An Introduction to Progressive Belief in the Twenty-first Century*, I. B. Tauris, London, UK.

Malm, W. P. (2000) *Traditional Japanese Music and Musical Instruments: The New Edition*, Kodansha International, Tokyo, Japan.

Margolin, V. (2002) *The Politics of the Artificial: Essays on Design and Design Studies*, The University of Chicago Press, Chicago, IL, USA.

Martin, C. (2006) *A Glimpse of Heaven*, Foreword by Cardinal Cormac Murphy-O'Connor, English Heritage, Swindon, UK.

Mascaró, J. (trans) (1965) *The Upanishads*, Penguin Books, London, UK.

McCabe, H. (2005) *The Good Life: Ethics and the Pursuit of Happiness*, Continuum, London, UK.

McDonough, W. and M. Braungart (2001) *Cradle to Cradle: Remaking the Way We Make Things*, Douglas & McIntyre, Vancouver, BC, Canada.

McGrath, A. E. (1999) *Christian Spirituality*, Blackwell Publishing, Oxford, UK.

Meisel, A. C. and del Mastro, M. L., (trans) (1975) *The Rule of St. Benedict*, Doubleday, New York, NY, USA.

Miller, V. J. (2005) *Consuming Religion*, Continuum, New York, NY, USA.

Moriguchi, Y. and Jenkins, D. (trans) (1996) *Hojoki: Visions of a Torn World*, Stone Bridge Press, Berkeley, CA, USA.

Muelder Eaton, M. (2001) *Merit: Aesthetic and Ethical*, Oxford University Press, Oxford, UK.

Musa, M. (trans) (1995,) *The Divine Comedy: Inferno, Canto I: 121-122*, in The Portable Dante, Penguin Books, London, UK.

Needleman, J. (1994) *The Indestructible Question: Essays on Nature, Spirit and the Human Paradox*, Arkana, Penguin Group, London, UK.

Nes, S. (2004) *The Mystical Language of Icons*, Canterbury Press, Norwich, UK.

Nhat Hanh, T. (1995) *Living Buddha, Living Christ*, Riverhead Books, New York, NY, USA.

Northcott, M. S. (2007) *A Moral Climate: The Ethics of Global Warming*, Darton, Longman and Todd, London, UK.

O'Doherty, B. (1986) *Inside the White Cube: the Ideology of the Gallery Space*, The Lapis Press, Santa Monica, CA, USA.

Okakura, K. (1906) *The Book of Tea*, Kodansha International, Tokyo, Japan (1989 edition).

Otto, R. (1923) *The Idea of the Holy*, Oxford University Press, Oxford, UK.

Papanek, V. (1996) *The Green Imperative*, Thames and Hudson, New York, NY, USA.

Polanyi, M. (1966) *The Tacit Dimension*, Doubleday and Company Inc, Garden City, NY, USA.

Porritt, J. (2007) *Capitalism as if the World Matters*, Earthscan, London, UK.

Proud, L. (2000) *Icons: A Sacred Art*, Jarrold Publ., Norwich, UK.

Ralston Saul, J. (2005) *The Collapse of Globalism and the Reinvention of the World*, Viking Canada, Penguin Group, Toronto, ON, Canada.

Ramakers, R. (ed) (2004) *Simply Droog: 10+1 Years of Creating Innovation and Discussion*, Droog Publishing, Amsterdam, The Netherlands.

245

Ratzinger, J. (2007) *Jesus of Nazareth*, Doubleday, London, UK.

Richie, D. (2007) *A Tractate on Japanese Aesthetics*, Stone Bridge Press, Berkeley, CA, USA.

Robèrt, K. H. (2002) *The Natural Step Story: Seeding a Quiet Revolution*, New Society Publishers, Gabriola Island, BC, Canada.

Robert Rauschenberg: On and Off the Wall (2006) [exhibition catalogue], Musée d'Art moderne et d'Art contemporain, Nice, France.

Scharmer, C. O. (2009) *Theory U: Leading from the Future as it Emerges*, Berrett-Koehler Publishers, Inc, San Francisco, CA, USA.

Schumacher, E. F. (1979) *Good Work*, Abacus, London, UK.

Senge, P., Scharmer, C. O., Jaworski, J., and Flowers, B. S. (2005) *Presence: Exploring Profound Change in People, Organizations, and Society*, Nicholas Brealey Publishing, London, UK.

Senge. P., Smith, B., Kruschwitz, N., Laur, J. and Schley, S. (2008) *The Necessary Revolution: How Individuals and Organizations Are Working Together to Create a Sustainable World*, Nicholas Brealey Publishing, London, UK.

Shibayama, Z. (1970) *A Flower Does Not Talk: Zen Essays*, Charles E. Tuttle Co. Inc, Tokyo, Japan.

Sim, S. (ed) (1998) *The Icon Critical Dictionary of Postmodern Thought*, Icon Books, Cambridge, UK.

Smart, N. and Hecht, R. D. (eds) (1982) *Sacred Texts of the World: A Universal Anthology*, Macmillan Publishers Ltd., London, UK.

Snow, J. (1977) *These Mountains are our Sacred Places: The Story of the Stoney*, Samuel Stevens, Toronto, ON, Canada.

Sparke, P. (1995) *As Long as it's Pink – The Sexual Politics of Taste*, HarperCollins, London, UK.

Sparke, P. (2004) *An Introduction to Design and Culture, 1900 to the Present*, second edition, Routledge, London, UK.

Steindl-Rast, D. and S. Lebell. (2002) *Music of Silence: A Sacred Journey through the Hours of the Day*, Seastone, Berkeley, CA, USA.

St. Paul, M. Sr. (2000) *Clothed with Gladness: The Story of St. Clare*, Our Sunday Visitor Inc, Huntington, IN, USA.

Stryk, L. (trans) (1985) *On Love and Barley: Haiku of Basho*, Penguin Books, London, UK.

Tarnas, R. (1991) *The Passion of the Western Mind: Understanding the Ideas that have Shaped Our Worldview*, Harmony Books, New York, NY, USA.

Taylor, C. (2007) *A Secular Age*, The Belknap Press of Harvard University Press, Cambridge, MA, USA.

Thackara, J. (2005) *In the Bubble: Designing in a Complex World*, MIT Press, Cambridge, MA, USA.

Thompson, D. (2006) *Tools for Environmental Management: A Practical Introduction and Guide*, University of Calgary Press, Calgary, AB, Canada.

Thoreau, H. D. (1854) *Walden and Civil Disobedience*, Penguin Books, New York, NY, USA, 1983.

Tredennick, H. and Tarrant, H. (trans) (1954) *The Last Days of Socrates* by Plato, Penguin Books, London, UK.

Van der Ryn, S. and Cowan, S. (1996) *Ecological Design*, Island Press, Washington DC, USA.

Verbeek, P.-P. (2005) *What Things Do: Philosophical Reflections on Technology, Agency and Design*, Penn State University Press, PA, USA.

Visocky O'Grady, J. and Visocky O'Grady, K. (2006) *A Designer's Research Manual*, paperback edition 2009, Rockport Publ Ltd, Beverly, MA, USA.

Von Hippel, E. (2005) *Democratizing Innovation*, The MIT Press, Cambridge, MA, USA.

Walker, J. A. and Chaplin, S. (1997) *Visual Culture*, Manchester University Press, Manchester, UK.

Walker, S. (2006) *Sustainable by Design: Explorations in Theory and Practice*, Earthscan/James & James Science Publishers, London, UK.

Waters, L. (2004) *Enemies of Promise*, Prickly Paradigm Press, Chicago, IL, USA.

WCED (1987) *Our Common Future*, World Commission on Environment and Development, Oxford University Press, Oxford, UK.

Weber, E. (1999) *Apocalypses: Prophecies, Cults and Millennial Beliefs Throughout the Ages*, Pimlico, Random House, London, UK.

Whittle, K. (2006) *Native American Fetishes, Carvings of the Southwest*, second edition, Schiffer Publ Ltd, Atglen, PA, USA.

Wilkinson, R. and K. Pickett (2009) *The Spirit Level: Why More Equal Societies Almost Always Do Better*, Allen Lane, Penguin Books, London, UK.

Williams, A. (trans) (2006) *Spiritual Verses: Rumi*, Penguin Books, London, UK.

Woodham, J. M. (1997) *Twentieth Century Design*, Oxford University Press, Oxford, UK.

247

Index

255